The
MARTIN
DUBERMAN
Reader

ALSO BY MARTIN DUBERMAN

The

MARTIN DUBERMAN

Reader

The Essential Historical, Biographical,
and Autobiographical Writings

Martin Duberman

THE NEW PRESS

NEW YORK
LONDON

Requests for permission to reproduce selections
from this book should be mailed to:
Permissions Department, The New Press,
38 Greene Street, New York, NY 10013.

Published in the United States by The New Press, New York, 2013
Distributed by Perseus Distribution

LIBRARY OF CONGRESS CATALOGING-IN-PUBLICATION DATA

Duberman, Martin B.
[Works. Selections. 2013]
The Martin Duberman reader : the essential historical, biographical, and
autobiographical writings / Martin Duberman.
pages cm
ISBN 978-1-59558-679-7 (pbk.)—ISBN 978-1-59558-890-6 (e-book) 1. Duberman,
Martin. 2. United States—History. 3. United States—Social
conditions. 4. United States—Politics and government. 5. Gay rights—United
States—History. 6. Gays—United States—History. I. Title.
HQ75.8.D82A25 2013
306.76'6092—dc23   2012041856

The New Press publishes books that promote and enrich public discussion and
understanding of the issues vital to our democracy and to a more equitable world.
These books are made possible by the enthusiasm of our readers; the support
of a committed group of donors, large and small; the collaboration of our many
partners in the independent media and the not-for-profit sector; booksellers,
who often hand-sell New Press books; librarians; and above all by our authors.

www.thenewpress.com

Composition by dix!
This book was set in Janson Text

Printed in the United States of America

2   4   6   8   10   9   7   5   3   1

If the misery of our poor be caused not by the laws of nature, but by our institutions, great is our sin.

—Charles Darwin, *Voyage of the* Beagle

To Ellen Adler

—my brilliant publisher
—my fine friend

Contents

Author's Note

To keep this *Reader* at a reasonable length, I've omitted the many footnotes that accompanied the original texts. Since those notes often cite archival sources and contain clarifying content, readers interested in confirming my statements should consult the full-length books themselves.

I'm grateful to Julie Enszer for her expert advice during the process of cutting down my original manuscript to manageable size, to Maury Botton for shepherding the manuscript through production, and to Ben Woodward of The New Press for fielding my many questions.

HISTORY

In order to preserve the integrity of the historical moment, I've had to bite my tongue and retain the usage current at the time these pieces were written. Thus, I haven't changed "Negro" to "African American" or "black," nor "men" to "men and women," "him" to "him and her," etc. It's precisely the social movements I write about that subsequently brought about these changes in vocabulary— which is really to say, changes in consciousness. The use of "men" to cover "men and women" is especially jarring in the first essay ("The Northern Response to Slavery") because so many women were active in the abolitionist movement, and quite a few held leadership positions.

The Northern Response to Slavery

The abolitionist movement never became the major channel of Northern antislavery sentiment. It remained in 1860 what it had been in 1830: the small but not still voice of radical reform. An important analytical problem thus arises: why did most Northerners who disapproved of slavery become nonextensionists rather than abolitionists? Why did they prefer to attack slavery indirectly, by limiting its spread, rather than directly, by seeking to destroy it wherever it existed?

On a broad level, the answer involves certain traits in our national character. Any radical attack on social problems, suggesting as it would fundamental institutional defects rather than occasional malfunctions, would compromise our engrained patriotism. And so the majority has generally found it necessary to label "extreme" any measures that call for large-scale readjustment. Our traditional recoil from extremism can be defended. Complex problems, it might be said, require complex solutions, or, to be more precise, complex problems have no solutions—at best, they can be partially adjusted. If even this much is to be possible, the approach must be flexible, piecemeal, pragmatic. Clear-cut blueprints for reform, with their utopian demand for total solutions, intensify rather than ameliorate disorder.

There is much to be said for this defense of the American way—in the abstract. The trouble is that the theory of gradualism and the practice of it have not been the same. Too often Americans have used the gradualist argument as a technique of evasion rather than as a tool for change, not as a way of dealing with difficult problems slowly and carefully but as an excuse for not dealing with them at all. We do not want time for working out our problems—we do not want problems, and we will use the argument of time as a way of not facing them. As a chosen people, we are meant only to have problems that are self-liquidating. All of which is symptomatic of our conviction that history is the story of inevitable progress, that every day in every way we will get better and better whether or not we make any strenuous efforts toward that end.

Before 1845, the Northern attitude toward slavery rested on this comfortable belief in the benevolence of history. Earlier, during the 1830s, the abolitionists had managed to excite a certain amount of uneasiness about slavery by invoking the authority of the Bible and the Declaration of Independence against it. Alarm spread still further when mobs began to prevent abolitionists from speaking their minds or publishing their opinions, and when the national government interfered with the mails and the right of petition. Was it possible, people began to ask, that the abolitionists were right in contending that slavery, if left alone, would not die out but expand, would become more, not less, vital to the country's interests? Was it possible that slavery might even end by infecting free institutions themselves?

The apathetic majority was shaken but not yet profoundly aroused; the groundwork for widespread antislavery protest was laid, but its flowering awaited further developments. The real watershed came in 1845, when Texas was annexed to the Union and war with Mexico followed. The prospect now loomed of a whole series of new slave states. It finally seemed clear that the mere passage of time would not bring a solution; if slavery was ever to be destroyed, more active resistance would be necessary. For the first time, large numbers of white Northerners prepared to challenge the dogma that black slavery was a local matter in which the "free" states had no concern. A new era of widespread, positive resistance to slavery had opened.

Yet such new resolve was not channeled into a heightened demand for the abolition of the institution but only into a demand that its further extension be prevented. By 1845, Northerners may have lost partial but not total confidence in Natural Benevolence; they were now wiser Americans perhaps, but Americans nonetheless. More positive action against slavery, they seemed to be saying, was indeed required, but nothing too positive. Containing the institution would, in the long run, be tantamount to destroying it; a more direct assault was unnecessary. In this sense, the doctrine of nonextension was but a more sophisticated version of the standard faith in time.

One need not question the sincerity of those who believed that nonextension would ultimately destroy slavery, in order to recognize that such a belief partook of wishful thinking. Even if slavery was contained, there remained large areas within the current borders of the Southern states into which the institution could still expand; even without further westward expansion, there was no guarantee that slavery would cease to be profitable; and even should slavery cease to be profitable, there was no certainty that the South, psychologically, would feel able to abandon it. Nonextension, in short, was far from a foolproof formula. Yet many Northerners chose to so regard it.

And thus the question remains: why did not an aroused antislavery conscience turn to more certain measures and demand more unequivocal action? To many, a direct assault on slavery meant a direct assault on private property and the Union as well. As devout Lockeans, Americans did believe that the sanctity of private property constituted the essential cornerstone for all other liberties. If property could not be protected in a nation, neither could life nor liberty. And the Constitution, many felt, had upheld the legitimacy of holding property in men. True, the Constitution had not mentioned slavery by name and had not overtly declared in its favor, but in giving the institution certain indirect guarantees (the three-fifths clause, noninterference for twenty-one years with the slave trade, the fugitive slave proviso), the Constitution had seemed to sanction it. At any rate, no one could be sure. The intentions of the Founding Fathers remained uncertain, and one of the standing debates of the antebellum generation (and since) was whether the Constitution had been designed as a pro- or an antislavery document. Since the issue was unresolved, Northerners remained uneasy, uncertain how far they could go in attacking slavery without at the same time attacking property.

Fear for property rights was underscored by fear for the Union. The white South had many times warned that if her rights and interests were not heeded she would leave the Union and form a separate confederation. The tocsin had been sounded with such regularity that some dismissed it as mere bluster. But there was always the chance that if the South felt sufficiently endangered, it might yet carry out the threat.

It's difficult today fully to appreciate the horror with which most white Northerners regarded the potential breakup of the Union. Lincoln struck a deep chord for his generation when he spoke of the Union as the "last best hope of earth." That the American experiment was thought the best hope may have been arrogant, a hope at all, naive, but such it was to the average American, convinced of his country's superiority and the possibility of the world learning by example. Americans, enamored of their own extraordinary success story, were especially prone to look on love of country as one of the noblest of human sentiments. Even those Southerners who'd ceased to love the Union had not ceased to love the idea of nationhood; they merely wished to transfer allegiance to a more worthy object.

The difficulty was compounded by the North's ambivalent attitude toward the Negro. The white Northern majority, unlike most of the abolitionists, did not believe in the equality of races. The Bible was read to mean—and the new science of anthropology was said to confirm—the view that the Negro had been a separate, inferior creation meant for a position of servitude. Where there was doubt on the doctrine of racial equality, its advocacy by the distrusted abolitionists helped to settle the matter in the negative.

It was possible, of course, to believe in Negro inferiority and yet disapprove of Negro slavery. Negroes were obviously men, even if an inferior sort, and as men they could not in conscience (the Christian democratic version) be denied the right to control their own souls and bodies. But if anti-Negro and antislavery sentiments were not actually incompatible, they were not mutually supportive either. Doubt of the Negro's capacity for citizenship continually blunted the edge of antislavery fervor. If God had intended the Negro for a subordinate role in society, perhaps a kind of benevolent slavery was, after all, the most suitable arrangement; as long as there was uncertainty, it might be better to await the slow unfolding of His intentions in His good time.

And so the average Northerner, even after he came actively to disapprove of slavery, continued to be hamstrung in his opposition to it by the competitive pull of other values. Should prime consideration be given to freeing the slaves, even though in the process the rights of property and the preservation of the Union would be threatened? Should the future of the superior race be endangered in order to improve the lot of a people seemingly marked by Nature for a degraded station? Ideally, the North would have liked to satisfy its conscience about slavery and at the same time preserve the rest of its value system intact—to free the Negro and yet do so without threatening property rights or dislocating the Union. This struggle to achieve the best of all possible worlds runs like a forlorn hope throughout the antebellum period—the sad, almost plaintive quest by the American Adam for the perfect world he considered his birthright.

The formula of nonextension did seem to many Northerners, for a time, the ideal formula for balancing these multiple needs. Nonextension would put slavery on the course toward ultimate extinction without producing excessive dislocation; since slavery would not be attacked directly, nor its existence immediately threatened, the South would not be unduly fearful for her property rights, the

Union would not be needlessly jeopardized, and a mass of free Negroes would not be precipitously thrust upon an unprepared public. Nonextension, in short, seemed a panacea: it promised in time to do everything while for the present risking nothing. But like all panaceas, it ignored certain hard realities: would containment really lead to the extinction of slavery? Would the South accept even a gradual dissolution of her peculiar institution? Would it be right to sacrifice two or three more generations of Negroes in the name of uncertain future possibilities? Alas for the American Adam, so soon to be expelled from Eden.

The abolitionists, unlike most Northerners, were not willing to rely on future intangibles. Though often called impractical romantics, they were in some ways the most tough-minded of Americans. They had no easy faith in the benevolent workings of time or in the inevitable triumphs of gradualism. If change was to come, they argued, it would be the result of man's effort to produce it; patience and inactivity had never yet solved the world's ills. Persistently, sometimes harshly, the abolitionists denounced delay and those who advocated it; they were tired, they said, of men using the councils of moderation to perpetuate injustice.

Historians have long assumed that the abolitionists were unified in their advocacy of certain broad policies—immediate emancipation, and without compensation—and also unified in refusing to spell out practical details for implementation. The abolitionists did agree almost unanimously (Gerrit Smith was one of the few exceptions) that slaveholders must not be compensated. One does not pay a man, they argued, for ceasing to commit a sin. Besides, the slaveholder had already been paid many times over in labor for which he had never given wages. Though told that public opinion would never support the confiscation of property, the abolitionists stood firm. They saw themselves as prophets, not politicians; they were concerned with what was right, not with what was possible, though they hoped that if men were made aware of what was right, they would find some practical way of implementing it.

The abolitionists were far less united on the doctrine of im-

mediate emancipation—that is, in the 1830s, before Southern intransigence and British experience in the West Indies convinced
almost all of them that gradualism was hopeless. During the 1830s,
there was a considerable spectrum of opinion as to when and how to
emancipate the slaves. Contrary to common myth, some of the abolitionists did advocate a period of prior education and training before the granting of full freedom. Men like Theodore Dwight Weld,
James G. Birney, and Lewis and Arthur Tappan, stressing the debas-
ing experience of slavery, insisted only that gradual emancipation be
immediately begun, not that emancipation itself be at once achieved.
This range of opinion hasn't been fully appreciated. Indeed, it might
be well to ask whether the abolitionists, in moving steadily toward
immediatism, were not, at least in part, driven to that position by the
intransigence of their society in the preceding decade, rather than
by any inherent extremism in their own temperaments. It has been
convenient, then and now, to believe that all abolitionists always
advocated instantaneous freedom, for it thus became possible to denounce any call for emancipation as patently impractical.

By 1840, however, most abolitionists *had* become immediatists.
They had come to see that not even the most gradual plan for doing away with slavery held any widespread appeal in the country,
and had also come to feel the compelling moral urgency of immediatism. Men learned how to be free, the abolitionists had come to
believe by 1840, only by being free; slavery, no matter how attenu-
ated, was by its very nature incapable of preparing men for those
independent decisions necessary for adult responsibility. Besides,
they insisted, the Negro, though perhaps debased by slavery, was
no more incapacitated for citizenship than were many poor whites,
whose rights no one seriously suggested curtailing. If conditions for
emancipation were once established, they could be used as a standing rationale for postponement; the Negro could be kept in a condition of semislavery by the self-perpetuating argument that he was
not yet ready for his freedom.

Moreover, any intermediary stage before full freedom would
require the spelling out of precise plans, and these would give the

enemies of emancipation an opportunity to pick away at the impracticality of this or that detail. They would have an excuse for dis-
avowing the broader policy under the guise of disagreeing with the
specific means for achieving it. Better to concentrate on the larger
issue and force men to take sides on that alone, the abolitionists
argued, than to give them a chance to hide their opposition behind
some supposed disapproval of detail. Wendell Phillips, for one, saw
the abolitionists' role as exclusively that of agitating the broader
question. Their primary job, Phillips insisted, was to arouse the
country's conscience rather than to spell out to it precise plans and
formulas. *After* that conscience had been aroused, it would be time
to talk of specific proposals; let the moral urgency of the problem
be recognized, let the country be brought to a determination to rid
itself of slavery, and ways and means to accomplish that purpose
would be readily enough found.

No tactical position could really have saved the abolitionists
from the denunciation of those hostile to their basic goal. If the
abolitionists spelled out a program for emancipation, their enemies
could nitpick it to death. If they did not spell out a program, they
could then be accused of vagueness and impracticality. Hostility
can always find its own justification.

A second mode of attack on the abolitionists has centered on
their personalities rather than their policies. The stereotype that
has long had currency saw the abolitionist as a disturbed fanatic, a
man self-righteous and self-deceived, motivated not by concern for
the Negro, as he may have believed, but by an unconscious drive to
gratify certain needs of his own. Seeking to discharge either individual anxieties or those frustrations that came from membership
in a displaced elite, his antislavery protest was, in any case, a mere
disguise for personal anguish.

Underlying this analysis is a broad assumption that has never
been made explicit—namely, that strong protest by an individual
against social injustice is ipso facto proof of his disturbance. Injustice itself, in this view, is apparently never sufficient to arouse unusual ire in "normal" men, for normal men, so goes the canon, are

always cautious, discreet, circumspect, self-absorbed. Those who hold to this model of human behavior seem rarely to suspect that it may tell us more about their hierarchy of values than about the reform impulse it pretends to describe. Argued in another context, the inadequacies of the stereotype become more apparent: if normal people do not protest "excessively" against injustice, then we should be forced to condemn as neurotic all those who protested with passion against Nazi genocide.

Some of the abolitionists, it is true, *were* palpable neurotics, men who were not comfortable within themselves and therefore not comfortable with others, men whose "reality testing" was poor, whose lifestyles were pronouncedly compulsive, whose relationships were unusual compounds of demand and fantasy. Such neurotics were in the abolitionist movement—the Parker Pillsburys, Stephen Symonds Fosters, Abby Folsoms. Yet even here we should be cautious, for our diagnostic accuracy can be blurred if the lifestyle under evaluation is sharply different from our own. Many of the traits of the abolitionists that today put us off were not peculiar to them but rather to their age—the declamatory style, the abstraction and idealization of issues, the tone of righteous certainty, the religious context of argumentation. Thus the evangelical rhetoric of the movement, with its thunderous emphasis on sin and retribution, can sound downright peculiar (and thus neurotic) to the twenty-first-century skeptic, though in its day common enough to abolitionists and nonabolitionists alike.

Then, too, even when dealing with the "obvious" neurotics, we must be careful in the link we establish between their pathology and their protest activity. It is one thing to demonstrate an individual's disturbance and quite another then to explain all of his behavior in terms of it. Let us suppose, for example, that Mr. Jones is a reformer; he is also demonstrably insecure. It does not necessarily follow that he is a reformer *because* he is insecure. The two may seem logically related (that is, if one's mind automatically links protest with neurosis), but we all know that many things can seem logical without being true.

Even if we establish the neurotic behavior of certain members of a group, we have not, thereby, established the neurotic behavior of all members of that group. To leap from the particular to the general is always tempting, but because one benighted monsignor has been caught with a Boy Scout does not mean we have conclusively proven that all priests are pederasts. Some members of every group are disturbed; put the local police force, the Medal of Honor winners, or the faculty of a university under the Freudian microscope, and the number of cases of palpable disturbance would probably be disconcertingly high. But what precisely does their disturbance tell us about the common activities of the group to which they belong—let alone about the activities of the disturbed individuals themselves?

Actually, behavioral patterns for many abolitionists do *not* seem notably eccentric. Men like Birney, Weld, James Russell Lowell, Edmund Quincy—abolitionists all—formed good relationships, saw themselves in perspective, played and worked with zest and spontaneity, developed their talents, were aware of worlds beyond their own private horizons. They all had their tics and their traumas—as who does not?—but the evidence of health is abundant and predominant. Yet most historians have preferred to ignore such men when discussing the abolitionist movement. And the reason, I believe, is that such men conform less well to the assumption that those who become deeply involved in social protest are necessarily those who are deeply disturbed.

Yet recent work in psychology suggests that the very definition of maturity may be the ability to commit oneself to abstract ideals, to get beyond the selfish, egocentric world of children. This does not mean that every man who reaches outward does so from mature motives; public involvement may also be a way of acting out disturbed fantasies. The point is only that political commitment need not be a symptom of personality disorder. It is just as likely to be a symptom of maturity and health.

It does not follow, of course, that all abolitionists protested against slavery out of mature motives; some may have been, indeed were, seeming neurotics. But if we agree that slavery was a fearful injustice, and if it's acknowledged that injustice will bring forth protest from mature people, it seems reasonable to conclude that at least some of those who protested strongly against slavery must have done so from healthy motives.

The hostile critic will say that the abolitionists protested too strongly to have been maturely motivated. But when is a protest too strong? For a defender of the status quo, the answer (though never stated in these terms) would be: when it succeeds. For those not dedicated to the status quo, the answer is likely to be: a protest is too strong when it is out of all proportion to the injustice it indicts. Could any nonviolent protest have been too strong morally against holding fellow human beings as property?

In this regard, there has been a persistent confusion of two separate indictments against the abolitionists: first, that they disrupted the peace, and second (in the classic formulation given by Daniel Webster), that they "bound more firmly than before" the bonds of the slave. It is undeniably true that the abolitionists contributed to the polarization of public opinion and, to that extent, to the disturbance of the peace.

But it does not follow that because they stirred up passions, they made freeing the slaves more difficult. This would be true only if it could be shown that the slaves could have been freed without first arousing and polarizing opinion. The evidence doesn't support such an argument. In all the long years before the abolitionists began their campaign, the North had managed to remain indifferent to the institution, and the South had done almost nothing, even in the most gradual way, toward ameliorating it. Had the abolitionists not aroused public debate on slavery, there is no guarantee that anyone else would have; and without such a debate it is most unlikely that measures against the institution would have been taken.

The fact that the debate became heated, moreover, cannot be explained by the terms in which the abolitionists raised it; what must also be taken into account is the fact that the white South, with some possible exceptions in the border area, reacted intransigently to any criticism of the institution, however mild the tone or gradual the suggestions.

When discussing the abolitionists we must, at a minimum, cease dealing in blanket indictments, in simpleminded categorizing and elementary stereotyping. Such exercises may satisfy our own hostility to reformers, but they do not satisfy the complex demands of historical truth. We need an awareness of the wide variety of human beings who became involved in the abolitionist movement, and an awareness of the complexity of human motivation sufficient to save us from summing up men and movements in two or three unexamined adjectives.

Surely there is now evidence enough to suggest that commitment and moral concern need not be aberrational; they may represent the profoundest elements of our humanity. Surely those who protested strongly against slavery were not all misguided fanatics or frustrated neurotics—though by so believing it becomes easier to ignore the injustice against which they protested. Perhaps it's time to ask whether the abolitionists, in insisting that slavery be ended, were indeed those men of their generation furthest removed from reality, or whether that description should be reserved for those Northerners who remained indifferent to the institution, and those Southerners who defended it as a positive good. From the point of view of these men, the abolitionists were indeed mad, but it is time we questioned the sanity of the point of view.

Those white Northerners who were not indifferent to slavery—a large number after 1845—were nonetheless prone to viewing the abolitionist protest as excessive, for it threatened the cherished values of private property and Union. The average Northerner may have found slavery disturbing, but convinced as he was that the Negro was an inferior, he did not find slavery monstrous. Certainly he did not think it an evil sufficiently profound to risk, by precipitous action, the nation's present wealth or its future power. The abolitionists were willing to risk both. They thought it tragic that men should weigh human lives on the same scale as material possessions and abstractions of government. It is no less tragic that we continue to do so.

—from *The Antislavery Vanguard* (1965)

Postscript

Beginning with *The Antislavery Vanguard*, continuing with Lewis Perry and Michael Fellman's *Antislavery Reconsidered* (1979), and culminating in Timothy Patrick McCarthy and John Stauffer, *Prophets of Protest* (2006), the reputation of the nonviolent abolitionist movement has by now been thoroughly rehabilitated. Not so John Brown, who utilized violence in attempting to free the slaves. Most African Americans have long regarded John Brown as a heroic figure, but few whites have, and even fewer white historians. With the notable exception of David S. Reynolds's 2005 biography, most white historians have continued to denounce Brown as a dangerous psychopath. The distinguished and influential C. Vann Woodward portrayed him as a "monomaniac," a man whose family history was riddled (in fact it wasn't) with insanity. Others have assailed him on grounds ranging from incompetence in business dealings to being a tyrannical father.

Few mention Brown's remarkable lack of racism, rare in his own day among whites, still not commonplace in ours. Perhaps more remarkable still, Brown practiced what he preached. He forbade his family to discriminate against blacks, had close friendships with many, admired black culture, and insisted on social integration, on living and working among them.

None of which necessarily justifies his resort to violence against slavery, but his actions both in Missouri and at Harper's Ferry raise a profound set of questions. Who, if anyone, has the right to kill? And from what source does that right derive? When does (or should) taking another life bring honor, and when disgrace? Is there such a thing as a just war—the American Revolution? World War II? Or—since war always involves the slaughter of innocents, including innocent young soldiers misled or forced into battle— should every resort to violence, whether between nations or individuals, be denounced?

What of the right to self-defense? On what grounds would one deny the right of Jews earmarked for destruction in the Warsaw

Ghetto or while being led to the gas chambers to violently resist? What of the right of black slaves—Nat Turner? Toussaint L'Ouverture? Denmark Vesey?—their lives stolen, their bodies brutalized, to slit the throats of their self-designated masters? Does the same exculpation extend to revolutionaries (Americans? Algerians? Cubans? Egyptians? Libyan?) who take up arms against tyrannical regimes? What about a woman who stabs her rapist? A gay person assaulted by a fag basher? A sex worker abused and threatened by a customer?

Should we validate self-defense solely for those directly in jeopardy? Or is it also legitimate to fight on behalf of the liberation of others? If the answer to the latter is "no," then do we automatically denounce the International Brigades that fought against fascism in Spain? If the answer is "yes," then on what grounds do we exempt John Brown, who fought to liberate blacks?

Perhaps the only consistent possible reply is to deny, under any and all circumstances, the right to commit violence. That's the stance of the War Resisters League, and of any number of other groups committed to nonviolence. Before signing up, be sure to understand that what's at stake would include the right to spank your child.

Black Power and the
American Radical Tradition

The slogan "Black Power" has caused widespread confusion and alarm. This is partly due to a problem inherent in language: words necessarily reduce complex attitudes or phenomena to symbols that, in their abbreviation, allow for a variety of interpretations. Stuart Chase has reported that in the thirties, when the word "fascism" was on every tongue, he asked a hundred people from various walks of life what the word meant and got a hundred widely differing definitions. And in 1953 when the *Capital Times* of Madison, Wisconsin, asked two hundred people, "What is a communist?" not only was there no agreement, but five out of every eight admitted they couldn't define the term at all. So it is with Black Power. Its definition depends on whom you ask, when you ask, where you ask, and, not least, who does the asking.

Yet the phrase's ambiguity derives not only from the usual confusions of language but from a failure of clarity (or is it frankness?) on the part of its advocates and a failure of attention (or is it generosity?) from its critics. The leaders of the Student Nonviolent Coordinating Committee (SNCC) and Congress of Racial Equality (CORE) who invented the slogan, including Stokely Carmichael and Floyd McKissick, have given Black Power different definitions on different occasions, in part because their own understanding of the term continues to develop, but in part, too, because their explanations have been tailored to their audiences. The confusion has been compounded by the press, which has frequently distorted the words of SNCC and CORE representatives, harping on every connotation of violence and reverse racism, minimizing the central call for racial unity.

For all these reasons, it is still not clear whether Black Power is to be taken as a short-term tactical device or a long-range goal—that is, a postponement or a rejection of integration; whether it has been adapted as a lever for intimidating whites or organizing blacks, for instilling race hate or race pride; whether it necessitates, permits, or encourages violence; whether it is a symptom of Negro despair or of Negro pride, a reaction to the lack of improvement in the daily lives of Negro Americans or a sign that improved conditions are creating additional expectations and demands. Whether Black Power, furthermore, becomes a constructive psychological and political tactic or a destructive summons to separatism, violence, and reverse racism will depend at least as much on developments outside the control of its advocates (like the war in Vietnam) as on their conscious determination. For all these reasons, it is too early for final evaluations; only time, and perhaps not even that, will provide them. At most, certain limited and tentative observations are possible.

If Black Power means only that Negroes should organize politically and economically in order to improve self-regard and to exert maximum pressure, then the new philosophy would be difficult to fault, for it would be based on the truisms that minorities must argue from positions of strength rather than weakness, and that the majority is far more likely to make concessions to power than to justice. To insist that Negro Americans seek their goals as individuals and solely by appeals to conscience and love, when white Americans have always relied on group association and organized protest to achieve theirs, would be yet one more form of discrimination. Moreover, when whites decry SNCC's declaration that it is tired of turning the other cheek, that henceforth it will actively resist white brutality, they might do well to remember that they've always considered self-defense acceptable behavior for themselves: our textbooks view the refusal of the revolutionaries of 1776 to sit supinely by as the very essence of manhood.

Although Black Power makes good sense when defined to mean further organization and cooperation within the Negro community, the results that are likely to follow in terms of political leverage can easily be exaggerated. The impact is likely to be greatest at the county level in the Deep South and in the urban ghettos of the North. In this regard, the Black Panther Party of Lowndes County, Alabama, is the prototype.

There are roughly twelve thousand Negroes in Lowndes County and three thousand whites, but until 1964 there was not a single Negro registered to vote while white registration had reached 118 percent of those eligible. Negro life in Lowndes, as Andrew Kopkind has graphically recounted, was—and is—wretched. The median family income for whites is $4,400, for Negroes, $935; Negro farmhands earn three to six dollars a day; half of the Negro women who work are maids in Montgomery (which requires a forty- to sixty-mile daily round-trip) at four dollars a day; few Negroes have farms, since 90 percent of the land is owned by about eighty-five white families; the one large industrial plant in the area, the new Dan River Mills textile factory, will employ Negroes only in menial capacities; most Lowndes Negroes are functional illiterates, living in squalor and hopelessness.

The Black Panther Party set out to change all this. The only path to change in Lowndes, and in much of the Deep South, is to take over the courthouse, the seat of local power. For generations the courthouse in Lowndes has been controlled by the Democratic Party; indeed, there is no Republican Party in the county. Obviously it made little sense for SNCC organizers to hope to influence the local Democrats; no white moderates existed and no discussion of integration was tolerated. To have expected blacks to "bore from within" would have been, as Carmichael has said, "like asking the Jews to reform the Nazi party."

Instead, Carmichael and his associates established the separate

Black Panther Party. After months of work SNCC organizers (with almost no assistance from federal agents) registered enough Negroes to hope for a numerical majority in the county. But in the election of November 1966, the Black Panther Party was defeated for a variety of reasons that include Negro apathy or fear and white intimidation. Despite this defeat, the possibility of a better life for Lowndes County Negroes does at last exist, and should the Black Panther Party come into power at some future point, that possibility could become a reality.

Nonetheless, even on the local level and even in the Deep South, Lowndes County is not representative. In Alabama, for example, only eleven of the state's sixty-seven counties have black majorities. Where these majorities do not exist, the only effect independent black political parties are likely to have is to consolidate the whites in opposition. Moreover, and more significant, many of the basic ills from which Negro Americans suffer—inadequate housing, inferior education, limited job opportunities—are national phenomena requiring national resources to solve. Whether these resources will be allocated in sufficient amounts will depend, in turn, on whether a national coalition can be formed to exert pressure on the federal government—a coalition of civil rights activists, church groups, campus radicals, New Class technocrats, unskilled, un-unionized laborers, and certain elements in organized labor, such as the United Auto Workers or the United Federation of Teachers. Such a coalition, of course, would necessitate Negro-white unity, a unity Black Power at least temporarily rejects.

The answer that Black Power advocates give to the coalition argument is of several pieces. The only kind of progressive coalition that can exist in this country, they say, is the mild, liberal variety that produced the civil rights legislation of recent years. And that kind of legislation has proven itself grossly inadequate. Its chief result has been to lull white liberals into believing that the major battles have been won, whereas in fact there has been almost no change, or even change for the worse, in the daily lives of most blacks.

Unemployment among Negroes has actually gone up in the past ten years. Title VI of the 1964 Civil Rights Act, with its promising provision for the withdrawal of federal funds in cases of discrimination, has been used in limited fashion in regard to the schools but not at all in regard to other forms of unequal treatment, such as segregated hospital facilities. Under the 1965 Voting Rights Act, only about forty federal registrars have been sent into the South, though many areas have less than the 50 percent registration figure that would legally warrant intervention. In short, the legislation produced by the liberal coalition of the early sixties has turned out to be little more than federally approved tokenism, a continuation of paper promises and ancient inequities.

If a radical coalition could be formed in this country—that is, one willing to scrutinize in depth the failings of our system; to suggest structural, not piecemeal, reforms; to see them executed with sustained rather than intermittent vigor—then Black Power advocates might feel less need to separate themselves and to concentrate on local, marginal successes. But no responsible observer believes that in the foreseeable future a radical coalition on the Left can become the effective political majority in the United States; we will be fortunate if a radical coalition on the Right does not. And so to SNCC and CORE, talk of further cooperation with white liberals is only an invitation to further futility. It is better, they feel, to concentrate on encouraging Negroes everywhere to self-respect and self-help, and in certain local areas, where their numbers warrant it, to try to win actual political power.

As an adaptation to present realities, Black Power thus has a persuasive logic. But there is such a thing as being too present-minded; by concentrating on immediate prospects, the new doctrine may be jeopardizing larger possibilities for the future, those that could result from a national coalition with white allies. Though SNCC and CORE insist that they are not trying to cut whites out of the movement, that they merely want to redirect white energies into organizing whites so that at some future point a truly meaningful coalition of Negroes and whites can take place, there are grounds for doubting whether they really are interested in a future reconciliation, or if they are, whether some of the overtones of their present stance will allow for it. For example, SNCC's so-called "position paper" on Black Power attacks white radicals as well as white liberals, speaks vaguely of differing white and black "psyches," and seems to find all contact with all whites contaminating or intimidating. ("Whites are the ones who must try to raise themselves to our humanistic level.")

SNCC's bitterness at the hypocrisy and evasion of the white majority is understandable, yet the refusal to discriminate between degrees of inequity, the penchant instead for wholesale condemnation of all whites, is as unjust as it is self-defeating. The indictments and innuendos of SNCC's position paper give some credence to the view that the line between Black Power and black racism is a fine one easily erased, that, as always, means and ends tend to get confused, that a tactic of racial solidarity can turn into a goal of racial purity.

The philosophy of Black Power is thus a blend of varied, in part contending, elements, and it cannot be predicted with any certainty which will assume dominance. But a comparison between the Black Power movement and the personnel, programs, and fates of earlier radical movements in this country can make some contribution toward understanding its dilemmas and its likely directions.

Any argument based on historical analogy can, of course, become oversimplified and irresponsible. Historical events do not repeat themselves with anything like regularity; every event is to a large degree embedded in its own special context. An additional danger in reasoning from historical analogy is that in the process we'll limit rather than expand our options; by arguing that certain consequences seem always to follow from certain actions and that therefore only a set number of alternatives ever exist, we can prevent ourselves from seeing new possibilities or from utilizing old ones in creative ways. We must be careful when attempting to predict the future from the past that in the process we don't straitjacket the present. Bearing these cautions and limitations in mind, some insight can still be gained from a historical perspective. For if there are large variances through time between roughly analogous events, there are also some similarities, and it is these that make comparative study possible and profitable. In regard to Black Power, I think we gain particular insight by comparing it with the two earlier radical movements of abolitionism and anarchism.

Because they called for an immediate end to slavery everywhere in the United States, the abolitionists represented the left wing of the antislavery movement (a position comparable to the one SNCC and CORE occupy today in the civil rights movement). Most Northerners who disapproved of slavery weren't willing to go as far or as fast as the abolitionists, preferring instead a more ameliorative approach. The tactic that increasingly won the approval of the Northern majority was the doctrine of nonextension: no further expansion of slavery would be allowed, but the institution would be left alone where it already existed. The principle of nonextension first came into prominence in the late 1840s when fear developed in the North that territory acquired from our war with Mexico would be made into new slave states. Later the doctrine formed the basis of the Republican Party, which in 1860 elected Lincoln to the presidency. The abolitionists, in other words, with their demand for immediate (and uncompensated) emancipation, never became the major channel of Northern antislavery sentiment. They always remained a small sect, vilified by slavery's defenders and distrusted even by allies within the antislavery movement.

The parallels between the abolitionists and the current defenders of Black Power seem to me numerous and striking. It's worth noting, first of all, that neither group started off with so-called "extremist" positions (the appropriateness of that word being, in any case, dubious). The SNCC of 1967 is not the SNCC formed in 1960; both its personnel and its programs have shifted markedly. SNCC originally grew out of the sit-ins spontaneously begun in Greensboro, North Carolina, by four freshmen at the all-Negro North Carolina Agricultural and Technical College. The sit-in technique spread rapidly through the South, and within a few months SNCC was formally inaugurated to channel and encourage further activities. At its inception, SNCC's staff was interracial, religious in orientation, committed to the American Dream, chiefly concerned with winning the right to share more equitably in that dream, and optimistic about the possibility of being allowed to do so. SNCC placed its hopes on an appeal to the national conscience, and this it expected to arouse by the examples of nonviolence and redemptive love, and by the dramatic devices of sit-ins, freedom rides, and protest marches.

The abolitionist movement, at the time of its inception, was similarly benign and sanguine. It, too, placed emphasis on moral suasion, believing that the first order of business was to bring the iniquity of slavery to the country's attention, to arouse the average American's conscience. Once this was done, the abolitionists felt, discussion then could, and would, begin on the particular ways and means best calculated to bring about rapid, orderly emancipation. Some of those abolitionists who later became intransigent defenders of immediatism—including William Lloyd Garrison—were willing, early in their careers, to consider plans for preliminary apprenticeship. They were willing, in other words, to settle for gradual emancipation immediately begun instead of demanding that freedom itself be instantly achieved.

But this early flexibility received little encouragement. Neither the appeal to conscience nor the willingness to engage in debate over means brought results. In the North, the abolitionists encountered massive apathy; in the South, massive resistance. Thus thwarted, and influenced as well by the discouraging British experiment with gradualism in the West Indies, the abolitionists abandoned their earlier willingness to consider a variety of plans for prior education and training, and shifted to the position that emancipation had to take place at once and without compensation to the slaveholder. They also began (especially in New England) to advocate such doctrines as Dis-Union and No-Government, positions that directly parallel Black Power's recent advocacy of separation and decentralization, and that, then as now, produced discord and division within the movement, anger and denunciation without.

But the parallel of paramount importance I want to draw between the two movements is their similar passage from moderation to extremism. In both cases, there was a passage, a shift in attitude and program, and it's essential that this be recognized, for it demonstrates the developmental nature of these movements for social change. Or, to reduce the point to individuals (and to clichés): "Revolutionaries are not born but made." Garrison did not start his career with the doctrine of immediatism; as a young man, he even had kind words for the American Colonization Society, a group devoted to deporting Negroes to Africa and Central America. And Stokely Carmichael did not begin his ideological voyage with the slogan of Black Power; as a teenager he was opposed to student sit-ins in the South. What makes a man shift from reform to revolution is, it seems to me, primarily to be explained by the intransigence or indifference of his society: either society refuses reforms or gives them in the form of tokens. Thus, if one views the Garrisons and Carmichaels as extremists, one should at least place the blame for that extremism where it belongs—not on their individual temperaments, their genetic predispositions, but on a society that scorned or toyed with their initial pleas for justice.

In turning to the anarchist movement, I think we can see between it and the new turn taken by SNCC and CORE (or, more comprehensively still, by much of the New Left) significant affinities of style and thought. These are largely unconscious and unexplored; I've seen almost no overt references to them either in the movement's official literature or in its unofficial pronouncements. Yet the affinities seem to me important.

But first I should make clear that in speaking of anarchism as if it were a unified tradition, I'm necessarily oversimplifying. The anarchist movement contained a variety of contending factions, disparate personalities, and differing national patterns. The peasant anarchists, especially in Spain, were fiercely anti-industrial and antiurban and wished to withdraw entirely from the state to live in separate communities based on mutual aid. The anarcho-syndicalists of France put special emphasis on the value of a general strike and looked to the trade unions as the future units of a new society. Michael Bakunin advocated violence; Leo Tolstoy abhorred it. Pierre-Joseph Proudhon believed in retaining individual owner-ship of certain forms of property; Enrico Malatesta called for its ab-olition in every form. Max Stirner's ideal was the egotist engaged in the war of "each against all"; Prince Peter Kropotkin's was human solidarity, a society based on the union of voluntary communes.

These are only some of the divisions of strategy, personality, and geography that characterized the anarchist movement. What bound these disparate elements together—what makes plausible the term "anarchism" in reference to all of them—is their hostility to authority, especially that embodied in the state, but including any form of rule by man over man, whether it be parent, teacher, lawyer, or priest. The anarchists were against authority, they said, because they were for life—not life as most men had ever lived it but life as it might be lived. Anarchists argued, in a manner reminiscent of Rousseau, that human aggression and cruelty were the products of imposed restraints. They insisted that the authoritarian upbring-ing most children were subjected to stifled spontaneity, curiosity, initiative, individuality—in other words, prevented possession of themselves. If they could be raised free—freed economically from the struggle for existence, intellectually freed from the tyranny of custom, emotionally freed from the need to revenge their own mutilation by harming others—they could express those "natural" feelings of fraternity and mutual assistance innate to the human species.

The anarchists' distrust of the state as an instrument of oppres-sion, as the tool by which the privileged and powerful maintained themselves, is generally associated with nineteenth-century classi-cal liberalism, with John Stuart Mill and, in this country, with the Jeffersonians. But by the end of the nineteenth century and increas-ingly in the twentieth, liberals began to regard the state as an ally rather than an enemy; only the national government, it was felt, had the power to accomplish regulation and reform, to prevent small groups of self-interested men from exploiting their fellows.

Today the pendulum has begun to swing back again. In the liberal—but more especially in the radical—camp, the federal government has lost some of its appeal; veneration is giving way to distrust; from an instrument of liberation, the central government is once more being viewed as a threat to individuality. This shift is the result of accumulated disappointments. The regulatory agencies set up to supervise the monopolists have been discovered to be operating in the interests of the monopolists; farm-subsidy programs have been exposed as benefiting the richer operators while dispossessing tenant farmers and sharecroppers; the urban renewal program seems to be aggravating rather than alleviating the housing problems of low-income groups; civil rights legislation has added to the sheaf of paper promises without making any notable dent in existing inequities; the poverty program begins to look like one more example of the fallacy of treating symptoms as if they were causes; and the traditional hostility between big government and big business has given way to a cozy partnership whereby the two enterprises have become almost indistinguishable in their interests.

The anarchists believed that man was a social creature, that he needed the affection and assistance of his fellows, and most anarchist versions of the good life (Max Stirner would be the major exception) involved the idea of community. The anarchists insisted, moreover, that it was not their vision of the future but rather society as presently constructed that represented chaos; with privilege the lot of the few and misery the lot of the many, society was currently the essence of *dis*order. The anarchists envisioned a system that would substitute mutual aid for mutual exploitation, voluntarism for force, individual decision making for centralized dictation.

All of these emphases find echo in SNCC and CORE. The echoes are not perfect: Black Power is above all a call to organization, and its acceptance of politics (and therefore of "governing") would offend a true anarchist—as would such collectivist terms as "black psyche" or "black personality." Nonetheless, the affinities of SNCC and CORE with the anarchist position are substantial.

There is, first of all, the same belief in the possibilities of community and the same insistence that community be the product of voluntary association. This, in turn, reflects a second and still more basic affinity: the distrust of centralized authority. SNCC's and CORE's energies, and also those of other New Left groups like Students for a Democratic Society (SDS), are increasingly channeled into local, community organizing. On this level, it's felt, participatory democracy, as opposed to the authoritarianism of representative democracy, becomes possible. And in the Black Panther Party, where the poor and disinherited do take a direct role in decision making, theory becoming reality at least in part—as, on the economic side, in the Mississippi-based Poor People's Corporation, which to date has formed some fifteen cooperatives.

Then, too, SNCC and CORE, like the anarchists, talk increasingly of the supreme importance of the individual. They do so, paradoxically, in a rhetoric strongly reminiscent of that long associated with the Right. It could be Herbert Hoover (or Booker T. Washington), but in fact it is Rap Brown who now reiterates the Negro's need to stand on his own two feet, to make his own decisions, to develop self-reliance and a sense of self-worth. The two ends of the political spectrum in this country have started to converge—at least in terms of vocabulary if not in terms of interests or goals. But the anarchist tradition is not of equal relevance to the New Left and to the traditional Right, except that it feeds their shared distrust of centralized power. The Right, however, has never been so much antiauthority as simply anti-one-kind-of-authority—that associated with the federal government. To the Right, authority has been bad when it emanates from Washington but good when associated with the Church, the Law, the schoolroom, the home, the Anglo-Saxon way. Far from being hostile to established opinion, the Right galvanizes its legions in its defense.

A final, more intangible affinity between anarchism and the entire New Left, including the advocates of Black Power, is in the area of personal style. Both hold up similar values for highest praise and emulation: simplicity, spontaneity, naturalness, and primitivism. Both reject modes of dress, music, personal relations, even of intoxication, which might be associated with the dominant middle-class culture. Both, finally, tend to link the basic virtues with "the people," and especially with the poor, the downtrodden, the alienated. It is this *lumpenproletariat*—long kept outside "the system" and thus purportedly uncorrupted by its values—that is looked to as a repository of virtue, an example of a better way. The New Left, even while demanding that the lot of the underclasses be improved, implicitly venerates that lot; the desire to cure poverty co-habits with the wish to emulate it.

The anarchist movement in the United States never made much headway. A few individuals—Benjamin Tucker, Adin Ballou, Lysander Spooner, Stephen Pearl Andrews, Emma Goldman, Josiah Warren—are still, in most cases faintly, remembered, but more for the style of their lives than for any impact on their society. It isn't difficult to see what prevented them from attracting a large following. Their very distaste for organization and power precluded the traditional modes for exerting influence. More important, their philosophy ran directly counter to the national hierarchy of values, a system of beliefs, conscious and otherwise, that has always impeded the drive for rapid change in this country. And it is a system that constitutes a roadblock at least as formidable today as at any previous point in our history.

This value structure stresses, first of all, the prime virtue of accumulation, chiefly of goods, but also of power and prestige. Any group—be it anarchists or New Leftists—that challenges the soundness of that goal, that suggests that it interferes with the more important pursuits of self-realization and human fellowship, presents so basic a threat to our national and individual identities as to invite almost automatic rejection.

A second obstacle that our value structure places in the path of radical change is its insistence on the benevolence of history. To the average American, human history is the story of automatic progress. Every day in every way we have gotten better and better. Ergo, there is no need for a frontal assault on our ills; time alone will be sufficient to cure them. Thus it is that many whites today consider the "Negro Problem" solved by the recent passage of civil rights legislation. They choose to ignore the fact that the daily lives of most Negroes have changed but slightly—or, as in the case of unemployment or imprisonment, for the worse. They ignore, too, the group of hard-core problems that have only recently emerged: maldistribution of income, urban slums, disparities in education and training, technological unemployment—problems that show no signs of yielding to time but that will require concentrated energy and resources for solution.

Without a massive assault on these basic ills, ours will continue to be a society where the gap between rich and poor widens, where the major rewards go to the few (who are not to be confused with the best). Yet it seems highly unlikely that the public pressure needed for such an assault will be forthcoming. Most Americans still prefer to believe that ours is either already the best of all possible worlds or will shortly, and without any special effort, become such. It is this deep-seated smugness, this intractable optimism, that must be reckoned with—that, indeed, will almost certainly destroy any call for substantive change.

A further obstacle facing the New Left, Black Power advocates and otherwise, is that their anarchist style and mood run directly counter to prevailing tendencies in our national life, especially those of conformity and centralization. The conformity has been commented on too often to bear repetition, except to point out that the young radicals' unorthodox mores (sexual, social, cultural) are in themselves enough to produce uneasiness and anger in the average American. In insisting on the right of the individual to please himself and to rely on his own judgment (whether in dress, speech, music, sex, or stimulants), SNCC and SDS may be solidly within the American tradition—indeed may be its mainstream—but this tradition is now more central to our rhetoric than to our behavior.

The anarchist focus in SNCC and SDS on decentralization, on

participatory democracy, and on community organizing likewise runs counter to dominant national trends. Consolidation, not dispersion, is currently king. There are some signs that a counterdevelopment has begun but as yet the overwhelming pattern continues to be consolidation. Both big government and big business are getting bigger and, more ominous still, are coming into ever-closer partnership. As Richard J. Barber has documented, the federal government not only is failing to block the growth of huge conglomerate firms by antitrust action but is contributing to that growth through procurement contracts and the exchange of personnel. The traditional hostility between business and government has rapidly drawn to a close. Washington is no longer interested in restraining the giant corporations, and the corporations have lost much of their fear of federal intentions. The two, in happy tandem, are moving the country still further along the road to oligopoly, militarism, economic imperialism, and greater privileges for the already privileged. The trend is so pronounced and there is so little effective opposition to it that it begins to take on an irrevocable, even irreversible quality.

In the face of these monoliths of national power, Black Power in Lowndes County is minuscule by comparison. Yet while the formation of the Black Panther Party in Lowndes brought out paroxysms of fear in the nation at large, the announcement that General Motors's 1965 sales totaled $21 billion—exceeding the gross national product of all but nine countries in the world—produced barely a tremor of apprehension. The unspoken assumption can only be something like this: it is less dangerous for a few whites to control the whole nation than for a local majority of Negroes to control their own community. The Kafkaesque nature of life in America continues to grow.

Black Power is both a product of our society and a repudiation of it. Confronted with the continuing indifference of the majority of whites to the Negro's plight, SNCC and CORE have lost faith in conscience and time, and have shifted to a position that the white majority finds infuriating. The nation as a whole—as in the case of the abolitionists over a hundred years ago—has created a climate in which earlier tactics no longer seem relevant, in which new directions become mandatory if frustration is to be met and hope maintained. And if the new turn proves a wrong one, if Black Power forecloses rather than animates further debate on the Negro's condition, if it destroys previous alliances without opening up promising new options, it is the nation as a whole that must bear the responsibility. There seems little likelihood that the American majority will admit to that responsibility. Let us at least hope it will not fail to recognize the rage that Black Power represents, to hear the message at the movement's core:

> *Sweethearts, the script has changed*
> *And with it the stage directions which advise*
> *Lowered voices, genteel asides.*
> *And the white hand slowly turning the dark page.*

—from *Partisan Review*, Winter 1968

Black Mountain College
and Community

To the extent that Black Mountain is known today it's as the site of a now-defunct experimental college/community located in the foothills of North Carolina, the forerunner and exemplar of much that is currently considered innovative in art, education, and lifestyle. It's known, too, as the refuge, in some cases the nurturing ground, for many of the singular, shaping talents of our time: John Cage, Merce Cunningham, Buckminster Fuller, Willem de Kooning, Franz Kline, Charles Olson, Josef Albers, Anni Albers, Paul Goodman, and Robert Rauschenberg. The life of Black Mountain and the work of these people have often been discussed as if they were interchangeable parts; the tendency has not been to delineate a relationship but to contrive a parable.

During Black Mountain's twenty-three-year existence (1933–1956), the famous were indeed there—sometimes for long periods (fifteen years in the case of Josef and Anni Albers) and sometimes engaged in exploring dimensions of their work (like John Cage's mixed-media event in 1952) that have significantly affected the actuality as well as the mythology of American cultural life. Such individuals did much to create the aura of originality and flamboyance ever since associated with Black Mountain's name. But in most cases—Albers and Olson are the chief exceptions—they were only peripherally connected with the continuities of daily life in the community.

A full history of Black Mountain is more intricate and poignant than a recitation of the famous names associated with it. It's the story of a small group of men and women—ranging through time from a dozen to a hundred, most of them anonymous as judged by standard measurements of achievement—who attempted to find some consonance between their ideas and their lives, who risked the intimacy and exposure that most of us emotionally yearn for and rhetorically defend but in practice shun. Black Mountain shifted focus, personnel, definitions, and strategies so often that its history is unified by little more than a disdain for life as usually lived and some unsettled notions—sometimes confused and self-glamorizing, sometimes startlingly courageous—as to how it might be made different and better.

At its best, Black Mountain showed the possibilities of a disparate group of individuals committing themselves to a common enterprise, resilient enough to absorb the conflicts entailed, brave enough, now and then, to be transformed by its accompanying energies. At its worst, the community consisted of little more than a group of squabbling prima donnas—many professional, others in training. Black Mountain proved a bitter experience for some, a confirmation of Emerson's view that "we descend to meet"— that close human association compounds rather than obliterates the drive toward power, aggression, and cruelty. For others Black Mountain provided a glimpse—rarely a sustained vision—of how diversity and commonality, the individual and the group, are reinforcing rather than contradictory phenomena.

As I went through the 100,000 documents relating to the community that are housed in The State Archives at Raleigh, North Carolina, and as I traveled the country tape recording interviews with people, the particularity of each experience startled—even overwhelmed me. I consider such diversity a tribute to Black Mountain—to the innumerable possibilities it called out. But others may prefer to ascribe it to my conceptual deficiencies, or to my temperamental distrust of sociological generalization. In any case, this is yet another individual response to Black Mountain; it is not the last word or the whole word, but *my* word. Researching the history of Black Mountain has generated feelings in me that have subtly affected the balance I've struck on every page. Since all balances are to some extent a betrayal, I've felt the final responsibility of letting *myself* be known. My conviction is that when historians allow more of themselves to show—feelings, reactions, fantasies, not merely skills at information-retrieval, organization and analysis—they are *less* likely to contaminate the data simply because there is less pretense that they and it are one.

Some will take exception to that last as self-indulgence. Yet the issue is not, I believe, *whether* the individual historian should appear in his books, but *how* s/he should appear—covertly or overtly. Every historian knows that s/he manipulates the evidence to some extent simply because of who s/he is (or is not), of what s/he selects (or omits), of how well (or badly) s/he empathizes and communicates. Those fallibilities have been frequently confessed in the abstract. Yet the process by which a particular personality intersects with a particular subject matter has rarely been shown, and the intersection itself almost never regarded as containing materials of potential worth. Because "objectivity" has been the ideal, the personal components that go into historical reconstruction have not been candidly revealed, or made accessible to scrutiny.

I believe it's time historians put their personalities as well as their names to their books—their personalities are in them anyway, however disguised and diluted by the profession's deceptive anonymities. To my mind the harshest indictment that can be made of academic historical writing is its refusal to acknowledge, other than in the most pro forma way, that a person is writing about other people—a person, not an IBM machine or a piece of blotting paper.

To say that a historian is inescapably in his/her own books and that s/he has the obligation to admit it, is not yet to show how s/he could include themselves in a way that might better serve the documentation and the reader. This book is an effort at such a demonstration.

There have been many pitfalls along the way. The most constant struggle has been to avoid mere self-revelation, belaboring the personal to the point where it eclipses the narrative. I've preferred to run that risk, however, rather than adhere to the traditional pretense of nonexistence. I believe (to paraphrase Fritz Stern) that although we may not learn from history, we *might* learn from historians—might, that is, if historians put themselves into relationship with their materials whereby each is explored in conjunction with the other.

For historians to use themselves in such a way, would make historical writing a considerably more risky enterprise than is currently the case. Risky not because the subject would be revealed less, but because the historian would be exposed more. To try to show up in one's work instead of distancing oneself from it, to remove the protections of anonymity, can be searing. Yet harnessing one's emotional resources to one's academic work can help to release them in one's life—or can make one aware for the first time of how limited those resources in fact are.

The 1930s: John Andrew Rice

If the charge that John Andrew Rice wore a jockstrap on the beach had come earlier in the hearings, it might have seemed bizarre. But it was so much of a piece with the preceding allegations that it hardly caused a ripple. Among the charges already leveled at Rice was that he had called a chisel one of the world's most beautiful objects, had whispered in chapel, had proposed that male and female students be paired off on arrival at college, had labeled public debates "a pernicious form of intellectual perversion," had put "obscene" pictures on the walls of his classroom, had an "indolent" walk, had left fish scales in the sink after using the college's beach cottage, and—*reductio ad absurdum*—had helped to alienate one young lady from her sorority.

Hamilton Holt, president of Rollins College, read these and other complaints aloud, hour after hour, before a two-man investigating committee from the American Association of University Professors (AAUP) in 1933. No one doubted that Rice was iconoclastic and outspoken (Rice paid others the great compliment of acting as if they, like him, were eager to question the guiding assumptions of their lives, and to that end would be willing to dispense with the usual protective discretion of polite conversation), but Holt had fired Rice as professor of classics on the grounds that he was "disruptive of peace and harmony" on the campus. Rice had appealed his case to the AAUP, and, after prolonged deliberations, the AAUP representatives decided in his favor, concluding that Rice had been "an unusually stimulating and effective teacher."

Rice nonetheless concluded that he had no place in a conventional college and decided, along with a small group of dissident faculty and students, to start a new college in which they could try out their innovative ideas. Nestled in the low hills overlooking the town of Black Mountain they discovered a set of buildings, dominated by the huge, white-columned Lee Hall and with an extraordinary view over the valley, available for a modest annual rental of $4,500. The religious group, the Blue Ridge Assembly, owned the buildings but used them only during the summer as a resort-conference site for its members. "Mac" Forbes, who came from a wealthy New England family and had been on the Rollins faculty, came up with the needed funds.

Classes, however, couldn't begin until it first became clear how the community saw its purposes and then decided what procedures would best implement them. The process of clarification began immediately, since living, unlike classes, couldn't wait. A variety of vague ideas were afloat as to how an ideal community should organize itself, and in the opening weeks these were presented, argued about, and voted on—though in fact votes were few, since it was widely agreed that organization and structure should be kept to a minimum lest Black Mountain go the way of most institutions, achieving codification at the expense of aliveness.

It was intended from the start that the students share in the power and responsibility for running the community. The search for ways to implement this began immediately. By spring of the first year, formal amendments had been introduced into the bylaws entitling any member of the college to inspect all records of the corporation, establishing the right of the student body to adopt a constitution for its own governance, guaranteeing all student officers the right to be present and heard at regular faculty meetings, and assigning its chief officer (the student moderator) actual membership on the Board of Fellows.

There was no pretense, at least on Rice's part, that this amount of student representation was the equivalent of pure democracy. Though students from the start had a larger formal voice in decision making than was (or is) true at most colleges, they didn't have an equal voice with the faculty—indeed some faculty members, namely those on the Board of Fellows, were more equal than others. All that Black Mountain College (BMC) ever claimed was that in at least one sense Black Mountain came as near to a democracy as possible: individual economic status had nothing to do with one's standing in the community. The guiding ideal was the Quaker "sense of the meeting": the community achieving consensus on a given issue, and the decision then implemented by its chosen representatives. As long as the community felt an identity of interests—as long as faculty and students felt their views were genuinely represented by the governing board—no major problems would arise.

From the first, there were few rules at Black Mountain and no social regulations beyond the implicit and difficult injunction to "behave intelligently," to assume individual responsibility for all relationships entered into—regardless of their duration or intensity. A "Do Not Disturb" sign on a study door was all that one needed to guarantee privacy—that and the limitless woods. Sex was not one of Black Mountain's major preoccupations during the thirties either as a topic or an activity. Testimony on that account is pretty much unanimous. There were, of course, romances and pairings-off, and also, of course, the usual intense speculations about them. One male student who arrived at Black Mountain in the late thirties put the matter to me flatly: there was "practically no casual or promiscuous sex at BMC the years I was there—we were much too serious about everything, including each other, and I think there was a certain puritan quality about much of the life." Continual contact between males and females probably helped to put sex into perspective: when so many facets of living are shared, when affection and energy find numerous outlets, sex is asked to do fewer duties, is more likely to become an aspect of relating.

But before many months had passed, the local people of Black Mountain village let it be known that they were upset by the "goings-on" at the college. To the suspicion that the community was a godless place practicing free love was soon added the rumor that it was a nudist colony as well: students often wore shorts in warm weather, and several appeared in town, at a movie, a square dance, or while shopping wearing sandals that revealed bare feet.

Although there were few rules—legislated procedures—freedom was circumscribed by a strong sense of what was or was not acceptable form. A favorite comment, widely and approvingly quoted in the community, was that Black Mountain stressed "informality within a form." Unspoken canons proved as strongly regulative in some areas of community life as any formal set of rules would have. It was understood (though never formally agreed to in a community or student meeting) that on Saturday evening everyone would dress up for dinner; that one would regularly attend classes unless actually sick; that one would not leave the college while it was in session for more than an afternoon or an evening; and that one would not indulge sexual appetites promiscuously, homosexually, or bisexually.

The BMC community was so small and its intentions as yet so undefined that opinion could be sounded and accommodated with ease. And the enthusiasm that comes with any new venture— especially if touched, as in Black Mountain's case, with the peril and joy of shared experimentation, poverty, and isolation—helped to overcome differences and to encourage generosity toward fellow pioneers. They felt, in those early days, that they were starting life anew, that in some uncertain way they were part of a revolutionary vanguard.

Within little more than a month, the Black Mountain community had established rough guidelines for governance and some tentative beginnings of a lifestyle. Few wanted more than that. Detailing, most agreed, was best left to the future, after the community had had more chance to formulate and test its purposes. Where and how community organization might require modifying would depend on what needs developed; by keeping structure to a minimum, values would have a chance to shape institutional features rather than, as is more usually the case, the institution molding the values.

This was felt with special force with regard to education, which was, after all, central to Black Mountain's founding and to its sense of common purpose. Their guru, John Dewey, understood that "to arrive at a conclusion was not to arrive at a conclusion, it was to arrive at a pause. And you would look at the pause, you would gaze at the plateau, and then you would see another thing to climb." Education, in this view, was never completed.

The one most common attitude was that living and learning should be intertwined. All aspects of community life were thought to have a bearing on an individual's education—that is, his or her becoming aware of who they were and wanted to be. Education should proceed everywhere, not only in classroom settings—which, in fact, at least as usually structured, were considered among the worst learning environments imaginable. A favorite slogan at Black Mountain was that "as much real education took place over the coffee cups as in the classrooms." The usual distinctions between curricular and extracurricular activities, between work done in a classroom and work done outside it, were broken down. Helping to fight a forest fire side by side with faculty members, participating in a community discussion on whether the dining hall should serve two or three meals on Sundays, discovering that a staff member was a homosexual or that married life included arguments as well as (and sometimes during) intercourse, taking part in an improvisational evening of acting out grudges against other community members—all these and a hundred more experiences, most of them the more vivid for being unplanned, contributed at least as much to individual awareness and growth as did traditional academic exercises.

This didn't mean that disparities of age, interest, knowledge, and experience between, say, a twenty-year-old and a fifty-year-old weren't recognized, or that it was thought either possible or desirable to merge all members of the community into some false concord of "buddyhood." But it did mean that many at Black Mountain believed that differences in age need not preclude communication, that interests could be shared, that the perspective of the young also had value. It meant, too, that while information, analytical skills, and reason were prized, they were considered aspects rather than equivalents of personal development; they were not confused, in other words—as they are in most educational institutions—with the whole of life, the only elements of self worthy of development and praise.

A central aim was to keep the community small enough so that members could constantly interact in a wide variety of settings—not only at meals, but on walks, in classes, at community meetings, work programs, dances, performances, whatever. Individual lifestyles, in all their peculiar detail, could thereby be observed, challenged, imitated, rejected—which is, after all, how most learning proceeds, rather than through formal academic instruction. "You're seeing people under all circumstances daily," as Rice put it, "and after a while you get to the point where you don't mind being seen yourself, and that's a fine moment."

It was hoped that a double sense of responsibility would emerge out of the varied contacts and opportunities Black Mountain provided: that which an individual owes to the group of which s/he is a member, and that which is owed to oneself—with neither submerging the other. From the beginning Black Mountain emphasized the social responsibilities that come from being part of a community, yet tried to see to it that personal freedom wouldn't be sacrificed to group needs. Rice, for one, liked to stress how different each person was from every other and how expectations of performance should vary accordingly. In trying to strike a balance between the needs of an individual and those of the group, Rice's instinct was to give preference to the individual.

Adults tended to bring out Rice's peremptory side more than students did. He showed greater patience with twenty-year-olds because he had greater faith in their ability to change, and where growth was possible Rice preferred to issue invitations rather than commands. He realized that many young people had already given up on themselves by the time they reached college. The wreckage could be terrible, the stupefaction total—and for Rice it was always harder to be nice to the stupefied than to the merely stupid, for the stupefied, as he put it, had "collaborated to a certain extent."

But he tried. He tried hard, because he deeply believed, despite his occasional cynicism to the contrary, that almost every young person could be salvaged. First create a climate of liberty, Rice would say—that is, remove the usual lists of dos and don'ts—and then "surround the person with one invitation after another," not only invitations to literature, art, music, and the like, but also "to be a good, pleasant, respectable person to have around, and that's a very nice invitation; it's not beyond most people." It might take a long time before those who'd grown up in a poverty-stricken environment, who'd been severely deprived or damaged, would respond, and some few would never respond, but Rice (like his contemporary A.S. Neill, the founder of the Summerhill School in England) firmly believed that in time the large majority would. His faith was based on the premise that at birth "we are all artists, every one of us: we are free to create the kind of world in which we choose to live, and we're equal in that freedom." For the artist in each person to develop, freedom from manipulation was a prerequisite; the student should be placed in competition with himself, not others.

In consonance with that philosophy, there were no fixed regulations at Black Mountain—no required courses, no system of frequent examinations, no formal grading. For the first ten days of classes, students were encouraged to "shop around," to sit in on classes, sample possibilities, and then decide on a schedule. Responsibility, in other words, was placed on the students themselves for deciding what shape their education would take—though the faculty made itself available for consultation.

Classes at Black Mountain were always small. Every teacher had complete freedom in choosing his classroom methods. Occasionally someone would lecture, but the overwhelming preference was for small discussion groups. There was also greater adherence in the beginning to a prescribed schedule: classes met between eight-thirty and twelve-thirty (usually for an hour) in the morning and again between four and six in the afternoon. The period from lunchtime until four was deliberately kept free so that people could get out of doors. Some would take part in the work program, cutting wood, digging on the farm, helping to improve the college road. There was no organized sports program, but there were tennis courts, an outdoor pool, a small lake on the college property, a fairly well-equipped gym with handball and basketball courts, horses for rent in the village, and everywhere mountain trails for hikes and walks. At about three-thirty every day, most of the community would gather in the huge Lee Hall lobby for tea and talk before resuming classes. An invention of the second or third year was the "interlude"—a periodic announcement, without advance warning, that all classes would cease for a week so that everyone could have a chance to try something they'd had to defer because of lack of time, whether reading George Bernard Shaw, attempting to write poetry, or sitting in the sun.

The arts, it was felt, were essential in developing individuals capable of choosing because "they are, when properly employed, least subject to direction from without and yet have within them a severe discipline of their own." They taught, in other words, that the worthwhile struggle was the interior one—not against one's fellows but against one's "own ignorance and clumsiness." The integrity an artist learns when dealing with materials translates into an integrity of relationship with oneself and with other people.

The 1940s: "Community"

In the spring of 1945, John Wallen, completing his doctorate at Harvard in psychology, arrived to teach at Black Mountain. He was young (twenty-seven) and glad of it, youth being one leg of a trinity completed by "enthusiasm and idealism"; and he'd had enough experience teaching in a traditional university to be pretty much convinced that they were "a dead end as far as making a genuine contribution to the growth of the students is concerned . . . the mechanized, mass-production university system does not have room in it for human values."

Everywhere, Wallen continued, he'd found segmented specialties, compartmentalized people, and a bureaucratic structure that emphasized grades, requirements, and subject matter at the expense of helping an individual to integrate—make personal sense out of—his experiences. Everywhere he'd found men who prated of democracy while exercising autocratic control, who talked fluently of man's noble potential but in fact doubted its existence. He'd therefore decided, Wallen wrote, that life in a standard university wasn't what he wanted for himself, his wife and baby—or for his students. He wanted to teach at a place that gave actual rather than rhetorical allegiance to individual growth. He'd heard that Black Mountain was such a place.

A successful teacher, in Wallen's view, set in process a cycle of "readjustment and reevaluation" that was lifelong. Which meant, obversely, that a teacher's function was *not* to encourage the mere accumulation of information, nor to decide the comparative value of different kinds of knowledge on the basis of his own rather than the student's needs. The student must not be "drawn aside from real-life experiences and carefully nurtured in a high-pressure, hot-house existence," for that would separate him from understanding "what creative living can be. Living is an end in itself; all other activities are—to a greater or lesser degree—means to that end. The prime function of knowledge and education, then, is to make living meaningful—both in terms of personal values and of interpersonal relations (if there is any distinction)."

John and his wife Rachel Wallen's initial impressions of the college were very favorable. They liked almost everything they heard: that there was no formal code of rules, the entire community agreeing at the beginning of each year what its guiding principles were to be; and that there were no organized athletics, but instead a work program vital to the college's continued survival—hence *meaningful* work, instilling group responsibility for a common fate. Life and learning were closely integrated, with constant contact between students and faculty; no degrees, no grades, no requirements—" 'the student is the curriculum'—and the teacher free to teach what he wants in any way he wants." The emphasis was on the *person*, with various means of communication and self-expression—not simply the verbal—utilized: painting, music, dance, weaving, theater. "The whole community—college life implies an integration and purpose that is sadly lacking in our culture."

He wasn't seeking a utopia, Wallen insisted. He was excited at the prospect of "a free, informal, and exploratory setting," the chance to work "hunches and ideas through in group give-and-take." Here at last seemed a chance to face the problems that "lie submerged under the morass of accumulated tradition in the wider culture." "I despise the values underlying our present society," Wallen wrote his friends, "I am disgusted by the cheap, careless, vulgar uses to which man puts his 'marvelous' achievements. . . . Somebody wrote that a cynic criticizes out of disillusion while a skeptic criticizes out of a belief in something better. Then I am a skeptic. I have a belief . . . I have a faith."

Black Mountain had become used to critics (both within and without the community) mocking its ideals. It had not yet had to deal with someone who took those ideals, quite literally, at face value.

The Wallens's stay at Black Mountain has raised some large questions for me. His career there as resident "collective visionary" (the phrase is Arthur Penn's) focuses many of the questions that originally attracted me to a study of the place: Is there a conflict between "individualism" and community? Can an "artist" survive—would he want to survive—the innumerable petty issues and responsibilities that come with communal living? Can one live fully and well with others and at the same time "produce"? What do people need? Do their needs differ? Does everyone, despite his "neurotic" distancing, want closeness, or is the desire for closeness itself a cultural phenomenon? Would most people seek solitude—along with intermittent contact with a few significant others—if the culture didn't tell them that solitude is the equivalent of disturbance or, alternately, that a capacity for continuous intimacy is the surest gauge of "health"?

Are there specific techniques of "group process" that can be utilized for improving communication—thus detoxifying tensions that arise between people of divergent tastes and goals? Does "honesty" aid in working out aggressions—or does it compound them? Why does anyone want to live in a "community" anyway? Why does the impulse continually reassert itself historically—and with special force in the United States? Is the impulse merely negative, as is often claimed—that is, in the nineteenth century, an "escape *from* industrialization" or today, a retreat *from* materialism and manipulation? Or do people look to communes to satisfy positive yearnings for contact and sharing? If so (or even if not) what kinds of people develop the impulse? Those whose gifts happen to be in the area of personal relationships rather than, say, in composition, color, mechanics or words? Do communities draw people who want to be "nice" and repulse people who want to be "distinctive"? Can (must?) a community serve only one kind of impulse? Is it incompatible with other "drives"—competition, personal aggrandizement, privacy and variety (the last two not necessarily contradictory, if one assumes, as I do, that people can derive special pleasure from alternating between, or even mixing together, supposed opposites)?

So many questions, most of them obviously unanswerable given how little anyone knows about human needs—indeed whether they exist, apart from what the culture (itself ever-changing) happens to say they are, or should be, at a given moment.

Wallen enjoyed his classes at Black Mountain more than any he'd ever had. Given complete freedom to teach as he wished, he used no text at all in the introductory class, and in the other, dispensed with the usual obligation to "cover" set topics in a set period of time; instead he let each discussion spin itself out, always emphasizing the people *present* in the room, the need to "develop skills in understanding and getting along with ourselves and others."

Wallen generally used the conceptual framework of Otto Rank, as adapted in the work of Fromm, Rogers, Allen, Horney, and others, stressing the

> dualisms that characterize personal lives, e.g., one's past—one's present; determinism—freedom of choice; thought—action; desire for predictability, similarity, certainty—desire for variety, difference, challenge; self (independence, striving for individuality, fear of being submerged by group)—others (dependence, striving for acceptance and belonging, fear of separation and aloneness). How a person copes with the inherent conflict between these polarities determines whether it is a source of creativity or of unproductive, repetitive behavior (neurosis). Acceptance and integration of both sides of the dualism leads to creative accomplishment. Rejection of and a continuing struggle to deny or avoid either side blocks achievement. This is applicable to a community, group or organization as well as to an individual.

For one session, the class read Sophocles's *Oedipus Rex*, discussed Freud's conception of the Oedipus complex and how it had been modified by the work of Malinowski, Horney, and Allen, and then analyzed the play (as Rank himself did) in terms of will-conflict, stressing the theme that "as an individual gains increased self-knowledge, he must accept increased responsibility for his own behavior."

The students, turned on by Wallen's youth and zeal, his knowledge of the latest literature, and his enormous interest in *them*, responded enthusiastically. Some of the older ones, returned GIs

who in several cases were close to Wallen in age, were a little uncomfortable with his easy dismissal of Freudian pessimism, with his
apparent belief that human competitiveness, violence, and power
strivings were not instinctive, but cultural. Wallen argued that
such traits resulted from learned social behavior and that human
"aggression"—that catchall term used by conservatives to cover and
confuse what in fact is a wide variety of biological mechanisms,
themselves variously shaped by the stimuli exerted upon them—
could, with the "right" kind of learning, be channeled into a drive
for self-mastery that complemented the simultaneous search for af-
filiative ties to other people.

Though not himself an original thinker (his formulations, in
fact, could be simplistic), Wallen was an early exponent of what has
been called the naive, American side of a debate on human aggression that has gathered increasing momentum since the mid-1940s
and has led to a large literature and to a pronounced split within the
ranks of behavioral scientists. The split has never been a clear-cut
one between "optimistic" Americans (Ashley Montagu, say, or Gor-
don Allport or Carl Rogers) arguing for genetic indeterminacy and
the possibilities of a cooperative society, and "pessimistic" Europeans (Konrad Lorenz, say, or Desmond Morris or Anthony Storr)
insisting that our appetites for competition and violence are instinctive. Indeed none of the work of even those individuals should be
simplemindedly categorized as pro- or antigenetic determinacy. Yet
despite the subtleties in position and the fact that some of the major
figures (B.F. Skinner, for example, or A.S. Neill) don't conform at
all to the standard "American" or "European" divisions, that polarity *has* been an essential element in the debate from its inception.

The German-born Josef Albers's distrust of Wallen was
grounded in the belief that one had to limit the number of ingredients in one's life, had to intensely preoccupy oneself with a few
concerns—like color—if one was ever to master them. Albers's hope
was that at Black Mountain everyone would become preoccupied,
that it would become a community of artists. And if it did, then
internal discipline would supersede the need for external rules. He

suspected those who elevated "dialogue" and cooperative enterprises into primary values; instead of eliminating disagreements,
they eliminated the concentration needed to produce art.

Wallen, on his side, was not against "art," and in fact was an
admirer of Albers's own work. Yet if it ever had to come to a choice
between, say, building a society that fulfilled the basic needs of most
people or one dedicated to producing "high art," Wallen would
doubtless have opted for the needs of the many as against the imaginative works of the few. The issues really did go that deep, though
when argued as they typically were at Black Mountain, in terms
of whether or not to package mountain laurel, it's as easy to understand the tedium and annoyance felt by those who focused on
the particulars of the debate as it is to understand the passion and
anguish of those who sensed, even if they couldn't articulate it, the
central thrust of what lay beneath.

"Community" was a word with a long history at Black Mountain, but it had almost always been used in a limited context: to
describe the set of relationships among the hundred-odd people in
residence at the college. The "other" community—the one beyond
the walls—was periodically acknowledged, but a blend of apprehension ("They'll burn us down") and disdain ("They're incapable of
understanding us") had kept contact minimal. A group of local music lovers from Asheville and its environs would attend concerts, and
during the war there was considerable contact with the veterans'
hospital in the area (itself, of course, another "foreign" enclave). But
the overwhelming, often self-conscious emphasis at Black Mountain
was interior. It centered on individual reality: "Am I growing?" "Am
I fulfilling my potential?" "Do November's drawings show an advance over September's?"

For Wallen, community meant what went on *both* within the college and between the college and its neighbors; and he viewed Black
Mountain's isolation from its local setting as a scandal. "At any moment," Wallen said to me, "you are some place in time and some
place in space. And it seems to me your experience ought to somehow reflect this and also manifest concern for that environment you

inhabit. . . . But Black Mountain was almost as if it wasn't any place in time and space."

Formulated in that way, Wallen's position sounds incontrovertible: *of course* people should be involved in whatever time and space they find themselves. In fact, though, the operative choice isn't *whether* to become active but in which areas and in what ways. Unless one equates the regional environment with the total sum of "time and space" (as Wallen tended to), it's clear that all of us are always involved in a variety of "spaces," interior as well as exterior, and that their demands often conflict. Indeed for some people—and I tend to think for *everyone*, potentially, were it not that most of us are conditioned to view ourselves as "ordinary"—the challenge is to create a time/space configuration never quite seen before, one representative of our own unique fantasies, needs, and talents. For people to concentrate their energies on reality as defined by the local social milieu (to picket the Lucky Strike plant, for example, because of its labor practices—an actual issue at Black Mountain during Wallen's stay) is perhaps to jeopardize their chance of developing that special configuration—one that needn't result in any product (like a painting or a poem) other than themselves, one that might make their own days richer and eventually, indirectly, depending on the force of that configuration, even end up by changing local "reality" as well.

Not that one can (or should) settle priorities on a fixed scale for all time. The focus of urgency shifts continuously, as now personal matters, now public ones, seem to demand primary consideration; ideally—if priorities haven't been rigidly set—energies can be readjusted accordingly. At Black Mountain, the priorities had earlier been set: individual "cultivation" took precedence over public issues, local or national, and to achieve status in the community one had to "cultivate" fiercely—to be *unusually* original, dynamic, fertile, cogent. For many—those either without special talent or long trained to believe they lacked it—terrible insecurity and a deep sense of worthlessness could develop.

Yet, oppositely, many students (*not* Albers's) could be overly indulgent of one another's pretensions. So long as one was going through the motions of "writing a novel" or "working in oils," s/he was often allowed the identity of artist. That could be enormously supportive for those who wanted to try on a role, a talent, or a commitment; Kenneth Noland, the painter, has often been cited to me as an example of a Black Mountain student who was allowed to conceive of himself as an artist at a time when he was not—thereby helping him to become one. Yet on the other hand, the students' willingness to validate each other's fantasies could be destructive for those who in fact lacked exceptional gifts and who might otherwise have made more realistic decisions about their life's work—thereby being saved, in the long run, a great deal of floundering and anguish.

In Wallen's view, the climate at Black Mountain could prevent authentic growth in yet another sense. People became known in such a wide variety of situations that it became difficult to separate them out, to recognize the changes someone might have undergone in one particular sector; experiences of each other were so continuous that despite their diversity, they tended to blend. Wallen put the problem this way: "The high degree of communication within the community binds you to your past, to your selves in other situations." That, in turn, could lead to defeatism, to passivity and indifference, to a decrease in the motivation and standards of work.

These were the students Wallen most cared about: the ones who lacked the gifts, courage, interest, or brass to compete for status as "artists," or whose tentative efforts to do so went unrecognized. They were also the students who migrated naturally to Wallen, seeing in him an alternative set of values wherein they might find some purpose, some validation of worth, which the established climate at Black Mountain denied them. One young student, who described herself to me as "more conventional than the rest" (though in her high school she had been considered the oddball), couldn't find any way to make a niche for herself at Black Mountain, not being sufficiently eccentric, original, or rebellious to attract attention; she doubted if she "would have gotten through it," she told me, if

Wallen hadn't been around to let her know that he liked her and valued her.

Because of what they thought of as an overemphasis on individual artistic achievement, the Wallenites tended to describe Black Mountain as "elitist" and to link that orientation to European "snobbery" and self-absorption. As a counterideal, they posited a cooperative democracy "in which the discovery of meaningful aspects of the self could take place through activities designated as socially useful," and they viewed that orientation, with its emphasis on "doing good," as peculiarly American. Despite the numerous exceptions and objections that can validly be cited against that duality, it does seem to me to contain some truth.

Yet I think another contrast could be made, one not dependent on national distinctions, that perhaps goes deeper: between those who see the world as a stage for shaping and dramatizing the self—a world whose events are in some ultimate sense illusory if they cannot be made an occasion for individual performance—and those who accept the *world's* definition of reality, internalizing its categories and laboring in its causes with a literalness that seems to have only peripheral relation to the effort of self-definition. Those primarily engaged with the self can be comfortably dismissed as narcissistic only if one believes that the world's issues (unlike selves) are nonrepetitive *and* capable of resolution. Those primarily committed to issues can be comfortably categorized as prosaic only if one's obsession with forging a self actually eventuates in a distinguishable shape.

Black Mountain had always been dedicated to two enterprises—establishing a community in which people shared common purposes and responsibilities, and creating a climate in which art of the highest excellence might flourish. The possible incompatibility of those enterprises had never been fully exposed until Wallen's arrival because no one had been as much of a purist on the community side as Albers had long been on the artistic side. As Wallen pushed his views, the sense began to grow that a choice did have to be made between the two enterprises, or at least a set of priorities established in which the one took clear precedence over the other.

Emerson once wrote in relation to Brook Farm that "[t]he only candidates who will present themselves will be those who have tried the experiment of independence and ambition, and have failed; and none others will barter for the most comfortable equality the chance of superiority. Then all communities have quarreled. Few people can live together on their merits." I, for one, see no reason why choice *had* to be viewed as a necessity; it can be argued that much of Black Mountain's previous history—indeed future existence as well—had demonstrated that no choice need be made, that "art" and "community" could coexist, could even be mutually supportive. But the self-consciousness and polarization produced by Wallen's presence (and above all, by Albers's negative reaction to him), for a time made "community" and "art" appear antagonistic forces. "Group process" became a dirty word to the art crowd, and "creativity" a selfish cop-out to the advocates of community.

Wallen sought to demonstrate that individual development in the arts and responsible group membership were complementary, not contradictory, goals. There's been a long history (the Swedish adventure playgrounds, for example)—and there would be many more examples in the sixties (Lama Foundation, Hog Farm, Woodstock)—of efforts to show that individuality and community can develop in tandem. That *any* such evidence exists in a Western culture that for centuries has stressed the supreme virtues of aggrandizement and competition can be considered remarkable. That the fugitives from middle-class life who made up the Black Mountain community could, more often than not, contribute their energies to a common enterprise, could regard their personal development as bound up with association, could try to negotiate (or at the least, ignore) the continual hostilities generated by the hothouse environment, is more astonishing than the fact that the community was sometimes characterized by those interpersonal antagonisms *central* to the social system from which it emerged—and from which it tried to separate.

Given the resistance within the college and the slow going he found in trying to implement change, Wallen increasingly turned his attention to his second communal concern—the relationship of the college to the surrounding area. Some people thought he ought to "let sleeping dogs lie," that since Black Mountain was a strange creature, establishing relations with the outside community could only lead to heightened antagonism (along with consuming valuable time and energy better put elsewhere). But Wallen preferred the observation of a friend of his that "treating a community as an oasis in the midst of a desert or wilderness is a rather futile endeavor. It becomes a refuge far more than a point of growth and development in the culture of the region."

In trying to increase points of contact with the neighboring area, Wallen "had no support from the faculty—none," one of his student admirers later insisted. Regardless, he continued to urge students to increase their experience of the surrounding world and to make concrete commitments to it. One student volunteered to serve as a companion two afternoons a week to a "schizophrenic" girl of about her own age who was a patient in a nearby mental hospital—and did so for a whole term, despite having to walk two miles each time to the bus stop. Other Wallen students got involved with the Southern Negro Youth Congress, took petitions around the region, and attempted to work on voter registration.

When Wallen would ask what kind of education Black Mountain stood for, he was usually told it didn't stand *for* anything—"They'd say, for instance, 'We don't have grades,' 'We don't have required courses,' etc., etc." Wallen did continue to feel that relationships between students and teachers at Black Mountain were "much more human" than at most places—people tended to meet as people rather than as pieces in the ancient mandarin game called Classroom. All that was to the good—but not good enough. Wallen's expectations were high—an occupational hazard with utopians; and he measured success not against the failures of preceding educational or communal enterprises but against his hopes for ideal future ones.

Intimate living conditions can militate against closeness if one's background has conditioned one to be wary of "closeness," to associate it with suffocation—a background common in a culture where parents are so likely to put the label "love" on what in fact are gestures of control. Many have started the effort at living together burdened by emotional memories that link intimacy with constriction. Whether close living ends by heightening trust or distrust finally depends on the particular values and skills of the particular people involved.

Wallen stuck it out at Black Mountain for several years, but finally concluded that the European faculty members especially were unwilling to make the needed investment in building human relations, were much less willing than the Americans to explore and share feelings on a personal level. Though he resigned from Black Mountain, Wallen for the rest of his life would persist in believing that "it's possible to have a group who would live closely together and would develop a relationship that would be a virtuous circle instead of a vicious circle. . . ."

The 1950s: The First "Happening": (or How History Is Really Written)

Of all the Zen texts John Cage had run across, the Huang Po seemed to him "the essential one." When he decided to read it aloud at BMC, several of the twenty to thirty people who attended (out of a community swelled to about seventy for the summer session) assisted him, especially in acting out the dialogue section where the teacher insults the student (a section Cage has since imitated in part of a text, "Experimental Music: Doctrine," printed in his collection *Silence*). Cage felt that the effect on those attending the reading was profound—especially for a Korean war vet "at his wits' end," and for another student "at a puzzled point" in his life circumstance.

Implicit in the Huang Po Doctrine of Universal Mind is the postulate that the centricity within each event is not dependent on other events. That same postulate is critical in the work of Antonin Artaud, who Cage had recently discovered. In Cage's mind, Huang Po and Artaud (along with Marcel Duchamp's doctrine that the work of art is completed by the observer) "all fused together into the possibility of making a theatrical event in which the things that took place were not causally related to one another—but in which there is a penetration, anything that happened after that happened in the observer himself." The idea developed in conversation between Cage and David Tudor—"and our ideas were so electric at that time," Cage told me, "that once the idea hit my head—and I would like to give David Tudor equal credit for it—I immediately then implemented it." Taking into account the resources of talent in the community, he outlined various time brackets, totaling forty-five minutes, on a piece of paper and invited various people to fill them. (Cage persists to this day in referring to his outline and organization as having been done "by means of chance operations"—reminding me of David Weinrib's comment that the strange thing about listening to ten of Cage's musical compositions is that despite his insistence on their "indeterminate" origins, all ten pieces could *only* have come from John Cage.

To fill the time brackets, Cage invited Charles Olson and Mary Caroline Richards to read their poetry, Rauschenberg to show his paintings and also to play recordings of his choice, David Tudor to perform on the piano any compositions he wanted, and Merce Cunningham to dance. Each person was left free, within his precisely defined time slot, to do whatever he chose to do. Cage's aim, in his words, was "purposeless purposefulness: it was purposeful in that we knew what we were going to do, but it was purposeless in that we didn't know what was going to happen in the total." In retrospect, he contrasts his procedure with those later "happenings" for which the 1952 event has been widely viewed as "prehistoric" pacesetter.

Yet by establishing rigid time brackets for each participant, and by scheduling the event for a particular time in a particular space (the dining hall), Cage had superimposed an intentional structure of considerable proportions, and to that extent had limited *some* of the possibilities for random development. And though he gave each individual absolute freedom to do what he or she wanted by way of composition or performance during their allotted time, each participant in turn—and the extent varied with the individual—preplanned what he or she would do. Cage himself knew that he would read from a lecture he had earlier prepared that had long silences in it; what he couldn't know was what would happen during the silences, or how much of what he did say would be heard over the volume generated by piano, records and voices. So in the upshot, the event, even while allowing for a variety of chance occurrences, was also full of controls and intentions—more so than Cage wanted to believe, and to a degree that makes his contrast between the 1952 occasion and later "happenings" less dramatic than he would like.

Cage also contrived the space carefully. The audience's seats were placed in the center of the performing area, facing each other, and broken by diagonals into four sections. When people arrived, they found an empty white cup on each seat. As others filed in, they asked what the cups were for, but were given no answer (at the end of the performance, as Cage tells it, "girls came in from the kitchen with pots of coffee and filled the cups," including those that had in the meantime been used as depositories for ashes and cigarette butts.)

Of the event itself, there are—one might even say, by design—varied accounts. Some of the variations must be ascribed to distortions of memory, rather than to differences in what was actually seen during the event itself. For example, one of my accounts has Cage reading from the top of a ladder, while another has him reading from a lectern—short of hallucination, or of a shift in position during the performance (neither of which I have evidence for), that kind of discrepancy must be due to the subsequent rearrangements and impositions of memory people have made during the intervening twenty years. Other descriptive variations, though, seem to have resulted from differences in perspective-sight lines, acoustical reception, etc. at the time of the event itself. One man, for example, recalls Cage reading lines from Meister Eckhart at some point; others deny such lines were read at any point.

Finally, though, there's no certain way of separating the memory distortions from the actual variations in perspectives—and that probably would please Cage. As he and his Zen masters know, events are too full of multiple sensory inputs and momentary variables ever to be reproduced with descriptive exactness; it's an insight historians, more than most people perhaps, need to incorporate. Yet as a historian I hold (tenuously) to the rationalist hope that when all variables are discounted, there will remain a residue of *agreed-upon* evidence that can thereby appropriately be called a "true," albeit partial, reconstruction of "what happened."

Let's try it both ways: first, five descriptions, partly contradictory, by those who actually attended that "first happening"; then, my own "objective" attempt to synthesize, to resolve or discard the material that conflicts and to salvage a version that, however unsatisfyingly skeletal, at least consists of data which all parties affirm. "All," of course, itself involves a major deception; it means, in fact, some eight to ten accounts. I have no list of everyone who attended the event, no way of getting one, no desire if I had such a list to spend another five years interviewing everyone on it, and no hope, even if I had the desire, of successfully contacting all those on the list who are still alive. And indeed, what should we do about those who have died? *Their* versions, were they but here to reveal them, might add exactly the material needed to confirm or deny critical elements in the composite picture presented by the living. I'm not being merely elfin, but trying to indicate why I believe historians should be more chary in their pretensions to objectivity. Most historians, of course, are fortunate in dealing with events long since past—events, that is, about which only limited evidence survives, and no live witnesses eager and willing to say "You've got it all wrong."

The first account is from the diary of Francine du Plessix, written the same evening of the event:

> At 8:30 tonight John Cage mounted a stepladder and until 10:30, he talked of the relation of music to Zen Buddhism, while a movie was shown. Dogs barked, Merce danced, a prepared piano was played, whistles blew, babies screamed, coffee

was served by four boys dressed in white [in Cage's account, you'll recall, *girls* came in with the coffee from the kitchen] and Edith Piaf records were played double-speed on a turn-of-the-century machine. At 10:30 the recital ended and Cage grinned while Olson talked to him again about Zen Buddhism. Stefan Wolpe bitched, two boys in white waltzed together, Tudor played the piano, and the professors' wives licked popsicles.

Next, an account from Carroll Williams, now a filmmaker, at the time part-student, part-instructor in printing. This account was recorded sixteen years after the event:

It was during the summer, early in the summer. . . . The chairs were arranged so that they faced in four different directions. In other words, they were divided with aisles. If you imagine a square, a perfect square of chairs, there was a cross shape dividing them into four separate units. And this permitted the dancers to dance down these two aisles through the audience any time. So that Merce Cunningham and a part of his then company—the company he had at that time, the group—were dancing. John Cage was reading. . . . He also was performing a composition which used radio . . . duck calls and various sound effects . . . that part of it had a composer named Jay Watt performing a piece back in the corner, utilizing some of the instruments from Lou Harrison's Pacific or Indonesian or Micronesia collection . . . There were still slides—35mm slides, both hand-painted on glass, and sometimes montages—or collages, using colored gelatins and other paints and pigments and materials, sandwiched between glass slides. And some photographs—abstract. I don't think there were any objective—all non-objective materials in the slides. I can't remember whether there was a motion picture projector used or not. Somehow I think there was. A short piece, perhaps; motion picture material. There were the limited theatrical lights that the school had, jelled in different colors, and on different dimmer and on-off switch circuits. I don't know what other things were going on. There was a lot of activity, all of these things were going simultaneously, for several hours. I think that everybody sat all the way through it except Stefan Wolpe, the composer, who was very upset by the whole thing. Angered by the whole thing. Got up and left—in protest. Most people who sat through it felt that it was great, that it had been an interesting experience and a worthwhile effort on the part of everyone who was taking part. I think I had something to do with the projected materials. . . . That was followed that same summer by another party—I think of these things as much as parties in some cases as a concert—a get-together for an experience.

The third account is from an interview with David Weinrib, the potter/sculptor. I include some of the questions and remarks I myself made during our talk, since they affected the shape of the "reality" that Weinrib was attempting to re-create:

WEINRIB: There were a lot of people looking at clocks. And there was a podium, I mean a lectern, and Cage was at it. . . . It was to the side. . . . And he started to lecture. . . . He read it. And as he read it things started to happen. But he just kept reading, as I remember, all evening.

DUBERMAN: What was the content, do you remember?

WEINRIB: I don't remember. Except there was—there were some quotations from Meister Eckhart. . . . I don't remember much else of the content. It was cut into very often. But he just kept reading. And then there were a number of things that happened. And there was Rauschenberg with an old Gramophone that he'd dug up. And every now and then . . . he'd wind it up and play this section of an old record.

DUBERMAN: What was he playing?

WEINRIB: Just old hokey records, as I remember.

DUBERMAN: Old popular records?

WEINRIB: Old records I'm sure he bought with the machine. 1920s. 1930s. Then Cunningham danced. Around the whole area.

DUBERMAN: Around this core of chairs.

WEINRIB: Yes, danced. And—

DUBERMAN: Were there aisles between—

WEINRIB: No, I remember we all sort of sat together.

DUBERMAN: In the center.

WEINRIB: Yes. Might have gone out to one side, but I think we all sat around. So now . . . Cunningham . . . came out and danced pretty much, going around, and then I remember a small dog we had—helped the spirit of the happening by chasing Cunningham.

DUBERMAN: That was not programmed.

WEINRIB: No. Barking and chasing him around. And then M.C. Richards was up on a ladder—she mounted this ladder. I think she read sections of Edna St. Vincent Millay. Poems, from the ladder. And then Olson had done this very nice thing where he had written a poem which was in parts, it was given in parts to a section of the audience . . . had to do with fragments of conversation . . . all of a sudden somebody would get up from the audience and just say this little bit. And then sit down. And then somebody else in the audience would stand up and say their bit . . . I believe Olson had written the whole thing out before. And given them their parts. So this happened, this was again another—you know, fragment. That occurred.... I'm sure David Tudor, the pianist, also was part of it . . . I think he played Cage's Water Music . . . where you pour water from one bucket to another. And then David played, I believe, prepared piano, and also a number of noisemakers that were all part of this piece. So that also came into it.

DUBERMAN: These things were happening simultaneously or—

WEINRIB: No, no.

DUBERMAN: One at a time?

WEINRIB: One at a time. Sometimes an overlap, but, you know—

DUBERMAN: As a member of the audience you could concentrate on each one because there weren't too many things going on?

WEINRIB: But there were a number, and that was their idea—you know, they've often talked about that. It's a three-ring circus.

DUBERMAN: How long did it last?

WEINRIB: It was a long thing. Long.

DUBERMAN: And what impact?

WEINRIB: I really don't know.... Mrs. Jalowetz ... she had this funny thing, very much like Wolpe, you know? It's like these people, they come from your German radicalist tradition, you know, all related to Schonberg and those people. But they could never make the next step, the next leap . . . I remember her reaction. She sat there—and she was a beautiful woman. "Deep in the middle ages" . . . she just kept saying it like an incantation: "Deep in the middle ages." And she respected John and liked him.... Olson was sitting right next to her. . . . I felt with the poem he'd just gone along with the joke. . . . I remember he sort of played it cool. Because Mrs. Jalowetz was talking to him and trying to—and he just sort of played it cool.

DUBERMAN: Noncommittal.

WEINRIB: Yes, sort of.

DUBERMAN: "An interesting experiment."

WEINRIB: Yes . . . you know he had often talked about theater . . . he and Huss often talked about theater and what theater should be. . . . Their idea of what vital American theater was, you know, were those few pageants that went on in the South. You know, the Indian pageant, Cherokee—

DUBERMAN: Paul Green's stuff?

WEINRIB: Yes. . . . I remember at one point that came out as the greatest American drama.

DUBERMAN: That's weird.

WEINRIB: But that's the kind of thinking that often happened, you know, way-out thinking which was not way-out, really. Just extreme. But those pageants—I remember Huss talking to me about it once, you know, like that's where drama was.

DUBERMAN: Spectacle.

WEINRIB: Yes. Exactly. And of course in a certain way they might have been right. They might have picked the wrong heroes. Like the happenings, for better or worse, were—that's exactly what they were based on . . . afterwards I didn't say, "God, this is really new! . . . a new theatrical experience!" I'd seen M.C. read poetry and I'd seen Merce Cunningham dance. So in a funny way I didn't see it as that unique an act. . . . It didn't excite me, not that much.

The fourth account (recorded in 1968) is from the dancer Katherine Litz, who stayed on for a while after Cunningham arrived, though he took over the dance classes:

LITZ: They all got excited about these new ideas in music and so forth. Chance. And they did the happening. . . . I thought Merce wrote some music for it. I think he did. It was a little bit of everything. Merce was playing the piano at one point, as I remember.

DUBERMAN: Didn't Rauschenberg do the backdrops?

LITZ: He may have done something, yes.

DUBERMAN: And M.C. read—

LITZ: And M.C. was reading, and—

DUBERMAN: And Merce was back and forth in the aisles, I've heard . . . what else was going on?

LITZ: Oh, M.C. came in on a—something that they were dragging, or maybe someone was playing the part of a horse, I don't know. Or there was some structure that—like a little car, or a—maybe it was a big basket or something, I don't know. I can't remember. But I picture her coming in on a horse. . . . Some kind of a movable structure . . . it's like a dream to me now, you know . . .

DUBERMAN: You don't recall any details of the evening?

LITZ: No, except that it was in French and I didn't understand it. I didn't understand the words. I could see visually what was going on. But you weren't supposed to understand it literally.

And finally, here's an account by one of the participants, Merce Cunningham, taped by me on December 18, 1967:

CUNNINGHAM: It was just an evening of theater. Theatrical event. Arranged in that particular way . . . this involved not only music and sound and dancing but all those other things. And there was a dog who chased me around, I remember . . . it didn't bark . . . just started dancing up and down those aisles, and followed me around. . . . And there were some other things going on. Not constantly, you know, but other minor—I don't mean minor, but things that went on for a short period of time and then stopped, and then somebody else did something else . . . with no other relationship than that they went on at the same time. That is, the music didn't support the dancing and so on, and the visual thing over here wasn't to decorate what I was doing, nor was I to have anything to do with what anybody else was doing necessarily . . . movies and whatnot . . . one was on the ladder. I think that was either Bob or M.C. or Olson. I've forgotten which. Or perhaps they both were. And they may have moved the ladder during the course of the thing.

DUBERMAN: Did you actually rehearse for the evening?

CUNNINGHAM: No. We just did our things, so to speak, separately. I improvised the whole thing. What I did ahead of time was just to work a little bit in the aisles just to know the kind of—how much I could manage without kicking somebody. . . . But other than that I don't think any of us did any rehearsing . . . conventional music has a beat, which one feels subject to one way or another, you know—you go against it or with it, or some way. Whereas the music that I use—and I'm sure the music that David Tudor played that evening— would not have had a beat. It would have been perhaps Cage's music or other composers, I don't remember exactly what was played. . . . Cage and I had worked that way for a long, long time. With the music and the dance. But this of course involved more elements. This involved the poetry . . . and the visual things . . . there were movies, it seems to me. . . . No—

well, maybe there were paintings . . . I have a recollection of suddenly at the last minute something else being included . . .

DUBERMAN: Can you tell me a little about the theory, if there is any such thing as a theory, as to what value there is for these separate activities to be going on simultaneously.

CUNNINGHAM: I think the values—if you're going to use that word—is in respect to the way life itself is all these separate things going on at the same time. And contemporary society is so extraordinarily complex that way. Not only things going on right around you, but there are all the things that you hear instantly over the television, that are going on someplace else . . . that idea of separateness, of things happening even though they are separate, they're happening at the same time . . . Rauschenberg showed his paintings. I don't know whether they were the black paintings or the white paintings. But he showed them in it.

We now know there was a ladder—or at least a lectern—and if M.C. wasn't on it (and she probably wasn't, since she was riding a horse, or in a basket) then Rauschenberg or Olson was. Except that Olson was also in the audience. But possibly that was after he delivered his poem; or maybe he came down and sat in the audience in order to deliver his poem, since that, as you'll recall, was broken into parts and it may be that he himself delivered only one of those parts (the part that was in French, perhaps). As for Rauschenberg, we know he exhibited something, either as backdrop or foreground—and something he himself had made. Except, of course, for the Gramophone: clearly he couldn't have made that— nor those discs, which were something from the twenties, or thirties, or Piaf. Clearly, too, there was an audience, and clearly it was in the center, though its exact arrangement—whether broken into triangles, squares or not broken at all—is less clear. Yet it had to have aisles since, as everyone agrees, Merce danced down them, followed by either a barking or a silent dog (and maybe by the pre-visionary spirits of a dance company due to arrive the summer of 1953). We know that there were other activities as well: Cage read—something (yet another account insists it was Emerson and Thoreau); and David Tudor played—something (maybe even something by Cunningham, who might also himself have played); and visuals of some kind were definitely shown, like slides, or movies, or montages, or hand-painted glass. And we know everyone loved it. Except Wolpe and Johanna Jalowetz (who at least loved all the people involved in it).

That's about it. I mean, you *do* know it was a "mixed media" event, right? Possibly the very first anywhere. And we know it was one because it had all the elements that critics have told us make for such an event: varied activities happening independently of each other, though happening simultaneously with each other; few chance procedures (though much chance rhetoric); some, but not a lot of room allowed for performer improvisation and audience participation (*fortunately* not a lot, else the event wouldn't strictly qualify as "mixed media" at all); and a rigidly flexible format that ensures the impossibility of the occasion ever being repeated.

I do have a few bits left over: Franz Kline was in the audience. In fact he was there most of the summer, and everyone loved him, and he loved Black Mountain (though he worried if all those wonderful kids would learn anything that would help them make a living while trying to become painters and writers). And he made a remark during that summer that Cage says everyone thought "marvelous"; as Cage tells it, Kline stood in front of an exhibit of paintings and "said he was sure they were great paintings because he felt absolutely—we never could remember whether he said 'helpless' or 'hopeless.' In front of them, you know."

And one last item from my interview with Cage—one that might comfort those who have missed a certain *weight* in the preceding account:

CAGE: I think there's a slight difference between Rauschenberg and me. And we've become less friendly, although we're still friendly. We don't see one another as much as we did. . . . I have the desire to just erase the difference between art and life, whereas Rauschenberg made that famous statement about working in the gap between the two. Which is a little—Roman Catholic, from my point of view.

DUBERMAN: Meaning what?

CAGE: Well, he makes a mystery out of being an artist.

—from *Black Mountain: An Exploration in Community* (1972)

On Misunderstanding
Student Rebels

The young, it's becoming clear, are regarded with considerable hatred in our country. Resentment against them can't be explained simply as a reaction to the style of a particular generation, for in recent years the young have been attacked on such divergent grounds that the grounds themselves take on the appearance of pretext. In the 1950s we denounced students for their inertia, their indifference to public questions, their absorption in the rituals of fraternities and football, their dutiful pursuit of achievement. In the 1960s we condemn them for the opposite qualities: for their passion, their absorption in public questions, their disgust with the trivia of college parties and athletics, their refusal to settle for the mechanical processes of education.

Since the past two college generations have been denounced with equal vehemence for opposite inclinations, it seems plausible to conclude that it isn't those inclinations but the very fact of their youth that makes them the target for so much murderous abuse. This conclusion may seem to contradict the fact that American society, above all others, is known for its adoration of youth. But that itself, paradoxically, is one cause of adult hostility: our youth-obsessed elders resent the eighteen-year-old's easy possession of the good looks and high spirits they so desperately simulate.

Adult anger at the physical superiority of the young has usually been contained by the comforting assumption that eighteen-year-olds are at least the moral, intellectual, and emotional inferiors of their elders. College students have traditionally been viewed as apprentices, almost as supplicants. And until recently they accepted their role as dutiful petitioners for entry into the world of adult insight and skill. As no one needs reminding, they no longer accept that role, though most of their elders continue the struggle to confine them to it. Today's eighteen-to-twenty-year-old considers himself an adult, by which he doesn't mean (as so many fifty-year-olds unconsciously do) that he's ceased growing, but that he's grown up enough to make his own decisions. In every sense, even statistically, his case is a strong one.

The weight of recent physiological and psychological evidence establishes the student claim that today's eighteen-year-olds mature more rapidly than those of earlier generations. Physically, they're taller and heavier than their counterparts at the turn of the century. Boys reach puberty around age fourteen, and girls begin to menstruate at the average age of twelve years, nine months (in both cases almost two years earlier than in 1900). Moreover, there's much evidence that this earlier physical maturity is matched by emotional and intellectual precocity. According to Dr. C. Keith Conners, director of the Child Development Laboratory at Massachusetts General Hospital, both emotional and intellectual growth are today largely completed by age eighteen. By this Dr. Conners means that the difficult trials of adolescence are over, the basic patterns of personality have become stabilized, and the ability to reason abstractly—to form hypotheses and make deductions—has been established. This doesn't mean, of course, that no further maturity is possible after age eighteen. Additional information and experience do (or at least should) provide material for continuing reassessments. But that, of course, is (or should) be true of all of us.

It's bad enough that we've refused to extend to students the rights and responsibilities that their maturity warrants. What's perhaps worse is that many of those who hold positions of power or prestige in our universities have learned so little from the upheavals that the refusal has produced. A recent spate of books and articles by such men demonstrates anew their uneducability; they make it clear, by their continuing patronization and belittlement, that the young still have an uphill fight in their struggle to be taken seriously.

One case in point, though not the most egregious, is that of George F. Kennan. When Kennan's article "Rebels Without a Program" (aptly characterized by Richard Poirier as "a new containment policy for youth") appeared in the *New York Times Magazine* for January 21, 1968, it drew such an unprecedented reply from students and teachers (including a letter from me) that the Atlantic Monthly Press decided to issue the article, the replies, and a lengthy rebuttal by Kennan as a separate volume, *Democracy and the Student Left*.

Kennan insists that the students "lack interest in the creation of any real style and distinction of personal life generally." By which he means, as he goes on to specify, their lack of "manners," their untidiness, their disinterest in "personal hygiene," their refusal to cultivate the "amenities." It's not that the new generation lacks "any real style," but that Kennan is unable to perceive much of its distinctiveness. Kennan is a good eighteenth-century *philosophe*, distrustful of "enthusiasm," and preoccupied with the rationalist credo of restraint and temperance in all things. Since "passion" is suspect, it follows (albeit unconsciously) that no injustice warrants fervent disapproval. What the new generation believes and Kennan apparently does not is that "moderation" can itself become a form of paralysis, even of immorality—like the moderate protest of Pope Pius XII against the extermination of Jews.

If Kennan's condescension toward the different lifestyle of the young was peculiar to him, it could be more readily ignored. But in fact his attitude is the characteristic response of the older generation to the young. There are any number of other examples, but I'll mention only two of the more prominent: Sidney Hook and Jacques Barzun.

Hook has published two statements (that I know of) on the recent ferment at Columbia: a long article, "The Prospects of

Academe," in *Encounter* for August 1968, and a brief note in the *Psychiatry and Social Science Review* for July 1968. It's difficult to choose between them in deciding the high point to date for gray-bearded arrogance. In the shorter piece Hook flatly states that the Columbia rebels "had no grievances," and that they were interested solely in "violence, obscenity, and hysterical insult." In the longer article, Hook characterizes the protesters as "callow and immature adolescents," whose dominant mood, like that of all adolescents, is "irrationalism." While denouncing students for their passion, this self-appointed defender of "reason" and of the university as the "citadel of reason," himself indulges in a rhetoric so inflamed ("Fanatics don't lack sincerity. . . . They drip with sincerity—and when they have power, with blood—other people's blood") that by comparison the most apocalyptic students seem models of sobriety. The students mean it's acceptable to be passionately against war and racism. Hook means it is acceptable to be passionately against those who passionately protest war and racism.

Jacques Barzun, in his recent book *The American University*, begins his discussion of the college population by adopting the Olympian view: they are, after all, young men, and that means "turbulence is to be expected." In other words, a certain amount of inherent anger adheres to the condition of being young (it *is* a "condition," in Barzun's view), and anger must find its outlet. The nature of the outlet is almost a matter of indifference: if "the people of the town" do not provide a convenient target, well then, it might just as well be politics.

Barzun loves dismissing the young with casual irony. Its elegant offhandedness is a useful device for keeping a proper distance between the generations. It's also useful—though of this Barzun seems unaware—for expressing the savagery that he likes to think is confined to the student population. What the undergraduates really want, Barzun insists, is more, not less, discipline. When they speak of the impersonality of the university, they mean, it seems, "the looseness of its grip upon them." Kennan makes the same point in almost the same words: students are currently objecting to parietal rules, he asserts, because "the rules have relaxed too much rather than that they have been relaxed too little." According to both men, students are starved for structure, are desperate to be introduced to the rigors of logic. In Barzun's phrasing, they are looking for "order," for "intellectual habits"; they sense that this is the balance they need, for like all youngsters they are in a "fever and frenzy," "their mind is monopolized by their inner life."

To meet this "rage for order," Barzun and Kennan posit an appropriately antiseptic university, a place of "respite and meditation," whose "proper work," in Barzun's phrase, is "in the catacombs under the strife-torn crossroads." He fills this subterranean cemetery with properly lifeless figures; they are "somewhat hushed," they give pause, as at Chartres, to the "spiritual grandeur of their surroundings."

Barzun also shares with Kennan and Hook the proposition that "emotion" has no place on campus, and that since student rebels tend to be emotional, it can be safely assumed they are also unreliable. All three men equate (and thereby confuse) "emotion" with "irrationality," and all employ a vocabulary of neat opposites—"reason" versus "emotion"—that separates what our experience combines. They see education as "the cultivation and tempering of the mind" but fail to see that "enthusiasm" is one path by which tempering proceeds.

Barzun is also huffy at other "nonsense" currently being peddled about teaching, especially the idea that teacher and student should explore together, each learning from the other. This view, he asserts, has done "immense harm to both parties. The teacher has relaxed his efforts while the student has unleashed his conceit." And of what does that "conceit" consist? Barzun is quick to tell us: the conviction that they (the students) have something to contribute. "Only rarely," he declares, with a hauteur appropriate to the century from which most of his ideas spring, does a teacher "hear from a student a fact he does not know or a thought that is original and true . . . to make believe that their knowledge and his are equal is an abdication and a lie."

And so we are back, as always in Barzun's schema, to the confinement of his starting assumption: students are children and, usually, fools. His contempt for undergraduates is pervasive. They are, very simply, not to be trusted. "Student reliability is at a low ebb," he warns, and especially among radical students, who have but one purpose: to destroy. The evidence Barzun marshals to justify his contempt is so exasperatingly trivial (as well as suspect in its accuracy) that it demeans its compiler far more than the students. The undergraduates, he asserts, cheat a lot on exams and papers; they obtain pocket money by stealing books from the college bookstore; they keep library books out as long as they like and let fines go unpaid; they deny their roommates "the slightest considerateness"; students of both sexes live "pig-style" in their dormitories; their conversations "usually cannot follow a logical pattern," and so on.

The first thing to be said about these accusations is that Barzun has seized upon the occasional practices of a few undergraduates in order to damn a whole generation. The second is that even if these qualities did characterize a whole generation, they hardly seem heinous when compared with the sins of the fathers—when compared, that is, with racism at home and imperialism abroad. The distressing consequence of this obsession with the peccadilloes of the young is an avoidance of those genuinely important problems to which the young are calling attention. Mandarins like Barzun, Kennan, and Hook are so preoccupied with manners that they forget matter.

A dozen or so studies have been made of student activists at a variety of universities, and the group portrait that emerges is strikingly different from the slanderous one being peddled by Messrs. Barzun and Hook. The activists, first of all, constitute only a small minority of all college students; their number is put at about 15 percent. Second, there are important differences, in almost all measurable categories, between activists on the campus and other students. The activists score consistently higher on a wide variety of personality tests, including theoretical skills, aesthetic sensitivity, degree of psychological autonomy, and social maturity. They are also the better students, with significantly higher grade-point averages than the nonactivists.

One set of grievances on the campus centers on what does—or does not—go on in the classroom. As David Riesman has written, "Colleges on the whole have been very backward as compared with industry or the Army in their curiosity about their own inner processes." Until recently they've accepted lectures, grading, and examinations as part of the Natural Order of Things and have seen no reason to question the long-standing assumptions that Teacher is the possessor and arbiter of Truth, that his function is to transmit knowledge (narrowly defined as accumulated information) to students, and that their function is to memorize it. Any challenge to this conventional wisdom is still viewed with scorn by the vast majority of faculty and administrators—and of the student population as well.

Lectures, at their best, can be useful—a good lecture can provide a lucid introduction to some particularly difficult areas of study, or it can offer a fundamental reinterpretation not yet published or widely accepted. But such moments in the lecture room are rare, so rare that they do not justify the maintenance of a system that far more typically inculcates sloppiness, omniscience, plagiarism, and theatricality in the lecturer, and passivity, boredom, resentment, and cynicism in the student.

In assuming that the university's main, almost exclusive, function is to produce and transmit information, we've given top priority to promoting those faculty members most likely to assist in the manufacture of knowledge. This means, of course, that the university has come to be staffed chiefly by those concerned with research and writing rather than those concerned with educating the young— that is, with helping them to discover what their interests and talents are. As Alfred North Whitehead said long ago, "So far as the mere imparting of information is concerned, no university has had any justification for existence since the popularization of printing in the fifteenth century." Yet most professors do look on the imparting of information as the sum and substance of their responsibility. They make little or no effort to show, either in their subject or in their person, how knowledge can influence conduct and inform action.

Most professors are interested only in students who are themselves potential scholars; they're concerned with training future colleagues, not with helping the individual young person grow in his own directions. The lack of interest taken by most professors in most students, their refusal to reveal or engage more than a small share of their own selves, has made many of the best students cynical about knowledge and about those who purvey it. They hoped to find in their professors models on whom they might pattern their lives; instead they find narrow specialists busy with careers, with government contracts, with the augmentation of status and income.

Most of the powers within the academic community won't even acknowledge the right of students to complain, let alone the cogency of those complaints. To the request that they be allowed a voice in planning the curriculum, Jacques Barzun replies that they have done nothing to "earn" a voice. To the lament that their studies seem outmoded or irrelevant, Barzun retorts that "relevance is a relationship in the mind and not a property of things," which apparently means that although students might want to study urban affairs, if they will instead study cockle shells *in the right way*, they will discover all there is to know about life in the ghettos. And to the students' suggestion that they have some formal power in such matters as choosing faculty, passing on applications for admission, or helping to decide on the expansion of the physical plant, Barzun responds with hoots of derision and George Kennan with cold anger.

Both gentlemen remind the undergraduates that the university is not, and was never meant to be, a democracy. Kennan, in this instance, is the more peremptory of the two. "Even if university trustees and administrators had a right to shift a portion of their responsibilities for university affairs to the student, which they do not," he writes, the student would in any case "be unqualified to receive it." The very suggestion, he warns, is part of the current tendency of American society "to press upon the child a premature external adulthood."

The other argument most often heard for denying students any say in university affairs is that they are "mere transients." True, but so are many professors, and so (to change the context) are members of the House of Representatives, who are elected for only two years. Besides, the *interests* of the student population do not shift as often as the population itself. But even if the interests of the undergraduates did continually change (and they probably should), life does, after all, belong to the living, or, in the case of the universities, a campus to its *present* constituents.

In addition to student grievances over what happens in the classroom and on the campus, there is another major source of disaffection: the university's relationship to the world around it—its role as landlord of neighboring property, and, on the broader canvas, its role as the recipient of government largesse and provider of government expertise.

The upheavals of last spring at Columbia brought to focus the problem of the university's relationship to the society at large. One of two key issues during that upheaval was Columbia's pending construction of a gym in a public park used by Harlem residents. This issue by itself might be thought of minor importance (if, that is, one is not a resident of Harlem), but in fact it was the latest of a long series of encroachments by Columbia into the surrounding ghetto, an encroachment that usually involved evicting tenants with little concern for their wishes and welfare. (Columbia is still secretly extending its real estate holdings in Harlem, and its "relocation office" is still forcing families out of buildings it wants to tear down.)

Barzun goes so far as to deny the reality of issues like the gym construction. Universities must expand, he argues, and expansion inevitably brings conflict with the university's immediate neighbors. But shall the needs of several hundred citizens, he rhetorically asks, "prevail over the needs of . . . a national university?" Besides, the area around a university is usually a "deteriorating" one (as regards Columbia, Barzun has elsewhere referred to its surrounding neighborhood as "uninviting, abnormal, sinister, dangerous"), so it is a matter of simple "self-protection" for the university to take "steps." The "steps," as Barzun defines them, include "bringing in the police against crime and vice, hiring special patrols, and buying real estate as fast as funds and the market will permit." In his long book, Barzun has almost no discussion of Columbia's relations with Harlem; when I came to a chapter entitled "Poverty in the Midst of Plenty," I thought I had finally come to a detailed review of those relations, but the chapter turned out instead to be about the financial problems of the university.

It's one thing to defend the university theoretically as a research center and quite another to ask specifically "research in what and for what?" The multiple and tangled relationships that have developed between our leading universities and the large corporations and the federal government raise doubts about the proper boundaries of "research." More than two-thirds of university research funds come from agencies of the federal government closely connected with defense matters, and about one quarter of the two hundred largest industrial corporations in the country have university officials on their boards of directors. It is certainly an open question these days whether the university is engaged in research in order to pursue "truth" or to acquire status, power, and profit. Columbia's own farcical involvement with the Strickman cigarette filter is but one of many examples of the university's placing greed ahead of integrity.

Only rarely do we have a generation—or at least a minority of one—that engages itself so earnestly on the side of principled action; that values people so dearly and possessions so little; that cares enough about our country to jeopardize their own careers within it; that wants so desperately to lead open, honest lives and to have institutions and a society that would make such lives possible. For such a generation [and for the current Occupy Wall Street one as well], we should be immensely grateful and immensely proud. Instead, we tell them that they are frenzied children; that we will try to be patient with them but that they should not push us too far; that they too in time will grow to understand the *real* ways of the world. To say that this condescension or blindness on the part of the older generation is a pity does not fit the dimensions of the case. It is a crime.

—from the *Atlantic Monthly*, November 1968

The Stonewall Riots

Craig Rodwell, founder of New York City's first gay bookstore (the Oscar Wilde Memorial Bookshop), wanted militant activism to be the touchstone of New York's homophile movement. He wanted gays to empower themselves through confrontational action to build a proud, assertive movement. Craig was also fed up with the gay bar scene in New York, with the Mafia controlling the only public space most gays could claim, with the contempt shown the gay clientele, with the speakeasy, clandestine atmosphere, the watered-down, overpriced drinks, the police payoffs and raids. His anger was compounded by tales he heard from his friend Dawn Hampton, a torch singer who, between engagements, worked the hatcheck at a Greenwich Village gay bar called the Stonewall Inn. Because Dawn was straight, the Mafia men who ran the Stonewall talked freely in front of her—talked about their hatred for the "faggot scumbags" who made their fortunes.

Indeed, the Stonewall Inn, at 53 Christopher Street, epitomized for Craig everything that was wrong with the bar scene. When a hepatitis epidemic broke out among gay men early in 1969, Craig printed an angry article in his newsletter, *New York Hymnal*, blaming the epidemic on the unsterile drinking glasses at Stonewall. And he was probably right. Stonewall had no running water behind the bar; a returned glass was simply run through one of two vats of stagnant water kept underneath the bar, refilled, and then served to the next customer. By the end of an evening the water was murky and multicolored. Craig thought Stonewall was a dive, an awful, sleazy place personified by the figure of Ed Murphy, one of the bouncer-doormen who dealt drugs, made "introductions" (for which he accepted "tips"), and was involved in corruption, simultaneously taking payoffs from the Mafia and the New York Police Department.

Yet the Stonewall Inn had, in the course of its two-and-a-half-year existence, become the most popular gay bar in Greenwich Village. Many saw it as an oasis, a safe retreat from the harassments of everyday life, a place less susceptible to police raids than other gay bars, and one that drew a magical mix of patrons ranging from tweedy East Siders to street queens. It was also the only gay male bar in New York in 1969 where dancing was permitted.

The Genovese family operated Stonewall, the Tenth of Always (an after-after-hours place that catered to all possible variations of illicit life and stayed open so late it converted by 9:00 A.M. into a regular working-class bar), the Bon Soir on Eighth Street, and—run by Anna Genovese—the Eighty-Two Club in the East Village, which featured drag shows for an audience largely composed of straight tourists. The Washington Square bar (which opened at three in the morning and catered primarily—rather than incidentally, as was the case with Stonewall—to transvestites) was owned by the Joe Gallo family; it also controlled Tony Pastor's and the Purple Onion.

The Mob usually provided only a limited amount of money to Family members interested in opening a club; thereafter it became the individual's responsibility to turn a profit. That meant, among other things, not investing too heavily in liquor. When Washington Square first opened, the Mafia members who ran the place lost twelve cases of liquor and fifty cases of beer during the first police raid. Thereafter, only a few bottles were kept in the club and the rest of the liquor was stored in a nearby car; when the bartender was about to run out, someone would go around the corner to the parked car, put a few bottles under his arm, and return to the club. (Other bars had different strategies, such as keeping the liquor hidden behind a panel in the wall.) By thus preventing the police from confiscating large amounts of liquor during any one of their commonplace raids, it was possible—and also commonplace—to open up again for business the next day.

The Stonewall Inn had, in its varied incarnations during the fifties, been a straight restaurant and a straight nightclub. In 1966 it was taken over by three Mafia figures in Little Italy: "Mario" (the best-liked of the three), Zookie Zarfas, who also dealt in firecrackers, and "Fat Tony" Lauria, who weighed in at 420 pounds. Together they put up $3,500 to reopen Stonewall as a gay club; Fat Tony put up $2,000, which made him the controlling partner, but Mario served as Stonewall's manager and ran the place on a day-to-day basis. Tony Lauria was the best-connected of the three.

Fat Tony lived from 1966 to 1971 with Chuck Shaheen, an openly gay man in his midtwenties of Italian descent. The relationship was secretarial, not erotic. Shaheen acted as a man Friday, serving at different times as everything from a Stonewall bartender to the trusted go-between who "picked up the banks"—the accumulated cash—at the bar several times a night and carried the money home to his boss. According to Shaheen, Tony developed a heavy methamphetamine habit, shooting the crystal several times a day into his veins. Under the drug's influence, Tony lost about two hundred pounds, stayed up all night at clubs (at Stonewall, his favorite hangout, he'd embarrass his partners by insistently doing parlor tricks, like twirling cigarettes in the air), and began, for the first time in his life, to go to bed with men—though, to Shaheen's relief, not with him. Tony's father stopped speaking to him altogether and Shaheen had to carry messages between them. Increasingly shunned, Tony, so the rumor mill had it, was later killed by the Family.

Tony and his partners, Mario and Zookie, had opened the Stonewall as a private "bottle club." That was a common ruse for getting around the lack of a liquor license; bottles would be labeled with fictitious names and the bar would then—contrary to a law forbidding bottle clubs from selling drinks—proceed to do cash business just like any other bar. The three partners spent less than $1,000 in fixing up the club's interior. They settled for a third-rate sound system, hired a local electrician and his assistant to build a bar and raise the dance-floor stage, and got their jukebox and cigarette machines—had to get them—from the local don, Matty "the Horse" Ianello.

As the man who controlled the district in which the Stonewall was located, Ianello was automatically entitled to a cut in the operation. Shaheen never once saw Ianello in Stonewall, nor did he ever meet him, but Matty the Horse got his percentage like clockwork. The Stonewall partners also had to pay off the notoriously corrupt Sixth Precinct. A patrolman would stop by Stonewall once a week to pick up the envelopes filled with cash—including those for the captains and desk sergeants, who never collected their payoffs in person. The total cash dispensed to the police each week came to about $2,000. Despite the assorted payoffs, Stonewall turned a huge weekly profit for its owners. With rent at only $300 a month, and with the take (all in cash) typically running to $5,000 on a Friday night and $6,500 on a Saturday, Stonewall quickly became a money machine.

Some of the Mob members who worked gay clubs were themselves gay—and terrified of being found out. "Big Bobby," who was on the door at Tony Pastor's, a Mafia-run place on Third Street between Sixth Avenue and MacDougal Street, almost blew his cover when he became indiscreet about his passion for a Chinese drag queen named Tony Lee (who, though going lamentably to fat, was famed for her ballerina act). The Stonewall Inn seems to have had more than the usual number of gay mobsters. "Petey," who hung out at Stonewall as a kind of freelance, circulating bouncer, had a thick Italian street accent, acted "dumb," and favored black shirts and ties; he was the very picture of a Mafia mobster—except for his habit of falling for patrons and co-workers.

Most of the employees at Stonewall, and some of the customers, did drugs, primarily "uppers." Desbutal—a mix of Desoxyn and

Nembutal—was a great favorite (though later banned by the FDA), and the bar was also known as a good place to buy acid. The chief supplier was Maggie Jiggs, a famous queen who worked the main bar at Stonewall, along with his partner, Tommy Long. (Tommy kept a toy duck on the bar that quacked whenever someone left a tip.) They were a well-known team with a big following. Maggie, blond, chubby, and loud, knew everybody's business and would think nothing of yelling out in the middle of the crowded bar, "Hey, girl, I hear you got a whole new plate of false teeth from that fabulous dentist you been fucking!" But Maggie loved people, had good drugs, was always surrounded by gorgeous men, and arranged wonderful three-ways, so his outspokenness, and even his occasional thievery, were usually forgiven.

Maggie and Tommy were stationed behind the main bar, one of two bars in Stonewall. But before you could get to it, you had to pass muster at the door (a ritual some of the customers welcomed as a relief from the lax security that characterized most gay bars). That usually meant inspection through peepholes in the heavy front door by Ed Murphy, "Bobby Shades," or muscular Frank Esselourne. "Blond Frankie," as he was known, was gay, but in those years not advertising it, and was famous for being able to spot straights or undercover cops with a single glance.

If you got the okay at the door—and for underage street kids that was always problematic—you moved a few steps to a table usually covered by members of what one wag called the Junior Achievement Mafia team. That could mean, on different nights, Zookie; Mario; Ernie Sgroi, who always wore a suit and tie and whose father had started the famed Bon Soir on Eighth Street; "Vito," who was on salary directly from Fat Tony, was hugely proud of his personal collection of SS uniforms and Nazi flags, and made bombs on the side; or "Tony the Sniff" Verra, who had a legendary nose for no-goods and kept a baseball bat behind the door to deal with them.

At the table, you had to plunk down three dollars (one dollar on weekdays), for which you got two tickets that could be exchanged for two watered-down drinks. (According to Chuck Shaheen, all drinks were watered down, even those carrying the fanciest labels.) You then signed your name in a book kept to prove, should the question arise in court, that Stonewall was indeed a private "bottle club." People rarely signed their real names. "Judy Garland," "Donald Duck," and "Elizabeth Taylor" were the popular favorites.

Once inside Stonewall, you took a step down and straight in front of you was the main bar where Maggie held court. Behind the bar some pulsating gel lights went on and off—later exaggeratedly claimed by some to be the precursor of the innovative light shows at the Sanctuary and other gay discos that followed. On weekends, a scantily clad go-go boy with a pin spot on him danced in a gilded cage on top of the bar. Straight ahead, beyond the bar, was a spacious dancing area, at one point in the bar's history lit only with black lights. That in itself became a subject for camp, because the queens, with Murine in their eyes, all looked as if they had white streaks running down their faces. Should the police (known as Lily Law, Alice Blue Gown—Alice for short—or Betty Badge) or a suspected plainclothesman unexpectedly arrive, white bulbs instantly came on in the dance area, signaling everyone to stop dancing or touching.

The queens rarely hung out at the main bar. There was another, smaller room off to one side, with a stone wishing well in the middle, its own jukebox and service bar, and booths. That became headquarters for the more flamboyant contingent in Stonewall's melting pot of customers. There were the "scare drag queens" like Tommy Lanigan-Schmidt, Birdie Rivera, and Martin Boyce—"boys who looked like girls but who you knew were boys." And there were the "flame" (not drag) queens who wore eye makeup and teased hair, but essentially dressed in male clothes—though an effeminate version with fluffy sweaters and Tom Jones shirts.

Only a few favored full-time transvestites, like Tiffany, Spanola Jerry (a hairdresser from Sheepshead Bay), and Tammy Novak, who performed at the Eighty-Two Club, were allowed to enter Stonewall in drag. (Tammy sometimes transgressed by dressing as a boy.) Not even "Tish" (Joe Tish) would be admitted, though he'd been a well-known drag performer since the early fifties when he'd worked at the Moroccan Village on Eighth Street, and though in the late sixties he had a long-running show at the Crazy Horse, a nearby café on Bleecker Street. Tish *was* admitted into some uptown straight clubs in full drag; there, as he sniffily put it, his "artistry" was recognized.

The queens considered Stonewall and Washington Square the most congenial downtown bars. If they passed muster at the Stonewall door, they could buy or cajole drinks, exchange cosmetics and the favored Tabu or Ambush perfume, admire or deplore somebody's latest Kanekalon wig, make fun of six-foot transsexual Lynn's size-twelve women's shoes (while admiring her fishnet stockings and miniskirts and giggling over her tales of servicing the firemen around the corner at their Tenth Street station), move constantly in and out of the ladies room (where they deplored the fact that a single red lightbulb made the application of makeup difficult), and dance in a feverish sweat till closing time at 4:00 A.M.

The jukebox on the dance floor played a variety of songs, even an occasional "Smoke Gets in Your Eyes" to appease the romantics. The Motown label was still top of the heap in the summer of 1969; three of the five hit singles for the week of June 28—by Marvin Gaye, Junior Walker, and the Temptations—carried its imprint. On the pop side, the Stonewall jukebox played the love theme from the movie version of *Romeo and Juliet* over and over, the record's saccharine sound periodically cut by the Beatles' "Get Back" or Elvis Presley's "In the Ghetto." And all the new dances—the Boston Jerk, the Monkey, the Spider—were tried out with relish. If the crowd was in a particularly campy mood—and the management was feeling loose enough—ten or fifteen dancers would line up to learn the latest ritual steps, beginning with a shouted "Hit it, girls!"

The chino-and-penny-loafer crowd pretty much stayed near the main bar, fraternizing with the queens mostly on the dance floor, if at all. ("Two queens can't bump pussy," one of them explained. "And I don't care how beefy and brawny the pussy is. And certainly not for a relationship.") The age range at Stonewall was mostly late teens to early thirties; the over-thirty-five crowd hung out at Julius's, and the leather crowd (then in its infancy) at Keller's. There could also be seen at Stonewall just a sprinkling of the new kind of gay man beginning to emerge: hippie, long-haired, bell-bottomed, laid back, and likely to have "weird," radical views.

Very few women ever appeared in the Stonewall. Sascha L., who in 1969 briefly worked the door, flatly declares that he can't remember *any*, except for the occasional "fag hag" (like Blond Frankie's straight friend Lucille, who lived with the doorman at One-Two-Three and hung out at Stonewall), or "one or two dykes who looked almost like boys." But Chuck Shaheen, who spent much more time at Stonewall, remembers—while acknowledging that the bar was "98 percent male"—a few more lesbian customers than Sascha does, and, of those, a number who were decidedly femme. One of the lesbians who did go to Stonewall "a few times," tagging along with some of her gay male friends, recalls that she "felt like a visitor." It wasn't as if the male patrons went out of their way to make her feel uncomfortable, but rather that the territory was theirs, not hers: "There didn't seem to be hostility, but there didn't seem to be camaraderie."

The Stonewall management had always been tipped off by the police before a raid took place—this happened, on average, once a month—and the raid itself was usually staged early enough in the evening to produce minimal commotion and allow for a quick reopening. Indeed, sometimes the "raid" consisted of little more than the police striding arrogantly through the bar and then leaving, with no arrests made. Given the size of the weekly payoff, the police had an understandable stake in keeping the golden calf alive.

But the raid on June 28, 1969, was different. It was carried out by a mixed group of detectives from the First Division (only one of them in uniform), the Morals Squad, and even Consumer Affairs; the Sixth Precinct had been asked to participate only at the last minute as backup. Moreover, the raid had occurred at 1:20 A.M.— the height of the merriment—and with no advance warning to the

Stonewall management. (Chuck Shaheen recalls some vague tip-off that a raid *might* happen, but since the early-evening hours had passed without incident, the management had dismissed the tip as inaccurate.)

There have been an abundance of theories as to why the Sixth Precinct failed on this occasion to alert Stonewall's owners. One centers on the possibility that a payment had not been made on time or made at all. Another suggests that the extent of Stonewall's profits had recently become known to the police, and the Sixth Precinct brass had decided, as a prelude to its demand for a larger cut, to flex a little muscle. Yet a third explanation points to the possibility that Deputy Inspector Seymour Pine held a special grudge against the Mafia owners of Stonewall, and a fourth held that the new commanding officer at the precinct was out of sympathy with payoffs— or hadn't yet learned how profitable they could be.

But evidence has surfaced to suggest that the machinations of the Sixth Precinct were in fact incidental to the raid. Ryder Fitzgerald, a sometime carpenter who had helped remodel the Stonewall interior and whose friends Willis and Elf (a straight hippie couple) lived rent-free in the apartment above Stonewall in exchange for performing caretaker chores, was privy the day after the raid to a revealing conversation. Ernie, one of the Stonewall's Mafia team, stormed around Willis and Elf's apartment, cursing (in Ryder's presence) the Sixth Precinct for having failed to provide warning in time. And in the course of his tirade, Ernie purportedly revealed that the raid had been inspired by federal agents. The Bureau of Alcohol, Tobacco and Firearms (BATF) had apparently discovered that the liquor bottles used at Stonewall had no federal stamps on them—which meant they'd been hijacked or bootlegged straight out of the distillery. Putting Stonewall under surveillance, BATF had then discovered the bar's corrupt alliance with the Sixth Precinct. Thus when the feds decided to launch a raid on Stonewall, they deliberately kept the precinct in the dark until the unavoidable last minute. The exact combination of factors that led to the raid remains to this day uncertain.

When it did get going, the previous systems put in place by the Mafia owners stood them in good stead. The strong front door bought needed time until the white lights had a chance to do their warning work: patrons instantly stopped dancing and touching, and the bartenders quickly took the money from the cigar boxes that served as cash registers, jumped from behind the bar, and mingled inconspicuously with the customers. Maggie Jiggs, already known for his "two for the bar, one for myself" approach to cash, disappeared into the crowd with a cigar box full of money; when a cop asked to see the contents, Maggie said it contained her tips as a "cigarette girl," and they let him go. When questioned by his employers later, Maggie claimed that the cop had taken the box *and* the money. She got away with the lie.

The standard Mafia policy of putting gay employees on the door so they could take the heat while everyone else got their act together also paid off for the owners. Ed Murphy managed to get out ("Of course," his detractors add, "he was on the police payroll"), but Blond Frankie was arrested. There was already a warrant outstanding for Frankie's arrest (purportedly for homicide; he was known for "acting first and not bothering to think even later"). Realizing that this was no ordinary raid, that this time an arrest might not merely mean detention for a few hours at Centre Street, followed by a quick release, Frankie was determined not to be taken in [he later managed to escape]. Owners Zookie and Mario, through a back door connected to the office, were soon safely out on the street in front of Stonewall. So, too, were almost all of the bar's customers, released after their IDs had been checked and their attire deemed "appropriate" to their gender—a process accompanied by derisive, ugly police banter.

As for Fat Tony, at the time the raid took place he had still not left his apartment on Waverly Place, a few blocks from Stonewall. Under the spell of methamphetamine, he'd already spent three hours combing and recombing his beard and agitatedly changing from one outfit to another, acting for all the world like one of those "demented queens" he vilified. He and Chuck Shaheen could see the commotion from their apartment window, but only after an emergency call from Zookie could Tony be persuaded to leave the apartment for the bar.

Some of the campier patrons, emerging one by one from Stonewall to find an unexpected crowd, took the opportunity to strike instant poses, starlet style, while the onlookers whistled and shouted their applause-meter ratings. But when a paddy wagon pulled up, the mood turned more somber. And it turned sullen when the police officers started to emerge from Stonewall with prisoners in tow and moved with them toward the waiting van. Sylvia Rivera, the street-hustling part-time drag queen, was standing with her boyfriend Gary near the small park across the street from Stonewall, and Craig Rodwell was perched on top of the brownstone stairs near the front of the crowd. They, and others, sensed that something unusual was in the air; all felt a kind of tensed expectancy.

The police (two of whom were women) were oblivious to it initially. Everything up to that point had gone so routinely that they expected to see the crowd quickly disperse. Instead, a few people started to boo; others pressed against the waiting van, while the cops standing near it yelled angrily for the crowd to move back. As Sylvia remembered it, "You could feel the electricity going through people. You could actually feel it. People were getting really, really pissed and uptight." A guy in a dark red T-shirt danced in and out of the crowd, shouting, "Nobody's gonna fuck with me!" and "Ain't gonna take this shit!"

As the cops started loading their prisoners into the van—among them, Blond Frankie—more people joined in the shouting. Sylvia spotted Tammy Novak among the three queens lined up for the paddy wagon, and along with others in the crowd started yelling, "Tammy! Tammy!" Sylvia's shriek rising above the rest. But Tammy apparently didn't hear, and Sylvia guessed that she was too stoned to know what was going on. Yet when a cop shoved Tammy and told her to "keep moving! keep moving!" poking her with his club, Tammy told him to stop pushing and when he didn't, she started swinging. From that point on, so much happened so quickly as to seem simultaneous.

As the police, amid a growing crowd and mounting anger, continued to load prisoners into the van, Martin Boyce, an eighteen-year-old queen, saw a leg in nylons and sporting a high heel shoot out of the back of the paddy wagon into the chest of a cop, throwing him backward. Another queen then opened the door on the side of the wagon and jumped out. The cops chased and caught her, but Blond Frankie quickly managed to engineer another escape from the van; several queens successfully made their way out with him and were swallowed up in the crowd. Tammy was one of them; she ran all the way to Joe Tish's apartment, where she holed up throughout the weekend. The police handcuffed subsequent prisoners to the inside of the van, and succeeded in driving away from the scene to book them at the precinct house. Deputy Inspector Seymour Pine, the ranking officer, nervously told the departing police to "just drop them off at the Sixth Precinct and hurry back."

From this point on, the melee broke out in several directions and swiftly mounted in intensity. The crowd, now in full cry, started screaming epithets at the police—"Pigs!" "Faggot cops!" Sylvia and Craig Rodwell enthusiastically joined in, Sylvia shouting her lungs out, Craig letting go with a full-throated "Gay power!" One young gay Puerto Rican went fearlessly up to a policeman and yelled in his face, "What you got against faggots? We don't do you nuthin'!" Another teenager started kicking at a cop, frequently missing as the cop held him at arm's length. One queen mashed an officer with her heel, knocked him down, grabbed his handcuff keys, freed herself, and passed the keys to another queen behind her.

By now, the crowd had swelled to a mob, and people were picking up and throwing whatever loose objects came to hand—coins, bottles, cans, bricks from a nearby construction site. Someone even picked up dog shit from the street and threw it in the cops' direction. As the fever mounted, Zookie was overheard nervously asking Mario what the hell the crowd was upset about: the Mafia or the police? The *police*, Mario assured him. Zookie gave a big grin of relief and decided to vent some stored-up anger of his own: he egged on bystanders in their effort to rip up a damaged fire hydrant and he persuaded a young kid named Timmy to throw the wire-mesh garbage can nearby. Timmy was not much bigger than the can (and had just come out the week before), but he gave it his all—the can went sailing into the plate-glass window (painted black and reinforced from behind by plywood) that stretched across the front of Stonewall.

Stunned and frightened by the crowd's unexpected fury, the police, at the order of Deputy Inspector Pine, retreated inside the bar. Pine had been accustomed to two or three cops being able to handle with ease any number of cowering gays, but here the crowd wasn't cowering; it had routed the cops and made them run for cover. As Pine later said, "I had been in combat situations, [but] there was never any time that I felt more scared than then." With the cops holed up inside Stonewall, the crowd was now in control of the street, and it bellowed in triumph and pent-up rage.

Craig dashed to a nearby phone booth. Ever conscious of the need for publicity, for visibility, and realizing that a critical moment had arrived, he called all three daily papers—the *Times*, the *Post*, and the *Daily News*—and alerted them that "a major news story was breaking." Then he ran to his apartment a few blocks away to get his camera.

One young man dashed to the phones to call his straight radical-left friends, to tell them "people were fighting the cops—it was just like Newark!" He urged them to rush down and lend their support (just as he had long done for *their* causes). Then he went into the nearby bars, the Ninth Circle and Julius's, to try to get the patrons to join the melee outside. None of them would. Nor did any of his straight radical friends show up. It taught him a bitter lesson about how low on the scale of priorities his erstwhile comrades ranked "faggot" concerns.

Gary tried to persuade Sylvia to go home with him to get a change of clothes. "Are you nuts?" she yelled. "I'm not missing a minute of this—it's the *revolution*!" So Gary left to get clothes for both of them. Blond Frankie, meanwhile—perhaps taking his cue from Zookie—uprooted a loose parking meter and offered it for use as a battering ram against the Stonewall's door. At nearly the same moment somebody started squirting lighter fluid through the shattered glass window on the bar's façade, tossing in matches after it. Inspector Pine later referred to this as "throwing Molotov cocktails into the place," but the only reality *that* described was the inflamed state of Pine's nerves.

Still, the danger was very real, and the police were badly frightened. The shock to self-esteem had been stunning enough; now came an actual threat to physical safety. Dodging flying glass and missiles, Patrolman Gil Weisman was hit near the eye with a shard, and blood spurted out. With that, the fear turned abruptly to fury. Three of the cops, led by Pine, ran out the front door, which had crashed in from the battering, and started screaming threats at the crowd, thinking to cow it. But instead a rain of coins and bottles came down, and a beer can glanced off Deputy Inspector Charles Smyth's head. Pine lunged into the crowd, grabbed somebody around the waist, pulled him back into the doorway, and then dragged him by the hair inside. Ironically, the prisoner was the well-known—and heterosexual—folk singer Dave Van Ronk. Earlier that night, Van Ronk had been in and out of the Lion's Head, a bar a few doors down from Stonewall that catered to a noisy, macho journalist crowd scornful of the "faggots" down the block. Once the riot got going, the Lion's Head locked its doors; the management didn't want faggots moaning and bleeding over the paying customers. As soon as Pine got Van Ronk back into Stonewall, he angrily accused him of throwing dangerous objects—a cue to Patrolman Weisman to shout that Van Ronk was the one who had cut his eye and then to start punching the singer hard while several other cops held him down. When Van Ronk looked as if he was going to pass out, the police handcuffed him, and Pine snapped, "All right, we book him for assault."

The cops then found a fire hose, wedged it into a crack in the door, and directed the spray out at the crowd, thinking that would certainly scatter it. But the stream was weak and the crowd howled derisively, while inside the cops started slipping on the wet floor. A reporter from the *Village Voice*, Howard Smith, had retreated inside the bar when the police did; he later wrote that by that point in the evening "the sound filtering in [didn't] suggest dancing faggots any more; it sound[ed] like a powerful rage bent on vendetta." By now Stonewall's front door was hanging wide open, the plywood brace behind the windows was splintered, and it seemed only a matter of minutes before the howling mob would break in and wreak its vengeance. One cop armed himself with Tony the Sniff's baseball bat; the others drew their guns, and Pine stationed several officers on either side of the corridor leading to the front door. One of them growled, "We'll shoot the first motherfucker that comes through the door."

At that moment, an arm reached in through the shattered window, squirted more lighter fluid into the room, and then threw in another lit match. This time the match caught and there was a *whoosh* of flame. Standing only ten feet away, Pine aimed his gun at the receding arm and (he later said) was preparing to shoot when he heard the sound of sirens coming down Christopher Street. At 2:55 A.M. Pine had sent out emergency signal 10-41—a call for help to the fearsome Tactical Patrol Force (TPF)—and relief was now rounding the corner.

The TPF was a highly trained, crack riot-control unit that had been set up to respond to the proliferation of protests against the Vietnam War. Wearing helmets with visors, carrying assorted weapons, including billy clubs and tear gas, its two dozen members all seemed massively proportioned. They were a formidable sight as, linked arm in arm, they came up Christopher Street in a wedge formation that resembled (by design) a Roman legion. In their path, the rioters slowly retreated but—contrary to police expectations— did not break and run. Craig, for one, knelt down in the middle of the street with the camera he'd retrieved from his apartment and, determined to capture the moment, snapped photo after photo of the oncoming TPF minions.

As the troopers bore down on him, he scampered up and joined the hundreds of others who scattered to avoid the billy clubs, but then raced around the block, doubled back behind the troopers, and pelted them with debris. When the cops realized that a considerable crowd had simply re-formed to their rear, they flailed out angrily at anyone who came within striking distance. But the protesters would not be cowed. The pattern repeated itself several times: the TPF would disperse the jeering mob only to have it re-form behind them, yelling taunts, tossing bottles and bricks, setting fires in trash cans. When the police whirled around to reverse direction at one point, they found themselves face to face with their worst nightmare: a chorus line of mocking queens, their arms clasped around each other, kicking their heels in the air Rockettes-style and singing at the tops of their sardonic voices:

> *We are the Stonewall girls*
> *We wear our hair in curls*
> *We wear no underwear*
> *We show our pubic hair*
> *We wear our dungarees*
> *Above our nelly knees!*

It was a deliciously witty, contemptuous counterpoint to the TPF's brute force, a tactic that transformed an otherwise traditionally macho eye-for-an-eye combat and provided at least the glimpse of a different and revelatory kind of consciousness. Perhaps that was exactly the moment Sylvia had in mind when she later said, "Something lifted off my shoulders."

But the tactic incited the TPF to yet further violence. As they were badly beating up on one effeminate-looking boy, a portion of the angry crowd surged in, snatched the boy away, and prevented the cops from reclaiming him. Elsewhere, a cop grabbed "a wild Puerto Rican queen" and lifted his arm as if to club him. Instead of cowering, the queen yelled, "How'd you like a big Spanish dick up your little Irish ass?" The nonplussed cop hesitated just long enough to give the queen time to run off into the crowd.

The cops themselves hardly escaped scot-free. Somebody managed to drop a concrete block on one parked police car; nobody was injured, but the cops inside were shaken up. At another point, a gold-braided police officer being driven around to survey the action got a sack of wet garbage thrown at him through the open window of his car; a direct hit was scored, and soggy coffee grounds dripped down the officer's face as he tried to maintain a stoic expression. Still later, as some hundred people were being chased down Waverly Place by two cops, someone in the crowd suddenly realized the unequal odds and started yelling, "There are only two of 'em! Catch 'em! Rip their clothes off! Fuck 'em!" As the crowd took up the cry, the two officers fled.

Before the police finally succeeded in clearing the streets—for that evening only, it would turn out—a considerable amount of blood had been shed. Among the undetermined number of people injured was Sylvia's friend Ivan Valentin; hit in the knee by a policeman's billy club, he had ten stitches taken at St. Vincent's Hospital. A teenager named Lenny had his hand slammed in a car door and lost two fingers. Four big cops beat up a young queen so badly—there's evidence that the cops singled out "feminine boys"—that she bled simultaneously from her mouth, nose, and ears. Craig and Sylvia both escaped injury, but so much blood splattered over Sylvia's blouse that at one point she had to go down to the piers and change into the clean clothes Gary had brought back for her.

Four police officers were also hurt. Most of them sustained minor abrasions from kicks and bites, but Officer Andrew Scheu, after being hit with a rolled-up newspaper, had fallen to the cement sidewalk and broken his wrist. When Craig heard that news, he couldn't resist chuckling over what he called the "symbolic justice" of the injury. Thirteen people (including Dave Van Ronk) were booked at the Sixth Precinct, seven of them Stonewall employees, on charges ranging from harassment to resisting arrest to disorderly conduct. At 3:35 A.M., signal 10-41 was canceled and an uneasy calm settled over the area. It was not to last.

*   *   *

Word of the confrontation spread through the gay grapevine on Saturday. The *New York Times* buried a short piece that headlined police injuries and characterized the event as a "rampage" by "hundreds of young men," but the *Daily News* put the story on page one and local television and radio reported it as well. The *Voice* ran two separate articles: Lucian Truscott's smacked of homophobia but Howard Smith's mentioned police vandalism. The *New York Post*, then a liberal paper, did a follow-up piece headlined "The Gay Anger Behind the Riots," which responsibly discussed resentment over Mafia control of Stonewall (and most other gay bars), over the huge profits that never went back into the gay community, and over the huge payoffs that went to the police. And both *RAT* and the *East Village Other*, organs of the counterculture, also carried sympathetic accounts.

But those were marginal voices in coverage that overall reflected all too accurately the dominant bias of the culture. *Time* magazine summarized the majoritarian view when, some four months later and in response to the publicity generated, it published a lengthy "analysis" of gay life. The article characterized "the homosexual subculture [as] . . . without question, shallow and unstable," and warned its possibly wavering readership yet again that "homosexuality is a serious and sometimes crippling maladjustment." There was the authentic voice of mainstream America, circa 1969.

Coverage in the dailies the next day helped bring out the crowds that milled around the Stonewall Inn all day Saturday; curious knots of people gathered to gape at the damage and warily celebrate the implausible fact that, for once, cops, not gays, had been routed.

The police had left the Stonewall a shambles. Jukeboxes, mirrors, and cigarette machines lay smashed; phones were ripped out; toilets were plugged up and overflowing; and shards of glass and debris littered the floors. (According to at least one account, moreover, the police had simply pocketed all the money from the jukeboxes, cigarette machines, cash register, and safe.) On the boarded-up front window that faced the street, anonymous protesters had scrawled signs and slogans: THEY INVADED OUR RIGHTS; THERE IS ALL COLLEGE BOYS AND GIRLS IN HERE; LEGALIZE GAY BARS; SUPPORT GAY POWER, and newly emboldened same-gender couples were seen holding hands as they anxiously conferred about the meaning of these uncommon new assertions.

Something like a carnival, an outsized block party, got going by evening in front of Stonewall. While older, conservative chinos-and-sweater gays watched warily, and some disapprovingly, from the sidelines, "stars" from the previous night's confrontation reappeared to pose campily for photographs; handholding and kissing became endemic; cheerleaders led the crowd in shouts of "Gay Power"; and chorus lines repeatedly belted out the refrain of "We are the Stone-wall girls." But the cops, including TPF units, were out in force, weren't amused at the antics, and seemed grimly determined not to have a repeat of Friday night's humiliation. The TPF lined up across the street from Stonewall, visors in place, batons and shields at the ready. When the fearless chorus line of queens insisted on yet another refrain, kicking their heels high in the air, as if in direct defiance, the TPF moved forward, ferociously pushing their nightsticks into the ribs of anyone who didn't jump immediately out of their path.

But the crowd had grown too large to be easily cowed or controlled. Thousands of people were by now spilling over the sidewalks, including an indeterminate but sizable number of curious straights and a sprinkling of street people gleefully poised to join any kind of developing rampage. When the TPF tried to sweep people away from the front of Stonewall, the crowd simply repeated the previous night's strategy of temporarily retreating down a side street and then doubling back on the police. In Craig's part of the crowd, the idea took hold of blocking off Christopher Street, preventing any vehicular traffic from coming through. When an occasional car did try to bulldoze its way in, the crowd quickly surrounded it, rocking it back and forth so vigorously that the occupants soon proved more than happy to be allowed to retreat.

The cops had been determined from the beginning to quell the demonstration, and at whatever cost in bashed heads and shattered bones. Twice the police broke ranks and charged into the crowd, flailing wildly with their nightsticks; at least two men were clubbed to the ground. The sporadic skirmishing went on until 4:00 A.M., when the police finally withdrew their units from the area. The next day, the *New York Times* insisted that Saturday night was "less violent" than Friday (even while describing the crowd as "angrier"). Sylvia, too, considered the first night "the worst." But a number of others, including Craig, thought the second night was the more violent one; that it marked "a public assertion of real anger by gay people that was just electric."

Not all gays were pleased about the eruption at Stonewall. Those satisfied by, or at least habituated to, the status quo preferred to minimize or dismiss what was happening. Many wealthier gays, sunning at Fire Island or in the Hamptons for the weekend, either heard about the rioting and ignored it (as one of them later put it: "No one [at Fire Island Pines] mentioned Stonewall"), or caught up with the news belatedly. When they did, they tended to characterize the events at Stonewall as "regrettable," as the demented carryings-on of "stoned, tacky queens"—precisely those elements in the gay world from whom they had long since dissociated themselves. Coming back into the city on Sunday night, the beach set might have hastened off to see the nude stage show *Oh, Calcutta!* or the film *Midnight Cowboy* (in which Jon Voight played a Forty-Second Street hustler)— titillated by such mainstream daring while oblivious or scornful of the real-life counterparts being acted out before their averted eyes.

Indeed some older gays, and not just the wealthy ones, even sided with the police, praising them for the "restraint" they had shown in not employing more violence against the protesters. As one of the leaders of the West Side Discussion Group reportedly said, "How can we expect the police to allow us to congregate? Let's face it, we're criminals. You can't allow criminals to congregate." Others applauded what they called the "long-overdue" closing of what for years had been an unsightly "sleaze joint." There have even been tales that some of the customers at Julius's, the bar down the street from Stonewall which had long been favored by older gays ("the good girls from the fifties," as one queen put it) actually held three of the rioters for the police.

The Mattachine Society had still another view. Mattachine, the homophile group that had been started as a radical oppositional force in California in the early fifties, but had since turned more conservative and middle class, had its New York chapter headquarters right down the street from the Stonewall Inn. In 1969 Dick Leitsch was its leading figure—he'd shown considerable sympathy for New Left causes but none for challenges to his leadership. Randy Wicker, himself a pioneer activist and lately a critic of Leitsch, now joined forces with him to pronounce the events at Stonewall "horrible." Wicker's earlier activism had been fueled by the notion that gays were "jes' folks"—just like straights except for their sexual orientation—and the sight (in his words) "of screaming queens forming chorus lines and kicking went against everything that I wanted people to think about homosexuals . . . that we were a bunch of drag queens in the Village acting disorderly and tacky and cheap." On Sunday those wandering by the Stonewall saw a new sign on its boarded-up façade, this one printed in neat block letters:

WE HOMOSEXUALS PLEAD WITH

OUR PEOPLE TO PLEASE

HELP MAINTAIN PEACEFUL AND QUIET

CONDUCT ON THE STREETS OF

THE VILLAGE—MATTACHINE

The streets that Sunday evening stayed comparatively quiet, dominated by what one observer called a "tense watchfulness." Knots of the curious continued to congregate in front of Stonewall, and some of the primping and posing of the previous two nights were still in evidence.

The police on Sunday night seemed spoiling for trouble. "Start something, faggot, just start something," one cop repeated over and over. "I'd like to break your ass wide open." (A brave young man purportedly yelled, "What a Freudian comment, officer!"—and then scampered to safety.) Two other cops, cruising in a police car, kept trying to start a fight by yelling obscenities at passersby, and a third, standing on the corner of Christopher Street and Waverly Place, kept swinging his nightstick and making nasty remarks about "faggots."

At 1:00 A.M. the TPF made a largely uncontested sweep of the area and the crowds melted away. Allen Ginsberg strolled by, flashed the peace sign, and, after seeing "Gay Power!" scratched on the front of Stonewall, expressed satisfaction to a *Village Voice* reporter: "We're one of the largest minorities in the country—10 percent, you know. It's about time we did something to assert ourselves." Deputy Inspector Pine later echoed Ginsberg: "For those of us in public morals, things were completely changed . . . suddenly they were not submissive anymore."

In part because of rain, Monday and Tuesday nights continued to be quiet, with only occasional random confrontations; the most notable probably came when a queen stuck a lit firecracker under a strutting, wisecracking cop, the impact causing him to land on what the queen called his "moneymaker." But Wednesday evening saw a return to something like the large-scale protest of the previous weekend. Perhaps as a result of the appearance that day of the two front-page *Village Voice* articles about the initial rioting, a crowd of some thousand people gathered in the area. Trash baskets were again set on fire, and bottles and beer cans were tossed in the direction of the cops (sometimes hitting protesters instead); the action was accompanied by militant shouts of "Pig motherfuckers!" "Fag rapists!" and "Gestapo!" The TPF wielded their nightsticks indiscriminately, openly beat people up, left them bleeding in the street, and carted four off to jail on the usual charge of "harassment."

The Stonewall Riots had come to end. But their consequences would be far-reaching.

—from *Stonewall* (1993)

Feminism, Homosexuality, and Androgyny

Feminism had begun "erupting" in Barbara Deming when she first read Kate Millett's *Sexual Politics* in 1970. During her year of recovery from a car accident, Barbara had focused her limited ability to read on the radical feminist literature that had recently been coming off the presses. The two books she ranked highest in importance were Shulamith Firestone's *The Dialectic of Sex*, published in 1970, and the philosopher/theologian Mary Daly's *The Church and the Second Sex* (soon followed by her still more influential *Beyond God the Father* in 1973). Firestone was only twenty-five when she published *Dialectic*—a daring, brilliant book that called for the abolition of the nuclear family, a postpatriarchal society, and the use of cybernetics to free women from pregnancy and child rearing. Earlier, she had helped to found New York Radical Women and then, in 1969, along with Ellen Willis, the radical feminist group Redstockings. Daly, more than fifteen years older and something of a disciple of the existentialist theologian Paul Tillich, was, especially with the publication of *Beyond God the Father*, a foundational figure in feminist theology.

The books had a profound impact on Barbara, and led to her personal friendships with Daly, the poet Adrienne Rich, the feminist leader Robin Morgan, and, somewhat later, Ti-Grace Atkinson,

Karla Jay, and Andrea Dworkin as well. The initial contact was with Adrienne Rich, who'd read two of Barbara's recent articles, "Two Perspectives on Women's Struggles" and "On Anger," and had written to tell her that "your work has meant a great deal to me over years of my life."

"Two Perspectives" opened with a brief rereading of various women writers whom Barbara, over the years, had found most meaningful to her; she wanted to see what they might have in common, though the authors and their books were very different one from the other. Her conclusion was that all the books shared at least one theme: "The danger in which the Self within stands if one is a woman—the danger that it will be blighted, because of the authority of men." From that point in the essay, Barbara proceeded to argue that it had for too long been assumed that the human race was "naturally" split between men and women, as epitomized by the popular saying "*Vive la difference!*"

She begged to differ. Aside from the physical asymmetry in reproductive equipment, she believed that men and women shared a common humanity, and that no task was more crucial at the current time than boldly to question the so-called differences between the genders. Every individual, Barbara argued, "is born *both* to assert herself or himself," an attribute previously considered primary in males, "*and* to act out of sympathy for others trying to find themselves," presumably the preserve of women.

She felt it urgent to reclaim both attributes, aggression and compassion, for both genders, and as Carolyn Heilbrun had recently argued in her seminal *Toward a Recognition of Androgyny*, to hold out androgyny (combining in every individual all the traits previously and artificially parceled out to men *or* women) as the ideal state. Barbara advocated that fathers also needed to become mothers and that motherhood needed to be redefined so that it no longer represented the female parent "giving one's very life for the father, then the son, to feed upon." Everyone had to learn that "we must give of ourselves, we are members one of another." Mutuality needed to replace sacrifice (the woman) and dominance (the man).

The genius of nonviolent action, Barbara added, was that it combined two impulses long treated as distinctly masculine *or* feminine: self-assertion and sympathy. Recombined, they restore "human community. One asserts one's rights as a human being, but asserts them with consideration for the other, asserts them, that is, precisely *as* rights belonging to any person." Barbara's further conviction was that there existed between any two individuals ("if only they will allow themselves to be individuals") sufficient polarity "for desire to flourish." Love, she concluded, did not mean the woman "cleaving to the man" and the man "cherishing his so-called better self." There could be "deep eroticism in comradeship." Indeed, Barbara—long "out" as a lesbian—suspected that one significant reason why homosexuality was generally viewed as threatening was because "loving comradeship" *was* its ideal.

The second article, "On Anger," which deeply impressed Adrienne Rich, remains one of Barbara's most influential essays. She started from the proposition that many of the people who were struggling in liberation movements—blacks, welfare mothers, women, gay men and lesbians, vets, GIs, prisoners, etc.—were angry people. Yet the anger, she was convinced, had to be expressed nonviolently "if we want to make the changes that we need swiftly and surely . . . and if we want to see the fewest possible people hurt in the struggle." In regard to the women's movement, Barbara felt that men were so accustomed to the present state of things that they were almost bound to panic at the very idea of women's liberation. It was important, she felt, for women "to reassure men continually," as their singular entrenched privileges were removed, that the pleasures of relating to others as equals were greater than those of treating them as subordinates or appendages.

Barbara felt that one kind of anger was healthy: "It is the concentration of one's whole being in the determination: this must change." Such a state does involve agitation and confrontation, but is not in itself violent because it respects oneself *and* the other. Barbara recognized that it was difficult for pacifists to acknowledge anger, "to have to discover in ourselves murderers." Yet it was precisely when repressed anger surfaces that a movement for change begins to show signs of life. But what one does with the anger is all-important. If one disciplines it—takes the murder out of it—and uses it to join with others comparably oppressed, the anger is transmuted into a determination not to destroy the oppressor but to change one's subservient status through conscious solidarity with those who are similarly situated or at least sympathetic to one's plight—often because they recognize some tyrannized portion of their own lives.

Barbara and Adrienne Rich began to correspond a little, met once, and then soon after spent an evening together with Robin Morgan and Mary Daly ("whom I would name a genius," Barbara wrote), neither of whom Barbara had previously known. She was especially impressed with Daly's "wonderfully bold mind," just as she had already been excited by Daly's articles (". . . did not read your essays but ate them, and they are now part of my flesh and bone"). Daly and Barbara agreed that "a genuine psychic revolution" had begun, with androgyny as its goal and with what Daly had called "the sisterhood of man" central to that evolution.

To Robin Morgan, Barbara emphasized her conviction that women, because of their ability to give birth, understood "that we are members one of another, that nobody, nothing, is strictly *other*." But it's not that men can't learn about connectedness; "it seems to me that we have to insist they can." For Barbara, the truism that nobody is simply *other* lay at the very heart of the nonviolent struggle. Those aspects of oneself that we currently despise and cast out are the same ingredients central to an androgynous vision. Men cast out in fear "all that is 'womanish' in them, then long of course for that missing part of their natures, so seek to possess it by possessing us." Critical to the potential revolution in consciousness was the need to embrace those very elements we previously chose to disown—which would mean destroying maleness and femaleness as we currently know them. But if women claim that their powers are unique, "we defeat ourselves. . . . *Won't we* always be men's prey until they come to acknowledge that in each one of *them* is what Adrienne beautifully calls a 'ghostly woman' . . . ?"

Barbara had a much longer-standing relationship (some fifteen years) with David McReynolds, the War Resisters League (WRL) stalwart, than with any of the feminists she was now connecting with. She and David had worked together as nonviolent radical activists in a variety of organizations (like WRL) and movements (like the struggles for black rights and against the war in Vietnam). They also shared a same-gender sexual orientation. But in 1976, and then sporadically for another half dozen years, Barbara and David got intensely tangled up in disagreement. It began when Barbara asked David to sign a petition calling for censorship of the notorious film *Snuff*, which purportedly (though it was never proven) captured on camera the mutilation and murder of one of the actresses in the movie.

David refused—heatedly. Though he hadn't seen the film, he strenuously objected to what he rightly presumed was Barbara's underlying assumption that most men on the Left (as he wrote her) were "deserting women—or have always seen them as less than human." Besides, as he wrote Barbara, he himself, on principle, opposed "*any* censorship." Where would Barbara draw the line? He told her to walk through a porn shop one day and she'd see depictions of scenes they'd both deplore—young boys being violated by older men, bound and gagged women being raped, whip-wielding women beating men *and* women. He claimed to fully understand the outrage at *Snuff*, but "for women to protest *this* movie implied that they accept the brutalizing" of all the other ones. He insisted the broad issue was not that women's lives were held cheap, but that most lives were.

In saying as much, David strenuously denied that he was antifeminist: "The women's movement interests me much more than the gay liberation movement which, at least in the 'men's division,' I find more concerned with arranging dances than overturning a structure." He felt, moreover, that "there is a certain natural contour of nature which puts both of us, as homosexuals, at its edge and places the heterosexual much closer to the center." He'd decided that he was basically an "integrationist" and did not want to live within the context of a "gay community."

As regarded feminism, he wanted Barbara to know that his support was not unconditional: "When women tell me they know all about men or that men are such and such, I know they speak *part* of the truth." He reminded her that for some time now she'd talked of "waiting, of silence, of hoping left-wing men would change and see patriarchy as the enemy." Yet in his view, "the attack on the patriarchy is possible only because it is, in a sense, already over." He felt that Barbara's pain was "a human condition, not a female one," and believed she was edging away "from the over-arching humanity which is at the core of nonviolence," to which both of them had long been committed: "We need one another, our common humanity being more urgent in this short life than our blackness, whiteness, or elseness. That is a truth you once knew and I sense you have lost or are losing it somewhere along the way."

Barbara felt deeply hurt at David's vehemence, and his painful misunderstanding of her position. Yet characteristically—"We must *listen* to the Other" was central to her being—she began her reply by thanking him "for taking such care in writing me. I take it as an act of brotherliness." She asked him to take equal care in reading her response. And in the various exchanges by phone and mail that followed, she (and David as well) often reiterated their love and respect for one another—though that didn't prevent either from forcefully speaking their minds.

Barbara began by accusing David of making assumptions about her that were "inaccurate." She was *not* a "correct liner: I just try to act out the truth I feel as best I can." She did *not* believe that "men and women are different in essential nature." She did *not* want to turn the clock back and reinstall the Matriarchy though she did believe that eons ago women were either co-partners in power, or fully ruled. She was *not* a separatist: "I have never given myself that name"; it was true that she felt that women for a time must, in consciousness-raising groups, "talk above all among ourselves, act above all together" so that later—"may it be soon"—"we can come into each other's presence as distinct persons." Nor, as a corollary, did she to any degree repudiate her past. She remained proud of having worked side by side with David and other radical men—with "kindred spirits"—in WRL and against racism, the arms buildup, civil defense, and the war in Vietnam.

When, in the early seventies, she'd begun to read and encounter radical feminists, she'd been convinced, she wrote David, that her brothers "would welcome feminism and would come to see feminism and nonviolence as 'inextricable,' and would be quick to acknowledge that women have been oppressed by men." But only a few "have moved in this direction" and most had not. *Why* they had not had deeply puzzled and upset her, though she continued to regard her male comrades as "brothers." But how could they not understand that "under patriarchy *all* our natures are distorted. If patriarchy were dissolved, I think we would all of us," among much else, "be not heterosexual or homosexual but simply sexual." She was shocked at David's belief that the power of the patriarchy was "already over"—"you leave me wordless. Please do try to persuade me that it is so. And I'm not being sarcastic."

Barbara had become unhappily convinced, she told David, that the vast majority of men, including those on the Left, had no real feel for the profound power that (white) men continued to exert over all others. She now felt that "our lives, women's lives, are not real to you (and to men generally)—except insofar as they support the lives of men." Yet she felt strongly that those who called themselves "anti-imperialists" (as both she and David long had) needed to recognize "that *women* are treated as a colonized people—here and everywhere."

Barbara urged him to read—she knew only one man [Arthur Kinoy] on the Left who had—at least some of the "extraordinary" books that feminists had written over the last few years, and specifically named the works of Firestone, Millett, Rich, Daly, and Dworkin. David would have none of it, though he acknowledged his ignorance of the books Barbara cited—along with many other books he never seemed to have time enough to read. But he accused Barbara of "guilt-tripping" him and of setting "a bad example of communicating." Besides, he indignantly added, he refused to "read a book written by someone who won't attend planning meetings with men, someone who insists on separate demonstrations, separate book stores, separate bars" (none of which was true of some of the women Barbara had mentioned, including herself)—"They can bloody well have a separate audience for their writing."

They were at a stalemate—these longtime friends and political allies who shared so many values, as well as personally holding each other in high regard ("For all my disagreements and angers," David wrote in one letter, "I love and respect you"—and Barbara felt the same). Given the time frame, the divergence between them was hardly unique. The midseventies and early eighties were marked by sharp divisions among activists on the Left—which had always been true but was more pronounced during some periods than others—as well as between self-identified gay men and lesbians. Antagonism between the New Left and the Old went back to the sixties and hinged on whether or not one believed in the centrality of the class struggle. David had been one of the few older leftists—in 1970 he was forty-one—who strongly identified with the New Left (though not with its patronization of women's liberation).

Both feminism and the gay movement had also, from their inception in the late sixties, been marked by internal conflict, with the mid-to-late seventies marking a period of heightened infighting. Liberal feminists like Betty Friedan denounced "the lavender menace" specifically, and radicals generally, for putting the women's movement in the wrong light and jeopardizing its growth. Radical feminists were themselves split into divergent ideological factions, some wanting to retain their ties to the male Left and to broad social reconstruction—even while opposing male supremacy—and others arguing for an autonomous women's movement that focused on building alternative institutions and was grounded in the conviction (which mistakenly discounted significant variations in class,

race, and ethnicity) that all women shared a universal and biologically intrinsic identity different from that of men.

David made it clear to Barbara that he'd never laid claim to being
"an orthodox feminist," and insisted, probably accurately, that "very
few groups have taken feminism as seriously as WRL," in which
both were members, and the radical *WIN* magazine, for which
both wrote. Barbara remained unpersuaded: "I used to feel listened
to, there at the League," she responded, "but the painful truth I'm
trying to speak is that now that I'm a feminist, I *don't* feel listened
to." She spelled that out more fully in a one-page piece she entitled
"Should We Be Alarmed?" Although many whites, she wrote, "took
part in the black struggle, and paid close attention to the words of
black leaders, men on the Left have paid no comparable attention to
the words of feminists. They may speak up for the ERA, the Equal
Rights Amendment then pending, which would ultimately fail to
win over a sufficient number of states, but—here Barbara repeated
an earlier charge—they don't read any of "the many extraordinary
books feminists have written over the past few years."

Since Barbara had already recycled those charges several times
(which didn't mean they weren't true), the repetition got David's
dander up. He replied that, speaking only for himself, he had too
little time to read more than a few books, "often mysteries written
by women (but not by the right kind of women—I know)." Then he,
too, repeated a stale charge that Barbara had already answered—
that she'd "chosen a separatist road." In the face of that charge,
Barbara remained comparatively calm, but she did insist that David
was making "assumptions about what it is that I believe which are
inaccurate." (He'd also again accused her of wanting to restore, assuming it had ever existed, "matriarchy" and of believing that men
and women had essentially different natures.)

Since she'd earlier refuted those interpretations, Barbara settled
for citing some of her published essays that had argued the opposite.
She concentrated instead on David's charge that she was a separatist. "I have never given myself that name," she wrote him. "Yes,
I do feel strongly that *for a time* women must talk above all among

ourselves." But she assured him that she had *not* abandoned her old comrades: "Many of the actions I have taken and the actions WRL has taken have been the same actions. Do I repudiate my past? I do not. I will always be proud that we took those actions. And many actions indeed"—like protesting nuclear proliferation and demanding unilateral disarmament—that "we still take in unison." David, in turn, also tried to turn down the heat and to emphasize instead their commonalities. That marked the end of their latest quarrel. Another round of recriminations had ended. The friendship held.

—from *A Saving Remnant* (2011)

BIOGRAPHY

Paul Robeson

Growing Up Black

Robeson experienced overt racism less often when he entered high school in 1912 than most teenage black males, but the subtler variety—the kind that allowed him, through practice and forewarning, to keep his temper under wraps—was more frequent. A distinct social line was drawn. He often walked to and from school with a white girl in his class, but she acknowledges ("There never really was an occasion to ask him in") that he never entered her house. Though everyone was "very nice to Paul" and Paul in turn was famously nice to everyone, he and his classmates didn't exactly "pal around" together. As one of his teachers put it, "He is the most remarkable boy I have ever taught, a perfect prince. Still, I can't forget that he is a Negro." Another of his teachers did urge him to attend high-school parties and dances, but Paul himself knew better. "There was always the feeling," he later wrote, "that—well, something unpleasant might happen." Yet a third teacher applauded Paul's discretion: he remained an "amazingly popular boy" because "he had the faculty for always knowing what is so commonly referred to as his 'place.' " Early habituated to solitude, Paul would all his life seek it, deeply marked in the eyes of some by the melancholy of confirmed apartness. Yet he would never be a true loner. Unwilling ever to live by himself, he would prefer later in life to sleep on a friend's sofa rather than to stay alone. His ideal situation would always be to have loving friends in near proximity, but to be able to retreat at will to an inner monastic fortress.

He learned early that accomplishment can win respect and applause but not full acceptance—although he tried to follow the established protective tactic of African American life in America: to "act right," to exhibit maximum affability and minimal arrogance. Even while turning in a superior performance, he had to pretend it was average and that it had been accomplished offhand, almost absentmindedly. Any overt challenge to the "natural supremacy" of whites had to be avoided, and on any occasion when whites were surpassed, the accompanying spirit could never smack of triumph. "Above all," Robeson later wrote, as if repeating a litany drummed into his head by his father, "do nothing to give them cause to fear you, for then the oppressing hand, which might at times ease up a little, will surely become a fist to knock you down again!"

This balancing act required enormous self-control. Robeson could safely stay on one side of the exceedingly fine line that separated being superior from acting superior only by keeping the line in steady focus. The effort contributed to the development of an acute set of antennae that he retained all his life—he later told a reporter that he could size someone up immediately, could sense, when introduced to a stranger, "what manner of man he is," regardless of the words he spoke. But having to maintain constant self-control took its emotional toll. "I wish I could be sweet all the time," he once said when under intense pressure, "but I get a little mad, man, get a little angry, and when I get angry I can be awful rough." No young man of Robeson's energetic gifts could continuously sustain a posture of bland friendliness without the effort's exacting some revenge—especially since his father had also taught him to be true to himself. The tension was further heightened by a lifetime conviction that "in comparison to most Negroes" he had had an easy time of it growing up in white America, and complaint might appear, even to other blacks, as ungrateful and unwarranted. He preferred to "keep silent," a tactic for coping with emotional distress that he maintained throughout his life. As an adult he could never reflect with ease on his youth, once confessing to a friend that, when he did recall some of his experiences, they only "aroused intense fury and conflict within him."

Robeson's natural talents were so exceptional that he had to make a proportionately large effort in order to forestall resentment in others. He learned early: even as a boy he is remembered as "a shy kid who did everything well, but preferred to keep in the background." Had his warmth and modesty not been quite so engaging, the astonishing record he compiled at Somerville High might well have stirred more fear and envy. Several of his classmates swore he never took a book home at night—even as Paul sat each evening under his father Reverend William Drew Robeson's rigorous eye reviewing the day's lessons in Virgil and Homer. He was wise enough to appear occasionally less than thoroughly prepared, or to use humor to "take the teachers on a bit, in a nice way." Even so, one classmate confessed, "He used to get my goat, everything seemed so easy to him."

Indeed it did—in athletics especially. Robeson excelled in every sport he attempted. In baseball he played the positions of shortstop and catcher with equal facility, ran fast, and hit well. In basketball— in those days essentially a guarding game—his height and dexterity made him "good at stopping a man." He also ran track and (after school) played a fair game of tennis. But it was his skill as a fullback in football that gained him the most attention. Paul "had such a big strong hand," one contemporary said, that "he could almost wrap [it] around a football [somewhat rounder than the modern ball] and throw that thing just like a baseball."

Envy of such prowess (especially in someone of his race) did occasionally surface. In a game against the superior team of Phillipsburg High (known as "a rough bunch of kids" and outweighing Somerville ten pounds to a man), the opposition "lay for him" and piled on—but the attack energized him and he scored a touchdown;

still, "handicapped by the work of officials" (as the local paper put it), Somerville lost "the greatest game ever played" on the Phillipsburg grounds. Paul's father was often on hand for the games. A contemporary recalls that "he would keep his eyes upon Paul through every second of play." Far from disapproving of sports, he wanted his son to distinguish himself in that area, as in all others—and stood on the sidelines to remind him that, should adversity arise, he had to resist both the sin of lashing out and the sin of stunting his purpose.

In 1915, the seventeen-year-old Robeson took a statewide written exam for a four-year scholarship to Rutgers University. His family preferred all-black Lincoln University, from which both his father and his brother Bill had graduated, but the strain on his father's limited income made the possibility of a scholarship appealing. Besides, Paul himself did not prefer Lincoln. As his teacher Anna Miller recalled, "Several of the Negro colleges were suggested to him, but Paul had his heart set on a large school, and no hints as to the difficulties he might encounter on that path could daunt him. . . . 'I don't want to have things handed to me,' he declared. 'I don't want it made easy.' " The other students competing for the Rutgers scholarship had previously taken a test covering their first three years of high school; not knowing of the test in time, Robeson had to sit an exam that included the entire four-year course of work. Nonetheless, he won the competition. "Equality might be denied," he later wrote, "but I knew I was not inferior."

William Drew Robeson had passed on to his son an intricate strategy for survival. He had taught him to reject the automatic assumption that all whites are malignant, to react to individuals, not to a hostile white mass. At the same time, he knew the extent of white hostility—he had, after all, been born a slave—and he counseled his son to adopt a gracious, amenable exterior while awaiting the measure of an individual white person's trustworthiness. But he was no Uncle Tom; Paul was constantly reminded of his "obligation to the race," constantly reminded of its plight. Taught to be firm in his dedication to freeing his people, Paul was also taught to avoid gratuitous grandstanding. His job was to protest and to stay alive; outright rebellion against a slave system was as suicidal as subservient capitulation to it.

Founded in 1766, Rutgers was one of the country's oldest colleges; yet in 1915, when Robeson entered, it was still a private school with fewer than five hundred students, bearing scant resemblance to the academic colossus it subsequently became. Prior to the Civil War, Rutgers had denied admittance to African Americans (Princeton continued to refuse them admission until World War II), and only two had officially attended the school before Robeson—though rumor had it that an additional few had in another sense "passed" through its portals. The year after Robeson entered, a second black student, Robert Davenport, enrolled, and "Davvy" and "Robey" (as they were known during their undergraduate years) became good friends, joining a scattering of other black collegians from the Philadelphia–Trenton–New York corridor to form a social circle. They would need each other.

Robeson's path at Rutgers was centrally defined by his race, though not—thanks to his own magnetism and talent—circumscribed by it. The simple fact of his dark skin was sufficient to bring down on him a predictable number of indignities, but his own settled self-respect kept them from turning into disabling wounds.

When freshman Robeson walked onto the practice field to try out for Rutgers football, the team had no blacks on it—indeed, like almost every other top-ranked college, Rutgers had never in its history had a black player. The "giant's" reputation had preceded him. Rutgers coach G. Foster Sanford had seen him play for Somerville and had been duly impressed. The Rutgers first-stringers had also heard about Robey's athletic prowess—and skin color. Several of them set out to prevent him from making the team. On the first day of scrimmage, they piled on, leaving Robeson with a broken nose (which troubled him ever after as a singer), a sprained right shoulder, and assorted cuts and bruises. He could hardly limp off the field. That night (as Robeson described the incident thirty years later) "a very, very sorry boy" had to take to bed and stay there for ten days to repair his wounds. "It was tough going" for a seventeen-year-old and "I didn't know whether I could take any more." But his father had impressed upon him that "when I was out on a football field, or in a classroom, or anywhere else, I was not there just on my own. I was the representative of a lot of Negro boys who wanted to play football and wanted to go to college, and, as their representative, I had to show I could take whatever was handed out. . . . Our father wouldn't like to think that our family had a quitter in it."

Robeson went back out for another scrimmage. This time a varsity player brutally stomped on his hand. The bones held, but Robeson's temper did not. On the next play, as the first-string backfield came toward him, Robeson, enraged with pain, swept out his massive arms, brought down three men, grabbed the ball carrier, and raised him over his head—"I was going to smash him so hard to the ground that I'd break him right in two"—and was stopped in the nick of time by a yell from Coach Sanford. Robeson was never again roughed up—that is, by his own teammates. Sanford, a white New Englander committed to racial equality as well as to football prowess, issued a double-barreled communiqué: Robey had made the team, and any player who tried to injure him would be dropped from it. But it was only gradually that Sanford's attitude came to be adopted.

Several of his teammates have subsequently downplayed the amount of racial antipathy Robeson faced on the Rutgers squad—just as whites who knew him in Somerville later minimized town prejudice. One Rutgers teammate, "Thug" Rendall, insisted sixty years later that there had been no opposition to Robey's joining the team, and Steve White, a senior when Robeson was a freshman, flatly declared, "There was never any discrimination." Earl Reed Silvers, who graduated two years ahead of Robeson and was later a Rutgers faculty member, claimed to have "attended every football practice" during Robeson's freshman year and did not remember "any untoward incident on the field." Silvers further claimed to have checked his memory with four members of the varsity squad of that season and reported that not one of them could recall a deliberate attempt to injure Robeson. In any case, Silvers felt sure, "Paul would not . . . wish to question the integrity of his college or the sportsmanship of his friends."

But another member of the varsity squad, Robert Nash, flatly states that Robeson "took a terrific beating. . . . We gave him a tough time during the practices; it was like initiation. He took it well, though." And Mayne S. Mason, one of Robeson's teachers, remembers him coming into class one day with his hand bandaged; Mason later found out that someone on the team had spiked Paul's hand. Robeson had learned as a young man to muzzle his feelings, but that wasn't the equivalent of not having any, nor any guarantee that under special provocation they wouldn't surface.

By the end of his freshman year, Robeson was in the starting lineup; by his junior year, he had become the star of an exceptionally talented Rutgers team and had gained national prominence—a "football genius," raved one sportswriter, echoing many others; "the best all-round player on the gridiron this season"; "a dusky marvel." Twice, in 1917 and 1918, Walter Camp, the legendary Yale coach, put Robeson on his All-American football teams—the first Rutgers player ever named—calling him "a veritable superman." The phrase scarcely seemed overheated; by then, with a superfluity of skill, Robeson had also distinguished himself as center on the basketball team, catcher on the baseball team, and a competent javelin and discus thrower on the track team. By the time of his graduation, he had won fifteen varsity letters in four different sports.

All of which suggests, in bald outline, a triumphal procession, inexorable and uninterrupted. The reality was a good deal bumpier. If Coach Sanford had never been bigoted, and if the Rutgers football team had been taught not to be, that still left the outside world. One classmate remembers the shouts of "nigger" that would sometimes come from the stands, and Coach Sanford's son recalls that Robeson "was treated very badly by the opponents. . . . Everybody went after him, and they did it in many ways. You could gouge, you could punch, you could kick. The officials were Southern, and he took one hell of a beating, but he was never hurt. He was never out of a game for injuries. He never got thrown off the field; when somebody punched him, he didn't punch back. He was just tough. He was big. He had a massive, strong body, among other things. He felt the resentment but he managed to keep it under wraps." Among Rutgers's Southern opponents in football, William and Mary and Georgia Tech simply refused to play against a black man.

Because the feats of "the giant Negro" extended beyond football, they could not easily be dismissed as the mere by-products of "animal vitality." Robeson dominated not only the playing fields but the classroom—and the debating hall and the glee club and the honor societies as well. And he did so with a modesty that further disarmed would-be detractors. Robeson maintained such a consistently high grade average in his course work that he was one of four undergraduates (in a class of eighty) admitted to Phi Beta Kappa in his junior year. A speaker of exceptional force, he was also a member of the varsity debating team and won the class oratorical prize four years in succession. His bass-baritone was the chief adornment of the glee club—but only at its home concerts; he was not invited to be a "traveling" member and at Rutgers sang only with the stipulation that he not attend social functions after the performances. "There was a clear line," Robeson later wrote, "beyond which one did not pass"; college life was "on the surface marvelous, but it was a thing apart."

In that same spirit, Paul once let a teammate, Donald Storck, persuade him to go to a college dance—but positioned himself on the balcony, where, to wild applause, he serenaded the dancers below with "Roses of Picardy." Storck marveled at his friend's calm exterior but recognized that he was "roiling" inside. By others, however, Paul's prudent self-possession was often mistaken for nonchalance. An undergraduate two years behind him sent him myopic congratulations later in life on the attitude he'd shown: "I will never forget how much you seemed to enjoy watching, though never participating in, any of the social affairs of your contemporaries. . . . This was but one of your most typical, admirable qualities that endeared you to all who knew you. It was in keeping with your modesty. . . ."

As a young man Paul talked less guardedly only among his circle of black friends, a small group of collegians, male and female, drawn from the Philadelphia–New York area and (as one of them has put it) from "well-to-do middle-class homes. . . . We met regularly for dances, forums, picnics, athletic games, and the usual events that engage college students. There were also profound discussions about the Negro in our society." As one of the young black women in his circle told me many years later, "Paul was distinctly aware and disturbed" about racial questions. . . . He was race-conscious at an early stage," and "it showed when we met in groups together." He described his hope of someday being able "to do something about it"—though "he wasn't clear at that early age about what he might be able to do . . ."

Essie

Soon after graduating from Rutgers in 1919—he delivered the Commencement Oration—Paul met and became romantically involved with a young woman named Eslanda Goode, called by everyone "Essie." She came from a distinguished lineage of mixed racial stock. Her grandfather, Francis Lewis Cardozo, was descended from a Spanish-Jewish-black family and became a prominent racial spokesman. Essie had cream-colored skin, black hair, and Mediterranean features—with a slightly Oriental look around the eyes that gave her the overall aura of being a foreigner rather than black. When Paul met her, she'd graduated from Columbia as a chemistry major, and was known for her quick intelligence, energy, efficiency, and spunk. Paul was ambivalent about settling down, but Essie knew she wanted to marry him almost from the first, and some evidence suggests that she may have maneuvered him into it. They married in 1921.

Initially trained for the law, Paul's disinclination for legal work in combination with the overt racism of the profession led him to explore possibilities in concert work and theater. His association with the Provincetown Playhouse and Eugene O'Neill led to a meteoric rise; by 1930 he was starring opposite Peggy Ashcroft in a London production of *Othello*—and having an affair with his leading lady as well. It was hardly Paul's first extramarital fling, but this time Essie found a love letter, and the affair with Ashcroft ended.

But Paul's need for sexual expression outside his relationship with Essie continued. His next affair, with a free-spirited young white actress named Yolande Jackson, became a consuming passion, what he himself called "the great love" of his life. He took a separate apartment from Essie and their young son and gave serious thought to divorcing her. When she, in turn, learned about Yolande, she decided to write Paul a long letter.

In the no-nonsense manner on which she prided herself (and in which she thought Paul woefully, perhaps morally, deficient), she laid out options, imposed conditions, drew up systematic conclusions. "My dear P," she began, "I don't seem to be able to talk to you anymore. We don't seem to speak the same language. So I thought I'd better write." She was now entirely prepared, she continued, to give him a divorce, should he want one. "I shall be infinitely better off divorced from you, than married to you. . . . As your wife, I have rarely had the supposed pleasure and comfort of your company— except at very irregular meals and at odd hours late at night; and of course on those social occasions when you found it convenient or necessary. . . . All I really lose when I divorce you is a job; and divorces being what they are, I lose the job but keep the salary, with a raise."

She then reiterated her charge that he was a deficient father, uninterested in his own son, and defended herself from his long-standing complaint about her extravagance. "You deplore the number of ménages you must keep up," she wrote, but seem unwilling to forgo separate sleeping quarters. As for Yolande, Essie had "thought a great deal about this racial mixing business" and concluded that "when a white woman takes a Negro man as a lover, she usually lowers him and herself, too; white people and Negroes feel rather that she has a bull or a stallion or mule in her stable, her stable being her bed of course, and view the affair very much as if she had run away with the butler or the chauffeur; she is rarely—almost never—a first-class woman, and neither white nor black people think the Negro has won a prize." On her own behalf, Essie objected to the way he had publicly flaunted his affair with Yolande and his "lack of taste in emphasizing" the gifts Yolande had given him of a cigarette case, a locket, and a seal ring.

"If you had ever seriously tried to make love to me, I'm sure I don't know what might have happened. But we needn't worry about that—you never did. You made a pass or two at it—took me to a theater and were very pleased with such evidence of your devotion. I was, too—which makes it even funnier. [I] seriously doubt if you were ever in love with me. You liked me, were companionable, and I was thoughtful and considerate of you. I doubt now if I was ever in love with you—I admired you tremendously, and I was certainly interested in you."

But the past, she concluded, "is behind us. The question is, what should we do with the future? I know what I want to do, and shall do, with mine. There is no indecision about me, as you know. But about you—you have a great natural gift, and a magnificent body, neither of which you have done anything to preserve and improve. . . . You also have a terrific charm—but have rather overworked that. You have a fine mind. You have, as I said in 1921, the immediate possibility of becoming the greatest artist in the world—if you want to; and it wouldn't take much work, either—you have so much to start with. If you continue to drift along as you are doing now, refusing to face things out, you will degenerate into merely a popular celebrity. Which seems poor stuff when one thinks of being a really great artist, the thrill of having done something perfectly. . . . Well, it does seem that I fall naturally into place in the role of lecturer, doesn't it? All I can say in my defense is that I have decided what to try to make of my own life, and as we part, I should be very happy to know that you have decided upon something for yourself. I do so hate waste. And you will be a wicked waste if you don't step on it."

On the evening of November 28 [1931], Paul dropped by the flat to leave a Russian dictionary (Essie had also taken up the study), found she had gone out, and saw the pencil draft of her letter to him. Apparently it moved him, and he returned the next morning to have a talk with her. As she described it in her diary, it turned out to be "a red-letter day for me, perhaps one of the most important days in my whole life. . . . We got closer and more friendly than we have been. He says he wants to see me often, and urgently, and that we have something between us which no one else will ever be able to duplicate. He thinks he wants to marry Yolande, but he isn't sure, but he is sure he wants us always to remain close and friendly. . . . We had a lovely time, slept together, and enjoyed it enormously. I'm so glad things are pleasant and friendly. Most important of all, he has found his feet, so far as his work is concerned, and is through with slacking and sliding and muddling through. Thank God for that!" She sent a high-spirited version of their new arrangements to Carl and Fania Van Vechten: "He doesn't live here of course, but has reached the regular and often-calling stage, which is much more inconvenient. He is a dear, though, I must say, even though he is so funny and serious and absurd at times. I think no matter what happens to him, and I'm sure a great deal will happen to him, he'll always be a very nice person." [In the upshot, Yolande broke off with him, and Paul and Essie remained married, though uneasily . . .]

Robeson and Communism

In the late thirties, even such left-leaning CIO (Congress of Industrial Organizations) unions as the Transport Workers or the Hotel and Restaurant Workers didn't address racism seriously—though these unions were light-years ahead of most AFL (American Federation of Labor) affiliates in accepting blacks for membership. Mike

Quill of the Transport Workers Union never made any substantial effort to fight for expanded job opportunities for black workers, placing priority instead on issues of union recognition and the protection of the rights of those already enlisted in its ranks. Other left-wing labor leaders did have strong convictions about the need to change patterns of racial discrimination within industry, but were sometimes reluctant to push their more conservative memberships in a direction that might split their unions and jeopardize their own positions of leadership. And the Communist Party (CP) didn't exert much pressure in that direction on labor leaders sympathetic to its ideology.

Preoccupied with the international crisis, the CP by the late thirties placed more emphasis on maintaining its alliances than on pushing aggressively for the kind of action against job discrimination that might shake those alliances. In choosing to "Americanize" the Party, in other words, the CP's leaders had inescapably become enmeshed in the contradictions of American life: to maintain its influence within the labor movement, it had to compromise somewhat on its vanguard position regarding black rights. The comparative inaction of the CP and the CIO against racial discrimination during and after World War II (when measured against their earlier clarion calls) would lead black militants, in the late 1940s and early 1950s, to press for "black caucuses" within each union. Robeson's friend Revels Cayton would play a central role in that movement— and Robeson, who never sanctioned a backseat role for blacks for long, would also become involved.

The dilution of the CP's mission to press the issue of job rights for the economically depressed black working class, in combination with the CP's aggressively secular scorn for Christian institutions and values so central to the culture of African Americans, seriously constricted its appeal to the black masses. But if communism failed to ignite the enthusiasm of any significant segment of the black working class—the agency on which it theoretically relied for producing social change—it did turn out to have a broad appeal for black artists and intellectuals. When emphasizing the class struggle in the years before the Popular Front, the CP as a corollary had downplayed the specialness of black culture. But during the Popular Front years, with the centrality of class struggle deemphasized, the party threw itself into pronounced support for black arts, helping to sponsor a variety of efforts to encourage black theater, history, and music. Robeson was hardly alone among black artists in welcoming this uniquely respectful attitude toward black culture. Here was an "Americanism" that exemplified *real* respect for "differentness" rather than attempting, as did official mainstream liberalism, to disparage and destroy ethnic variations under the guise of championing the superior virtue of the "melting pot"—which in practice had tended to mean assimilation to the values of white middle-class Protestants.

Symbolizing this appreciation of black culture, the fraternal organization International Workers Order sponsored a pageant on "The Negro in American Life" (with the Manhattan Council of the National Negro Congress [NNC] as co-sponsor) dramatizing major events in African American history. Robeson enthusiastically offered his services. The pageant, written by the black playwright Carlton Moss, proved weak in its dramaturgy but strong in its emotional appeal. Its dedication "to the Negro People and to Fraternal Brotherhood Among All" roused a racially mixed audience of five thousand to an ovation—and then to an ecumenical frenzy of cheering when Robeson called for all minorities to unite in making "America a real land of freedom and democracy."

Hitler's invasion of the Soviet Union on June 22, 1941, and the Anglo-Soviet pact that followed soon after, created an international realignment that abruptly brought Robeson's views into greater consonance with mainstream patriotism. The Soviet Union was now hailed among the Western democracies—as Robeson had hailed it all along—as the front line of defense in the struggle against fascism. The image of the bullying Russian bear bent on aggression quickly gave way in the West to the image of a heroic homeland battling to preserve the integrity of its borders against fascist incursion. The communists and their pro-Soviet allies in the NNC and the left-wing CIO unions were no slower in repainting their political canvases. A year before the Nazi invasion, CP leader William Z. Foster had branded the British Empire "the main enemy of everything progressive," but after the invasion the main enemy rapidly became Hitler's Germany—so much so that, out of its concern for a unified war effort, the CP would support a "no-strike" pledge by labor and dilute its protest against racism in the armed forces, thereby partly compromising the vanguard position in the civil rights struggle that it had earlier staked out for itself.

Robeson, too, shifted his advocacy from nonintervention to massive aid for the Soviet Union. He urged the Roosevelt administration to help arm the now combined forces of antifascism— to support the Allies against the Axis (as the struggle soon came to be called, once the Japanese completed the diametric symmetry by bombing Pearl Harbor at the end of the year). He freely lent his voice in concerts and his presence at rallies in support of an all-out effort to assist the Soviet Union, Britain, and China, alternately joining fellow artists like Benny Goodman in presenting an evening of Soviet music, or co-signing a letter that deplored the "strikingly inadequate" information available in America about the Soviet Union and offering to make up the deficiency with free copies of *The Soviet Power*, a book by Reverend Hewlett Johnson (the "Red" Dean of Canterbury). At a time when Soviet military fortunes were at a low ebb and predictions of the Soviet Union's collapse widespread, Robeson insisted in statements to the press that the Russian masses, convinced they had a government that offered them hope, would never succumb to the Nazis.

With the Soviet Union now a wartime ally, the cause of Russian war relief became so entirely respectable by 1942 that, in a rally at Madison Square Garden on June 22, Robeson was joined on the podium by a full panoply of American life—Supreme Court Justice Stanley Reed, Mayor Fiorello La Guardia of New York, William Green (president of the AFL), Harry Hopkins, Soviet Ambassador to the United States Maxim Litvinov, the Jewish leader Dr. Stephen S. Wise, the opera star Jan Peerce, and the eminent pianist Artur Rubinstein. The shift in public opinion from antagonism to approval of the "heroic" Russian ally became dramatically complete over the next few years, with the mass-circulation magazines illustrating—and fostering—the changing image. *Collier's* in December 1943 concluded that Russia was neither socialist nor communist but, rather, represented a "modified capitalist set-up" moving "toward something resembling our own and Great Britain's democracy," while a 1943 issue of *Life* was entirely devoted to a paean to Soviet-American cooperation. Wendell Willkie's enormously popular *One World* contained glowing praise of Soviet Russia—and Walter Lippmann, widely considered the preeminent political analyst, in turn, praised the astuteness of Willkie's analysis. A nationwide poll in September 1944 asking whether the Russian people had "as good" a government "as she could have for her people" found only 28 percent replying in the negative. By 1945, no less a figure than General Dwight D. Eisenhower told a House committee that "nothing guides Russian policy so much as a desire for friendship with the United States."

None of this diluted the suspicion of Bolshevik intentions harbored by the right wing—and notably by its chief champion in the federal bureaucracy, FBI director J. Edgar Hoover—or its rising conviction that Robeson was playing a sinister role in Soviet councils. As early as January 1941, special agents were reporting to FBI headquarters in Washington that Robeson was "reputedly a member of the Communist Party" (which he was not, and never would be). Three months later, a zealous agent in Los Angeles sent a brown notebook to Hoover, "apparently belonging" to Robeson, that "contains Chinese characters"; the Bureau's translation section examined the notebook and concluded it was "clearly of significance to no one other than its owner." In the summer of 1942, an agent was present when Robeson visited Wo-Chi-Ca, the interracial camp for workers' children, and portentously reported that Robeson had signed "Fraternally" to a message of greeting and that "tears had rolled down his cheeks" when a young camper presented him with a scroll.

As Robeson stepped up his activities on behalf of the Allied war effort, Hoover stepped up surveillance of him. By the end of 1942, the Bureau had taken to describing Robeson as a communist functionary: "It would be difficult to establish membership in his case but his activities in behalf of the Communist Party are too numerous to be recorded." The FBI began to tap his phone conversations and to bug apartments where he was known to visit. Special agents were assigned to trail him and to file regular reports on his activities. By January 1943, Hoover was recommending that Robeson be considered for custodial detention (that is, subject to immediate arrest in the case of a national emergency); such a card was issued on him on April 30, 1943—the same month that he was being hailed in the press for a triumphal concert tour and just before he starred in a giant Labor for Victory rally in Yankee Stadium. By August 1943, "reputedly" was being dropped in special-agent reports to Hoover, with Robeson now being straightforwardly labeled "a leading figure in the Communist Party . . . actively attempting to influence the Negroes of America to communism." From this point on, the FBI fattened Robeson's file with "evidence" to support its view that he was in fact a dangerous subversive. During the war years, Robeson's secret dossier and his national popularity grew apace; their collision was still half a dozen years off.

For the time being, national and personal priorities coalesced. Roosevelt's reaffirmation of democratic values on the home front, in tandem with the country's joining hands internationally with a Russian ally Robeson believed free of racial and colonialist bias, meant that national purpose coincided with his own special vision more fully than he had ever imagined would be possible in his lifetime. The juncture galvanized him, releasing in him a torrent of energy and resolve. Over the next three years—until the death of Roosevelt in April 1945—Robeson operated at the summit of his powers, in an escalating spiral of activity and acclaim, and in the glow of a political optimism that would be as brutally shattered as it had been briefly, unexpectedly plausible.

Even at its height, Robeson's optimism was not unblinkered.

Roosevelt might now speak kindly of his "heroic" Russian ally, but Robeson hardly took that to mean the president had converted to socialism. In the same way, he didn't regard New Deal domestic policies, promising though he found them, as signifying the imminent attainment of social justice. The Roosevelt administration did much to excite the hopes of black Americans: it opened itself to the counsel of such notable black figures as Mary McLeod Bethune, Robert Weaver, William H. Hastie, and Walter White; it issued the president's Fair Employment Practices Committee (FEPC) order in 1941; it included blacks in the voting on cotton-control referendums sponsored by the Agricultural Adjustment Administration. Yet, as Robeson well knew, the Democratic Party remained tied to its racially unreconstructed Southern wing, and the actual execution of policy had produced only marginal changes in the oppressive pattern of daily life for the black masses. In the mid-forties, Robeson told a friend that he thought Roosevelt's reformism would have as its chief result the guarantee that capitalism would exist for another fifty years.

As Robeson crisscrossed the country in a whirlwind of rallies, concert appearances, meetings, dinners, and testimonials, he tempered his enthusiasm for the nation's wartime mission to defeat fascism with reminders about its obligation to combat oppression at home. The CP opted for primary attention to the war overseas, downplaying the black struggle in the U.S.; Robeson did not. He encouraged blacks to support the war effort, warning that the victory of fascism would "make slaves of us all"—but he simultaneously called on the administration to make the war effort worth supporting for blacks by destroying discriminatory practices in defense industries and the armed forces. "Racial and religious prejudices continue to cast an ugly shadow on the principles for which we are fighting," he told a commencement audience at Morehouse College in 1943. At the prestigious and widely broadcast annual Herald Tribune Forum that same year, he devoted most of his speech to warning that continuing economic insecurity, poll-tax discrimination, and armed forces segregation were arousing "the bitterest resentment among black Americans"; they recognized that under Roosevelt some progress was being made but rightly felt that the gains thus far had been "pitifully small" and that their own struggle for improved conditions was intimately bound up with "the struggle against anti-Semitism and against injustices to all minority groups."

In asserting his "respect and affection" for the people of the Soviet Union, Robeson rarely made any distinction between them and the government that ruled them—an equivalence that was common parlance in the world communist movement of the time, yet has opened him ever since to alternating charges of naiveté or rigidity. The *New Statesman and Nation* echoed the view of many in 1955 when it wrote, "Paul is courageous but not sophisticated about politics. . . . His personal warmth and generosity, his bigness and his kindness, made him everybody's friend—and many of those friendships have lasted despite the naïveté of his political activities in recent years. Even today, when Paul makes some outrageous statement, one which would seem silly or vicious in the mouth of a hard-boiled party official, one feels more embarrassment than anger."

But Robeson, in the words of Stretch Johnson (the entertainer and second-echelon black Communist Party USA leader), was "not so much naïve as trusting." He deeply believed in human nature, even though he'd learned deeply to distrust human beings—his faith was in the potential, not in current distortions of it. He'd seen, and come to expect, the world's every mean trick, yet in his heart he continued to believe that people were good and that socialism would create an environment that would allow their better natures to emerge.

The world has never had much tolerance for those who persist in arguing unseen possibilities against the abundant evidence of their eyes, for the champions of what might be as against what is. The powers that be, bent on inculcating narrow-gauged formulas about the "necessities" of human nature—and human society (on the acceptance of which the continuation of their hegemony depends) must always vilify those purveying a more sanguine message. This is not to say that Robeson never dealt in simplicities but, rather, that those making the charge usually did so on the basis not of greater sophistication, but of competing simplicities.

When Khrushchev revealed the full extent of Stalin's crimes at the Twentieth Communist Party Congress, early in 1956, Robeson read the complete text in the *New York Times* and put down the newspaper without comment. As his son Paul Jr., recalls, "He read it, he knew it was true," but "he never commented on it to my knowledge in public or in private to a single living soul from then to the day he died"—nor to his most intimate friends, Helen Rosen, Freda Diamond, and Revels Cayton. As early as the thirties Robeson had had some knowledge of the purges, and in the late forties some of his friends—Itzik Feffer, for one—had disappeared. He possibly regarded the trials of the thirties, as did many of those who were pro-Soviet, as necessary reprisals against the malignant "intrigues of the Trotskyists," believing that subsequent reports on the extent of the purges were exaggerations designed to discredit the Revolution.

He also adopted the standard argument "You can't make an omelet without breaking eggs," justifying the purges as *occasional* injustices, as the inevitable excesses inherent in any effort to create a new society, the excesses to be excused, if not sanctioned, on the basis of the principle that collective welfare takes precedence over the rights of individuals. Robeson would have approved the analogy offered by Andre Malraux: though Christianity has had its murderous inquisitions, few have demanded that Christians abandon their religion because of its past depravities. Still, Khrushchev's revelation of the sheer number of Stalin's crimes, his policy of *systematic* murder, shook the faith of many in the eggs-omelet analogy; and it suggested to some that brutality may have been endemic to the centralized authoritarianism that had come to characterize the Soviet system, displacing its earlier, visionary ideals.

There is no evidence that Robeson either disputed the accuracy of Khrushchev's revelations or discounted reportage of them in the Western press as exaggerated. His reaction *probably*—this must remain a "best guess," given the lack of concrete evidence—fell into the middle ground of disappointed acceptance: disappointment that the socialist experiment in which he believed had been derailed by the acts of an unsound leader, acceptance (and continuing faith) that in the long run the derailment would prove temporary and that socialism, still humanity's best hope, would triumph. Even this much he could have said had he wanted to clarify his position publicly. But he chose not to, chose silence instead, preferred to be called a stubborn dupe—naive at best, criminal at worst—rather than join the growing legion of Soviet detractors, rather than become himself (as he saw it) an obstacle to the eventual triumph of socialism.

However naive his continuing faith may have appeared to the world at large, it was an accurate reflection of one strain in Robeson's complex personality. While he essentially trusted no one, Robeson had, at the same time, a fundamental belief in the decency of most people, and held to the sanguine view that they were potentially as generous, as aware and as concerned about the sufferings of mankind as he was. He expected much of others—as he did of himself. He'd never learned as a youngster, as had almost all black Americans, to deal in limited expectations; treated in his own family like a god, he'd met in the outside world far fewer institutional humiliations than afflict most blacks attempting to make their way. Ingrained optimism had become a characteristic attitude; he expected *every* set of hurdles, with the requisite hard work and determination, to be cleared as handily as those of his youth had been.

But Robeson was hardly naive. Even as a young man he'd experienced enough discrimination in his own life, and seen enough desperation everywhere around him in the black world, always to have carried with him the knowledge that society was cruel and individuals frail. When awareness of the brutalities of daily life further deepened in adulthood, however, and disappointments over political attempts to mitigate them continued to mount, Robeson could somehow never entirely digest the world's bad news. "He was a softie," the black trade-unionist Sam Parks remembers with reproving admiration. "He never wanted to hurt anybody—it used to make me mad at him." With time, Robeson came to temper his faith only to the degree of accepting the view that social transformation would be a longer process than he'd originally thought simply because human nature had been more disabled than he'd once assumed. But he did remain full of faith—faith that one day humanity would rise to its better nature, that a cooperative social vision would supplant a ruthlessly competitive one, that human beings would somehow turn out better than they ever had, that the principle of brotherhood would hold sway in the world. There was no other attitude—with disappointments on every hand—that would have allowed him to persevere. Nor one, resting as it did on accumulated denial, more likely in the long run to produce an emotional breakdown (as it did).

Robeson's political identification was primarily with the Soviet Union in its original revolutionary purity, and not with its secondary manifestation, the American Communist Party. On the most obvious level, he was never a member of the CPUSA, never a functionary, never a participant in its daily bureaucratic operations (he told a close friend that its internecine warfare and rigidity made him miserable). He was a figure apart and above, his usefulness to the Party directly proportionate to the fact that his stature did not derive from it. The Party, as Eugene Dennis's widow, Peggy Dennis, has put it, "was just a small part of Paul's life." "I have a hunch," Dorothy Healey, the ex-Communist leader in California, has added, "that 90% of the inner-C.P. stuff was either unknown to Paul or, if known, considered unimportant."

He'd aligned himself with the Soviet Union by the late thirties because it was playing the most visible role in the liberation of American and colonial peoples of color; he'd aligned himself with the principles of black liberation and socialism, not with national or organizational ambitions. From his early visits to the Soviet Union, he'd taken away the overwhelming impression of a nation devoted to encouraging the independent flowering of the culture of different peoples—including nonwhite people—within its borders, a policy in basic opposition to the "melting-pot" view for which the United

States officially stood, The socialist principle could in practice be sabotaged or misdirected—as it was in the Soviet mistreatment of the Crimean Tatars—but to Robeson the principle remained uniquely attractive.

Despising American racism and viewing the Soviets as the only promising counterbalancing force to racism, Robeson was inclined to look away when the U.S.S.R. acted against its own stated principles, to look away fixedly as the perversions multiplied over the years, discounting them as temporary aberrations or stupidities ultimately justified by the long view, the overall thrust, the "correct" direction. Explaining Robeson's view (and her own), Dorothy Healey describes him as "well aware" of the Soviet Union's "terrible weaknesses" but nonetheless convinced that "it's going in a direction that you think is a proper direction. . . . You never settle it once and for all," but "you're not going to get caught in the company of the anti-Sovieteers." In ex-CP leader John Gates's comparable if more bellicose version, Robeson took "the classic point of view that all of us did. . . . This is a revolution, and you have to fight all kinds of people in revolutions, and sometimes innocent people get killed. It's a war."

—from *Paul Robeson* (1989)

Lincoln Kirstein and
George Balanchine

By 1933 Lincoln Kirstein's long-simmering search for a way to establish a classical ballet company in the United States picked up steam and intensity. In mid-May, he went up to Hartford to see his friend Chick Austin, the youthful head of the prestigious Wadsworth Atheneum, who showed him the half-completed new International Style addition to the museum; Lincoln noted in his diary that "his little auditorium is perfect for small ballets." Chick, like Lincoln, was a serious advocate of the arts and an audacious innovator. As director of the Atheneum, he'd transformed Hartford's reputation as the stodgy headquarters of the insurance business into an important center of cultural ferment.

Lincoln knew that although Chick was married, his erotic preference was homosexual, and he hinted to Lincoln, who also preferred men, about having recently indulged in "some highly irregular pleasures," saying that he'd tell him more some other time. Most people saw Chick as a charming, engaging, outgoing man, but Lincoln had a far different take on him. He intuited "glimpses of acute hysteria, like lightning in his conversation; a person of many splits whose energy could collapse at almost any moment, I think, if he was either confined or pressed. Really vicious: that is, unimaginative, morally repetitious and lazy." Lincoln's chief interest in Chick was to get him involved in some way, somehow, with his ballet plans. Lincoln suggested that the Atheneum host a "Ballet Demonstration," which he thought he could arrange for the following year. It was an idea Chick apparently "warmed up to." Lincoln said he'd provide more details soon.

Lincoln's interest in the ballet had initially quickened on his various trips as a teenager to Europe, where in 1929 he'd seen Sergei Diaghilev's Ballets Russes. Since then, with Diaghilev's death in that same year, the ballet world had become rent by factions. A number of émigré artists had been trying to lay claim to his mantle, and to find venues, patrons, and, they hoped, companies that might make their existence less precarious. George Balanchine, who'd been Diaghilev's last important choreographer, succeeded in putting together a group called Les Ballets 1933, a young company of some fifteen dancers, including Tamara Toumanova, Andre Derain, and Roman Jasinski. None of this would have come to pass had it not been for the events of a decade earlier, when Vladimir Dmitriev, a former baritone in the Mariinsky Theatre opera company, successfully engineered exit visas from the Soviet Union for a small group of artists, the so-called Soviet State Dancers. Among them were Balanchine, his first wife Tamara Geva, and Alexandra Danilova, who would become his "unofficial" second wife.

When in Europe during the summer of 1933, Lincoln—twenty-six years old at the time—met with Balanchine, and the two had "a long and satisfactory talk" in French; Lincoln thought him "wholly charming." A few days later, they had lunch, Balanchine arriving nattily dressed in a gray flannel suit, "his strong, delicate Caucasian face very animated" (as Lincoln wrote in his diary). They talked in some detail about the possibility of an American ballet, with Lincoln briefly mentioning Chick's museum at Hartford as a possible site. "We got frightfully excited about it all," Lincoln wrote. "I visualized it so clearly. He wants so much to come . . . says it has always been his dream. He would give up everything to come."

Lincoln then got "frightfully worked up" and, able to "think of nothing else," sat down and wrote his now-famous sixteen-page letter to Chick. It began with a grand theatrical flourish: "This will be the most important letter I will ever write you . . . my pen burns my hand as I write: words will not flow into the ink fast enough. We have a real chance to have an American ballet within three years' time. When I say ballet, I mean a trained company of young dancers—not Russians—but Americans with Russian stars to start with." Years later Lincoln claimed that he'd deliberately chosen "an optimistic style" in writing to Chick. But "calculated optimism" doesn't begin to capture a tone that singes with ardent intensity. Lincoln's words leap off the page with an almost libidinous passion. "You will adore Balanchine," he tells Chick. "He is, personally, enchanting—dark, very slight, a superb dancer and the most ingenious technician in ballet I have ever seen." Then, knowing his audience, Lincoln appealed to Chick's homoerotic side by describing the likely male star, Roman Jasinski, as "extremely beautiful—a superb body."

There had been earlier attempts to find a home for ballet in the United States, but although Anna Pavlova (from 1910 to 1925) and a few other internationally famous stars, as well as Diaghilev's Ballets Russes on its 1916–17 tours, had successfully drawn audiences, there'd been few opportunities to study classical technique and a scant tradition of indigenous choreography. Lincoln insisted to Chick that their planned-for school "can be the basis of a national culture as intense as the great Russian Renaissance of Diaghilev. We must start small. But imagine it—we are exactly as if we were in 1910. . . . Please, please, Chick, if you have any love for anything we do both adore, rack your brains and try to make this all come true. . . . It will mean a life work to all of us [and] incredible power in a few years." He assured Chick that he was not being "either over-enthusiastic or visionary."

But of course he was being both. Drunk on possibilities, perhaps feeling it might be now or never, Lincoln couldn't help throwing caution—along with absolute truthfulness—to the winds. Even if he'd been capable of a more modulated tone, it might not have appealed to Chick's own audacious nature. Bravado and amplitude were mother's milk to both men. If Chick was going to bite, the nervier the vision, the better.

Finally, on July 26, the long-awaited cable from Chick Austin arrived: GO AHEAD IRONCLAD CONTRACT NECESSARY STARTING OCTO- BER 15 SETTLE AS MUCH AS YOU CAN BRING PUBLICITY PHOTOGRAPHS MUSEUM IS WILLING CAN'T WAIT. Lincoln was elated and immedi- ately wired Balanchine in Paris. While in London, Lincoln received a further telegram from Chick announcing that he'd already raised $3,000 from some dozen people, with the architect Philip Johnson ($500), Jim Soby of MoMA ($500), and Eddie Warburg, scion of the wealthy Warburg clan ($1,000) giving the largest sums. The extraordinary Muriel Draper, already close to Lincoln, was also trying to raise money for the enterprise, though she confessed in a letter to him that she was having trouble envisioning the "poor Russians" in Hartford, "stopping for a Western at a lunch wagon." Her letter upset Lincoln because he knew she was at least "half true" about the cultural disjunction between the cosmopolitan Russians and the conservative business elite of Hartford.

Balanchine notified Lincoln that his friend Vladimir Dmitriev would be a necessary addition to any plans. When Lincoln met Dmitriev, he was immediately impressed with the older man's solid- ity and shrewdness. Aged forty, and with considerable experience, Dmitriev could be a formidable ally—or antagonist—depending on whether he felt Balanchine's interests (and his own) were being suf- ficiently protected. Lincoln could tell, he wrote in his diary, "how afraid they are to be left high and dry." The commercial failure in London of Les Ballets 1933, meant that Balanchine was feeling par- ticularly tender at the moment. He insisted that he did want, above all, to come to the United States, but as everyone agreed, it would be "a big risk and . . . very difficult to actualize." Besides, though he claimed a lack of interest in them, Balanchine had recently received several offers to stay in Europe, including an invitation to go to Copenhagen as *maître de ballet*, and to stage for the well-known and wealthy actress-mime Ida Rubinstein, an Igor Stravinsky–Andre Gide work for the Paris Opera.

Dimitriev, Lincoln wrote Chick, felt that the project fell into two distinct parts: a school to train dancers and a ballet company to perform; and at first "everything should be centered around the foundation of a school . . . nothing at all should be mentioned about a company or ballets." Lincoln urged on Chick the formation of a private corporation, arguing that it, and not the Atheneum trustees, must hold "the whiphand." He reiterated that "such a chance as now presents itself comes but once in a lifetime," and lamented that it should be at a time of such general economic distress. "When I think," he wrote Chick, "of the cash spent on the bushes and shrubbery of the Philadelphia Museum, of the people who collect stamps and matchboxes, I go mad. This will be no collection, but living art—and the chance for perfect creation. . . ."

Ready or not, the day of Balanchine's arrival was suddenly upon them. In the early evening of October 17, 1933, Lincoln, Chick, and Eddie Warburg gathered dockside to await Balanchine's and Dmitriev's debarkation from the *Olympic*. They went immediately to the duplex apartment he'd rented for them on the thirty-fourth floor of the Barbizon-Plaza at Fifty-Eighth and Sixth; Lincoln had decided to splurge on the steep twelve-dollars-a-night rental to help create a favorable first impression.

After dinner, Lincoln had the first of what would be many "heavy" talks with Dmitriev about plans for the school, Dmitriev telling him firmly that the importation of Pierre Vladimiroff, the prominent ballet teacher, was "a necessity." Dmitriev also made clear that the European offers Balanchine had had "would have paid him a lot had he accepted them." Lincoln boldly replied that he "knew Balanchine's services were not to be named in mere figures, but if it was money he wanted he wouldn't be here." Then, it was off, by car, to Hartford. On the way they talked politics, with Balanchine and Dmitriev expressing their grave fear about "the coming of communism" to the United States, and how no Russian "has any civil rights anywhere."

After seeing the museum's new theater, the Russians declared that it was "a big disappointment; there is no height; they couldn't use any scenery in it . . . the floor is too hard for dancing, the whole thing too small," that no more than twenty-four people at most could be put on that stage. Dmitriev said it might do well enough for rehearsals, "small ballets," or school performances, but no more than that. Dmitriev came quickly to the point: Hartford was impossible. It was too far away from New York, the facilities were unsuitable, the cost of living too high, and Chick's dilettantism (he'd made the mistake of remarking at one point that he himself would paint whatever scenery was needed) boded ill for a serious venture.

Was Hartford really a needed preliminary? Why waste time in a provincial backwater, and allied with a dilettante like Chick? Perhaps they could open the school straight off in New York under the auspices of MoMA—especially since Eddie Warburg had just given the museum a $100,000 check. Dmitriev felt that "Chick was wholly unimportant," and that they "never could work with him." Lincoln expressed his feeling that they had to have some sort of a sponsor in order to convince the public that this was not just another dancing school. The more everyone talked, the more Hartford faded into the background.

As they passed through Harlem on their way back to New York, Balanchine asked him if he'd "ever screwed a negress." No, Lincoln said, "but he'd always wanted to"—which would have come as surprising news to any number of Lincoln's closest friends. "*Alors*," Balanchine responded, "we will go together." Obviously Lincoln hadn't yet brought up the subject of his sexual preference, nor had Balanchine apparently surmised it for himself or heard about it from the many others who knew. Either that or Balanchine was playing cat and mouse. Dmitriev later confided to Lincoln that he "really didn't understand" Balanchine, that Balanchine "had no sentiment, liked casual fucking . . . no heart"; he was of "another generation."

As for MoMA, the director Alfred Barr read the prospectus Lincoln drew up "with great sympathy," and made several useful suggestions for improving it still further. But he told Lincoln frankly that he thought the whole idea was "utopian," that "no Americans could submit to the necessary discipline" for creating an

American ballet; in addition, Barr emphasized his belief that "European sources" were responsible for all American art—that there was "no possibility of calling anything primarily American."

Nonetheless, Lincoln notified Chick that the Russians had turned down Hartford as "unsuitable." Chick, in turn, "exploded" with resentment, and Eddie Warburg felt that "a definitive meeting" with him, without the Russians present, was necessary. Lincoln agreed and the two headed up to Hartford. The meeting *was* definitive—but hardly pleasant. Chick had already decided to save face by telling the local press that the venture had unexpectedly turned commercial and that the Atheneum could not possibly lend its good name to that sort of enterprise. He intended to announce publicly that he was voiding the contract with Balanchine and Dmitriev, apparently not realizing (or caring) that the contract was already void since neither man had as yet signed it.

When face-to-face with Chick in Hartford, Lincoln could feel his "just resentment." He told Chick how sorry he was that things had turned out the way they had, and made "several polite attempts to engage" him in conversation. They failed. Chick told him "bitterly" that he'd "hypnotized Eddie [Warburg] and betrayed him." Within twenty minutes the meeting was over. Lincoln felt that Eddie himself lacked any profound interest in ballet and it was questionable how long he would stick. Then there were all those people, from Archie MacLeish to Alfred Barr, who believed the project was misguided from its inception. And perhaps worst of all, despite a printed notice soliciting applications, no students were banging down the doors seeking instruction. That is, with one exception. A "boy" named Erick Hawkins, whom Lincoln remembered seeing in Harvard Yard, came by to say he'd already studied with the modern dancer Harald Kreutzberg and now wished to learn ballet from Balanchine. This was the same Erick Hawkins, of course, who would subsequently shift his allegiance to Martha Graham, become her lover, and play an aggressive role in her company before going on to found his own.

Then, just as Lincoln's gloom began to thicken, he and Dmitriev finally found "a dream place" for the school at 637 Madison Avenue, a space "better than anything [that] could be imagined." That same day they signed the papers for incorporation that they'd long been working on, with parity for all four participants: Lincoln, Eddie, Balanchine, and Dmitriev.

But these encouraging developments were paralleled by a sudden, sharp decline in Balanchine's health. After viewing his X-rays, Eddie's physician, Dr. H. Rawle Geyelin, came over to the hotel and said, in front of Balanchine (who was now running a high fever), that they had shown "an active tuberculosis spot" and he would have to go to Presbyterian Hospital for at least two weeks. Then, out of Balanchine's hearing, he notified Lincoln and Dmitriev that there was "another darker spot on his lung which might be a really serious thing. If so, he would have to go away for six months perhaps." In any case, "he could not live much longer than ten years, if that long." In response to Lincoln's direct question, Geyelin advised them not to sign any lease for the school—which, of course, they'd already done.

Though the number of students did begin to climb, by the end of 1933 only some seventeen of them (by Lincoln's estimate) were paying fees, which in total were projected to bring in about $10,000 during 1934. In the sketchy budget the four partners had drawn up, expenses came to roughly $22,000, with rent ($94 a week) and salaries the major items; Pierre Vladimiroff topped the list at $150 a week, and Balanchine and Dmitriev each got $100. (All these figures, in today's terms, would be approximately nine times higher.) That left a considerable projected deficit, even without factoring in any of the much-desired and discussed plans for performance and expansion.

Eddie's pledge of $12,000 a year and Lincoln's of $8,000 did, theoretically, cover the deficit. But Eddie would one day declare himself "satisfied with the way everything was going," and the next privately tell Lincoln that he was "consumed with apprehensiveness about the future finances of the ballet school," that he was wary of committing himself to what seemed like a bottomless pit, and that he doubted if Balanchine "understands American taste sufficiently to give them what they want."

Lincoln constantly had to play nursemaid to Eddie, reassuring him about everything from the school to his hemorrhoids to the endless crises attendant on his endless psychoanalysis with the brilliant but unscrupulous Russian émigré Gregory Zilboorg (George Gershwin was another of his patients). Lincoln thought Eddie essentially "soulless" and without any real commitment to anything. But out of both self-interest and friendship (at his best Eddie could be a charming companion), Lincoln played out his role of concerned confidant—half the time wanting to strangle him. One night, when Eddie had a bad cold, Lincoln stayed overnight in order to administer steady doses of tea and lemon. On another, Eddie asked Lincoln to talk him to sleep, and as he did (so Lincoln recorded in his diary), Eddie "became amorous and over a long sleepy period gradually worked "himself down and me up"—but Lincoln, "moist," stopped him. That seems to have been the only time Eddie attempted sexual contact, though Lincoln occasionally recorded other instances of Eddie's homosexual escapades.

Though his father Louis, a prominent partner in Filene's department store, was wealthy, Lincoln had no significant financial resources of his own, or none he could touch anyway, in order to meet his pledge to the school of eight thousand a year; in truth, as he wrote his father, "I have no idea how much money I own myself, that is, in my own name." Louis had grown accustomed to paying his son's bills and providing him with a monthly allowance to cover incidental expenses, but he constantly hectored him about his financial irresponsibility—even though it was Louis who'd set up the framework that perpetuated it: he'd kept Lincoln in the dark about his own assets, even after he'd turned twenty-one, and then, from his own pocket, had indulged his son's constant overdrafts. As a result Lincoln had become incorrigibly inept at keeping reliable financial records and had long since learned, when pressed, to turn to his parents to bail him out. . . .

Lincoln had seen himself as something of a co-creator with

Balanchine, and for months he'd been dreaming up ideas for new ballets based on American themes—*Flying Cloud* (about the clipper ships), *Custer's Last Stand*, *Pocahontas*, and (one that did interest Balanchine) a ballet based on the Rover Boys books. Still, Lincoln fully understood Balanchine's "righteous fear of dilettantism" and had no doubts about who the chief creative force was. But Dmitriev and Balanchine's combined remarks, sometimes cruelly overstated, made him increasingly feel like some sort of incompetent office boy, someone incapable of carrying out even the minor tasks assigned him. It rendered Lincoln upset and resentful. He tried to harden himself against feeling bitter toward the Russians, though (as he put it in his diary) "their iron lack of emollient words" did nothing to help his hurt pride. Lincoln had a habit, when feeling emotionally wounded, of believing that his current mood would be permanent ("I will never meet Balanchine or Dmitriev on friendly terms again," and so on), but he vowed to break the habit this time around, to work himself through his resentment. Yet the wound went deep, and he had trouble adjusting to what their harsh words had revealed about the diminished creative esteem in which they held him and the peripheral role they saw him playing in future plans.

Yet even during the worst of his pain, Lincoln recognized that he remained "influential," saw clearly enough that "Balanchine can be ably and efficiently influenced, if it is sufficiently indirect, flattering, and if the suggestions are validly imaginative. What my role would have been had I not been, as now, disappointed, I have, now, no idea. As a matter of fact I thought hardly at all of what I'd do, imagining only consecutive and charming collaboration." Yet instead of holding to his decision to be "cold-blooded" and coolly aloof while concealing his resentment, Lincoln in fact lurched quite quickly in the opposite direction, turning his anger inward, blaming himself for all that had gone wrong, indulging in an orgy of lacerating self-recrimination and a humiliating outburst of apologetics.

It was as if he couldn't manage to sustain an emotional middle ground, couldn't simply acknowledge where he may have made some mistakes or come up short, even as he justifiably held to account those who'd evaded their own inadequacies by trying to blame them on him. Instead he tended to lurch between fierce denunciation and savage self-blame. Always a man of extremes, he dealt all his life in hyperbole, crudely lashing out at others or holding himself infernally culpable and damned. What he called his "demons" rarely allowed, in personal relations as well, for a cool appraisal or for more than a fleeting sense of inner peace. . . .

Good news came from Dr. Geyelin; after examining Balanchine over the winter, a surprised Geyelin announced that it "might be the case to refute the old idea one could not get well from TB while in New York and working." All of which helped to dissipate months of gloomy apprehension and backbiting—though hardly ushering in an uninterrupted reign of harmony and sunny satisfaction. The School of American Ballet was, after all, a newborn; as with most infants, peaceful interludes were all but guaranteed to give way to some rude wailing and sudden spitting. Within weeks of the general rapprochement, Eddie was sitting Lincoln down for yet another lecture about his shortcomings and a renewed insistence that he go to see his analyst. "You aren't exactly mean," Eddie said, "but your nervous jumpings-about and your shortness with people gave a bad impression."

Dmitriev, having picked up on Lincoln's infatuation with the dancer Harry Dunham, decided to have the conversation that Lincoln had long been "dreading." He "couldn't understand Americans," Dmitriev announced to Lincoln when the two were alone one day. "He'd been here five-and-a-half months and he'd only met pederasts: Eddie and I never went out into the country, etc., with young girls: 'Were all Americans queer?' " Lincoln told Dmitriev he was right: "We are the nation of the great intermediates." (Lincoln had been reading Havelock Ellis.) "I was not apologetic or ruffled," Lincoln wrote in his diary, "but resentful at the arrogance with which he stated his position of . . . limitless normality."

Where Dmitriev could be openly abusive, Balanchine could be coolly dismissive. As Lincoln wrote in his diary, Balanchine could be "suggestible in small doses, in cafeteria intervals," but "a formal conversation tires him." After one talk between them about legal and financial matters, Lincoln could feel "Balanchine's slight contempt" and it left him all "loose and worried" and prone to nightmares; in one bad dream, "Balanchine a murderer; myself shipwrecked. Disaster and guilt all around."

During the winter of 1934 Lincoln and Balanchine did have at least a few discussions involving "creative" issues. What Balanchine primarily wanted from Lincoln was not creativity or collaboration but small-task efficiency—and large sums of money. Lincoln was perfectly willing to sweat and toil in the trenches, and did so prodigiously, but efficiency at niggling detail work wasn't well suited to his offhanded nature, his baronial sense of consequence, and his stirring dreams. Being relegated to treadmill routines amounted to an insulting misreading of his temperament and talent, of his high intelligence and genuine artistic sensitivity. Lincoln had envisioned himself as sitting at the helm of an ocean liner, not working the ropes on the assisting tugboat. Feeling unappreciated and underutilized, he turned increasingly to the ego-soothing pursuits of writing ("My bitterness against Balanchine and Dmitriev conveniently keeping me in my room"), lecturing, and socializing. . . .

Lincoln felt that he, more than Balanchine, knew what might be most special about "*American* dancing," about what he called the "unique, indigenous, and creative style of American dances, choreographers, and composers." "Instead of setting a stereotype of remoteness, spectral grandeur, and visionary brilliance," he wrote in an April 1938 column in *The Nation*, "Americans are volatile, intimate, frank. . . . The most important thing about American dancers is the retention of their amateur status and their nearness to the audience . . . the frontier spirit of spontaneous collective entertainment, where everybody got up and danced as they could, still persists. But with a difference. Our dancing artists have selected and amplified all that is most useful in the amateur spirit to make of it a conscious and brilliant frame for their individual theatrical projection"—and he explicitly included not merely ballet or modern dancers but also the can-do "hoofers" Fred Astaire, Paul Draper, Ginger Rogers, Eleanor Powell, Buddy Ebsen, and Ray Bolger.

"Volatile, intimate, frank" were shrewd if contestable definitions of the American essence (certainly in dance, "energy" and "athleticism" might just as easily serve), yet at the very least Lincoln had put his finger on some recognizable, canny half-truths, and throughout his life he'd continue to hone his definition of "American."

—from *The Worlds of Lincoln Kirstein* (2007)

Howard Zinn

Atlanta

It was raining and hot when the Zinn family arrived in Atlanta in August 1956. It immediately struck them that this felt different from a typical New York summer evening. Though late in the season, the air was still redolent with the sweet smell of the city's famed magnolias and honeysuckle. Having grown up amidst cramped, urban grit and gridlocked crowds filled with noisy humanity, the quiet of Atlanta felt strange, even a bit unnerving. Plus it was obvious at once that this wasn't similar to the diverse mingling found in New York. Here there was black and there was white, and skin color everywhere determined location and expectations. Atlanta in 1956 was nearly as rigidly segregated as it had been at the turn of the century—and that included public transportation, water fountains, theaters, and libraries.

Spelman College epitomized what was true of the city as a whole. Though near Atlanta's center, Spelman was an island apart. An eight-foot-high chain-link fence—topped in part with barbed wire—surrounded the campus; Howard joked that it looked like "they were trying to keep the students in rather than intruders out." The campus itself was an attractive collection of mostly nineteenth-century red-brick buildings. For the first year, the Zinns lived in a poor white district in Atlanta, then moved on campus into the first floor in the back of MacVicar Hospital, the college infirmary, the apartment overlooking the tennis courts. In 1956, the student body consisted entirely of young black women—it wouldn't be until 1960 that a trickle of white undergraduates would begin to arrive—and the faculty was about one-quarter white. The school's mission officially remained what it had been since its establishment by two white New England women in 1881: to graduate carbon copies—"sedate, quiet, careful"—of young white ladies from a genteel finishing school, with their capacity to pour tea gracefully.

Most of the students' routine was lockstep: the day began with each making her bed, cleaning her room, attending breakfast neatly dressed, and going daily to chapel at 8:00 A.M. When leaving the campus, students had to sign in and out, to be accompanied by at least two other students, to wear stockings, skirts, and dresses, and to carry gloves and a purse. Young black men from Morehouse College (of which Martin Luther King Jr. was an alumnus) and graduate students from Atlanta University Center (AUC), a consortium of six colleges—both directly across the street from Spelman—were allowed to come calling but only for one hour; Spelman women, however, could not visit male apartments. Occasionally there would be strictly chaperoned dances, but no male student was ever allowed to enter a Spelman woman's room, and she was given exactly fifteen minutes to get back to her dormitory after a dance ended. She had an unyielding curfew every night of 9:00 P.M.

Only some two hundred thousand African Americans were enrolled in college in the 1950s (there were thirty times as many whites), and about half of that number were in all-black or predominantly black schools. The black colleges essentially survived on crumbs, receiving only 2.7 percent of state money for higher education and a mere 0.66 percent of federal funds. Howard found that some of his students, coming as they did from segregated secondary schools, were ill-prepared for college, though hungry for knowledge. Ironically, it was some of the "worst" colleges that (according to Howard) produced "some of the finest youngsters in the country—courageous, idealistic, informed"—those who in 1960–61 would spark the black civil rights movement.

The atmosphere seemed airtight to the Zinns, both on the Spelman campus and in the city of Atlanta. But in fact by the time they arrived, entrenched conventions had been challenged on several fronts. Black Atlanta in the early 1950s was marked, unlike most Southern cities, by a significant number of black-owned businesses and organizations, an elite that had managed to clear a narrow footpath between the prickly brambles of segregation. Representative figures of that generation, like the minister Martin Luther King Sr. or the attorney A.T. Walden, had built up at least minimal, behind-the-scenes contact with the white establishment.

The 1954 Supreme Court decision *Brown v. Board of Education* had declared segregation in the nation's schools unconstitutional. Hope was initially high in black communities across the country, but under the double lash of "liberal" white detachment and Southern white hostility, that hope was soon dashed. President Eisenhower publicly stated his disapproval of the Supreme Court decision and made no effort to enforce it. Nor did Congress, dominated by influential Southern Democrats, pass a single enabling law. Instead of white schools throwing open their doors posthaste to black students, white Citizens' Councils, determined that desegregation never happen at all, rapidly spread fear through the South. And their threats were not rhetorical: when the Montgomery bus boycotts began in 1955, the leaders' homes were bombed; when the brave Autherine Lucy attempted to enter the University of Alabama, she was greeted by an angry mob, and three days later, on trumped-up charges, was expelled.

Soon after Howard arrived in Atlanta in 1956 and began to know his students and to mingle generally in the black community, he recognized that surface politeness toward whites concealed strong feelings of indignation; the brutal murder of young Emmett Till by white vigilantes the year before the Zinns arrived pushed that anger up several notches. This suppressed rage had sometimes

broken through the crust in the form of individual acts of resistance, usually punished severely. The coordinated action that had
produced victory in the 1955 Montgomery bus boycotts, as well as
the National Association for the Advancement of Colored People's
(NAACP's) court battles, strongly suggested that group organizing
was the prerequisite for successful change.

Even before Howard's arrival, Atlanta had seen a few earlier victories in the long struggle for desegregation: the 1940s had marked
the end of the white primary, the hiring of black policemen (though
only to patrol black neighborhoods), and the opening of the city's
golf courses at certain hours to blacks. As Howard would often say,
the accumulation of such small victories, usually accomplished by
people who never make it into the history books, is a necessary precursor to a more widespread upheaval.

Few of the young black women at Spelman had ever had a white
teacher, and it was predictable that they initially greeted "Mr. Zinn"
with polite shyness. But thanks to his warmth, his down-to-earth
style, and his obvious lack of racism, the students quickly realized
that they had a friend in Howard. During his first year at the college, he became faculty advisor to the student-run Social Science
Club, where issues of the day were discussed and debated and where
Howard made clear his view that the injustice of segregation should
be confronted head-on, though nonviolently.

In January 1957, a mere six months after arriving, he suggested
a visit to the Georgia state legislature to observe its workings
firsthand. The group of thirty included a few male students from
Morehouse—one of them named Julian Bond, who the Zinns would
come to know well—and their white apartment neighbors, Pat and
Henry West (he taught philosophy at Spelman). No intentional
disruption was planned, merely observation. But when the group
went to sit in the gallery, they were confronted by a sign marked
"Colored," designating a small section. The contingent conferred
and decided to sit instead in the largely empty "White" section.

That produced an immediate uproar from the floor of the legislature. Members stood in their seats and shouted up at the miscre-

ants, while the Speaker grabbed the microphone and yelled, "You nigras get over to where you belong!" Police quickly appeared and escorted the group out into the hall, where they again conferred and—the mass upheavals of the civil rights struggle hadn't yet begun—resentfully decided to return to the "Colored" section. At which point the Speaker called up to them through the microphone: "The members of the Georgia state legislature would like to extend a warm welcome to the visiting delegation from Spelman College." As long as the rigid separation of the races remained intact, so did white Southern graciousness.

At the beginning of 1957, nonviolent radical activists like Ella Baker and Bayard Rustin helped to organize the Southern Christian Leadership Conference (SCLC) led by activist ministers, including Martin Luther King Jr. Like most men at the time, the ministers held sexist views—women were regarded as subordinate helpmates; SCLC's mission was racial, not gender, equality—and neither Ella Baker nor Rosa Parks was invited to join the patriarchal inner circle (though in 1958 SCLC did hire Baker as a full-time staff member in Atlanta). Nor were relations particularly cordial between SCLC and the NAACP, which tended to view the upstart new organization as unnecessarily duplicating its own civil rights work.

During the year that she worked for SCLC, Baker's discontent grew. Somewhat blind to King's relative modesty in the face of so much adoration, she deplored SCLC's growing reliance on his celebrity and its concomitant emphasis on a top-down organizational strategy that had the double effect of discouraging participation among poor, grassroots blacks while encouraging the all-too-familiar kind of demeaning deference that already marked their relationship with whites.

Baker decided to leave SCLC and turned her attention to grass-roots activity; within the year, she and Howard would meet. In the interim Howard suggested to the Social Science Club early in 1959 that the group might find it interesting (in his words) "to undertake some real project involving social change." One of the students suggested trying to do something about the segregation of Atlanta's public library system. The idea was enthusiastically taken up and the target chosen was Carnegie, the main library in Atlanta.

Along with Howard, the students enlisted the help of Whitney Young, then dean of the School of Social Work at Atlanta University (in 1961 he became head of the National Urban League), and Dr. Irene Dobbs Jackson, professor of French at Spelman and the sister of Mattiwilda Dobbs, then a well-known coloratura soprano and the first black singer to be given a long-term contract at the Metropolitan Opera. (Irene Jackson's son, Maynard Jackson, would in 1974 become the first African American mayor of Atlanta.)

The group carefully discussed a strategy plan. That its tactics would be nonviolent went without saying. Beyond that, it was decided to rely on polite but persistent and repetitive requests from Carnegie for books with obviously relevant content: John Stuart Mill's *On Liberty*, Tom Paine's *Common Sense*, or John Locke's *An Essay Concerning Human Understanding*. Each request got the same response: "We'll send a copy of that book to your Negro branch." (Atlanta had three libraries for blacks, all of them inadequate.) To further heighten the library's uneasiness, hints were made that a lawsuit might well follow if black students continued to be denied access to use of the books at Carnegie itself, with Professor Irene Jackson as one of the plaintiffs.

Howard was sitting in Whitney Young's office talking about possible next moves when a phone call informed Young that the Library Board had just made the decision to end segregation throughout the Atlanta library system. That swift and substantial victory preceded by nearly two years the wave of sit-ins in 1960–61 for which Greensboro, North Carolina, became the symbol. It also confirmed Howard's developing view—which would ripen a few years later into his book *The Southern Mystique*—that the typical white Southerner cared about segregation, but cared about other matters *more*, including economic profit, peer approval, and political power.

Greensboro, in fact, wasn't the first instance of black resistance. There'd been several dozen flash points during the 1950s, including the frightening struggle in 1957 to integrate Central High in Little Rock. But the underground fires of resentment and anger weren't quite yet stoked to the level of erupting in a mass movement. The Greensboro sit-in did make a significant contribution to that end. On February 1, 1960, four black freshmen from North Carolina Agricultural and Technical College sat down at a Woolworth's lunch counter in Greensboro, asked for service, were refused, and then stayed put at the counter until the store closed at 5:30. The following day, they returned—along with twenty-three other students— and in the next few days the protest quickly expanded, with at least eight other sit-down strikes that week in North Carolina alone.

The time now *was* ripe. The earlier generation had relied on more traditional means—like court cases—for moving desegregation forward, means that now seemed too slow for the new generation of black college students. Far more than their elders, moreover, they were insistent on basing decision making in the movement on ground-level participation. In their intensity, the sit-in generation could sometimes forget or minimize the major contributions that the older black organizations had made—necessary precursors, perhaps, to the militant turn the movement was now taking. The NAACP had focused on litigation, the Congress of Racial Equality (CORE) on reducing Northern racism, and SCLC on operating through the most powerful of black institutions, the church. Several leaders of the older organizations—Roy Wilkins in particular—had their doubts about the confrontational style, the "aggressiveness," of the sit-ins, and feared they'd prove counterproductive.

But if some members of SCLC and the NAACP were caught by surprise and reacted with disapproval, others, including Martin Luther King Jr., welcomed the new energy that now infused the black struggle. The (partly) spontaneous and variable nature of the sit-ins did take many by surprise—and as well, many of the historians who later wrote about them. Historians tend to be logical-minded types not comfortable with the unexpected and spontaneous, and thus not likely to factor it into their rational and confident "explanations" of why a given event takes place—thus missing the opportunity to underscore the messy triggers of change, the mysterious and unpremeditated elements in human behavior.

The Greensboro sit-in was widely covered in the national media and a veritable firestorm of sit-ins followed. Within days, a group of AUC students went to talk with Benjamin Mays, the most liberal of the AUC college presidents. Mays gave them his blessing, but soon after, he got a phone call from Roy Wilkins, the conservative head of the NAACP, who'd somehow gotten wind of the students' plans. He told Mays, who relayed the message to the students, that they should stick to their studies and that the NAACP would continue the desegregation battle through the courts.

Student leaders from all six colleges of the AUC consortium decided to ignore Wilkins and to publish "An Appeal for Human Rights" in three Atlanta newspapers, including the *Atlanta Constitution*. Roslyn Pope, president of the Spelman student government and close to Howard and Roz (Pope was one of many students who used the Zinns' home as a combination sanctuary and planning center) wrote most of the first draft.

The reworked "Appeal for Human Rights" appeared on March 9 and was then reprinted in *The Nation* on April 2. Howard thought the students had produced a "remarkable" document. It itemized black grievances in eloquent detail and asserted the determination "to use every legal and nonviolent means at our disposal" to end the widespread suffering under segregation. "The students who instigate and participate in these sit-down protests," the appeal read, "are dissatisfied not only with existing conditions, but with the snail-like speed at which they are being ameliorated."

Ernest Vandiver, governor of Georgia, immediately branded the appeal "anti-American," claimed it could not have been written by students (talk about a backhanded compliment), and predicted that this "left-wing statement is calculated to breed dissatisfaction, discontent, discord, and evil"—apparently a reference to a line in the appeal stating, "We do not intend to wait placidly for those rights which are already legally and morally ours to be meted out to us one at a time."

Six days after Vandiver's outburst, several hundred students from AUC staged sit-in demonstrations at ten different eating places in the city—including restaurants in the state capitol and City Hall. Howard's role that day was to call the city's newspapers at exactly 11:00 A.M. and read to them the list of restaurants where the students planned to sit-in. Seventy-seven of the students were promptly arrested—fourteen from Spelman, nearly all of them from the Deep South. One of the fourteen, Marian Wright, was photographed sitting calmly in a cell reading C.S. Lewis's *The Screwtape Letters*—a photo widely reproduced. By April, the sit-ins had spread throughout the upper South, and there were even a handful in the Deep South (though none of those, unlike in the border areas, were successful). That same month students from various colleges gathered in Raleigh, North Carolina, to form the Student Nonviolent Coordinating Committee (SNCC).

By midsummer of 1961, an estimated fifty thousand students (some of them white, like Jane Stembridge, Bill Hansen, and Bob Zellner, who became well known in the movement) had participated in sit-ins—four thousand of whom spent time in jail—and 110 cities had desegregated their public facilities. Yet the Deep South still held firm. The arrested Spelman students were never brought to trial, but a remarkable change had come to pass. Even the school's cautious president, Alfred Manley, for a time shifted ground. At commencement that year, he spontaneously congratulated the senior class "for breaking the 'docile generation' label" with their demonstrations. That same year the first white students arrived at Spelman as part of an exchange program, and several liberal whites joined the faculty. Simultaneously, the amount of contact with white students from other Atlanta colleges (like Emory) escalated.

This shift in climate meant that a significant number of Spelman students would become or remain active in the series of protests that soon followed. The next target chosen was Rich's department store, Atlanta's largest. Again, Howard and his wife Roz played significant roles. Entering Rich's, they bought coffee and sandwiches at the counter and then sat down at one of the tables. By prearrangement, two black students then joined them. Another group of four followed (including, again, Pat and Henry West) using the same strategy. Instead of calling the police, Rich's simply turned off the lights and shut down the lunch counter. A few more black students also showed up and in the semidarkness they talked contentedly among themselves until closing hour. By fall 1961, Rich's ended its policy of segregation and nearly two hundred other Atlanta restaurants followed suit.

By 1961, Atlanta and Nashville had between them become a kind of epicenter for SNCC, with its Atlanta office staffed by two full-time people. By then, Ella Baker and Howard had been invited to serve as senior advisors to SNCC—a measure of the high regard the radical generation of young black students had for them. The spring and summer of 1961 also saw the phenomenon of Freedom Rides. Designed to put an end to segregated interstate travel, they were no sooner inaugurated than they were met with savage beatings, firebombs, arrests, and jailings. In Anniston, Alabama, the melee was so bloody that several Freedom Riders had to be hospitalized.

The federal government tut-tutted over the violence, but continued to do nothing to stop it, though Howard and others strenuously pointed out the several sections in the Constitution that allowed for, even mandated, intervention by President Kennedy and Attorney General Robert Kennedy. But if they had the justification for acting forcefully, the Kennedys lacked the will. When the Freedom Riders were beaten with iron pipes in Birmingham and one of their buses set afire, the passengers barely managing to escape with their lives, Robert Kennedy did nothing—though the Fourteenth Amendment to the Constitution gave him the right, even the obligation, to overrule the states and to use the power of the federal government to protect citizens against racial discrimination.

But in 1961, the Justice Department did succeed in sending a shock wave across the country by initiating a large-scale prosecution—not against racist white thugs who'd been attacking nonviolent protestors but against eight black leaders of the so-called Albany Movement (plus one white sympathizer).

While the administration, reliant on Southern white votes, continued to dither, the Interstate Commerce Commission (ICC) ruled (and here the Kennedys *did* exert some pressure) that interstate bus and train travel must henceforth be completely desegregated. Still, an abstract pronouncement from on high hardly guaranteed local compliance—and especially not in the Deep South. That became all too clear when Charles Sherrod and Cordell Reagon, both veterans of the Freedom Rides, decided—with unimaginable courage—to test the ICC ruling in Albany, Georgia. They set up workshops to train volunteers in nonviolent action and picked up a dozen or so recruits for the tryout run. The plan was to sit at the lunch counter in the Albany bus terminal and try to get served.

But FBI agents had in advance alerted Albany's notoriously racist sheriff, Laurie Pritchett, and he planned a painful reception for the protestors. Cleverly circumventing the ICC ruling, he arrested the students for "failing to obey the orders of an officer," and had them jailed. This didn't in itself overly alarm those arrested since "fill the jails" had become one of SNCC's key tactics, yet SNCC did notify the Department of Justice about the jailings. Again, nothing happened. SNCC next tried to target the railroads. Once again Pritchett had them arrested, shifting the rationale to "disorderly conduct."

Within Albany's black community, word of SNCC's ongoing defiance spread quickly. Grassroots black support for the students became so decisive that much of the community's middle-class leadership fell into line—which hadn't usually been the case elsewhere. Three weeks later, Martin Luther King Jr. arrived in Albany to join the protest. Mass meetings and marches followed, along with many arrests (the total at one point reached 737). This time the ever-inventive Pritchett cited the offense of "parading without a permit," and—somehow—he also got the city attorney to obtain a *federal* court order banning further demonstrations.

At the height of the ongoing struggle, Howard, who'd been in and out of Albany since December 1960, got a phone call from the Southern Regional Council (SRC), an organization in Atlanta that specialized in gathering data on race relations. The SRC asked him to go again to Albany and do a formal report on what was going on there. Howard immediately accepted the assignment. A number of SNCC organizers were already at work there and several of his students had been jailed; he hoped it would be possible to visit them, but as it would turn out, the authorities denied him access (refused the right of visitation, he stood outside the jail—a stone building topped with barbed wire—to shout up to students and friends who'd been arrested).

The day after Howard arrived in Albany, local officials and the Albany Movement reached a verbal agreement; but it in fact made few concessions to the black community and soon fell apart. Martin Luther King Jr. and his close associate in SCLC, Ralph Abernathy, were called back to Albany from Atlanta to stand trial for leading an earlier demonstration, were found guilty on July 10, 1962, and were sentenced to forty-five days in jail or the payment of a $178 fine. They chose jail.

The trial produced a sensation, even leading Burke Marshall, head of the Civil Rights Division of the Justice Department and previously resistant to intervention, to put in a number of strategic phone calls to Albany officials. As a result, King and Abernathy were released the following morning. Soon after, a number of high-powered lawyers, including William Kunstler of the American Civil Liberties Union, started to put together a series of court cases to challenge Albany's unbending defense of segregation.

Further marches, prayer meetings, and demonstrations—along with arrests and bloody beatings—followed. The Justice Department, besieged by delegations, letters, and telegrams, in August 1962 finally filed a friend-of-the-court brief in support of the Albany Movement. Up to then the department and its head, Robert Kennedy, had, through their inaction, essentially been collaborators with the segregationists.

Howard continued to go back and forth between Albany and Atlanta, and in December 1961, the FBI, which had let Howard's file go dormant since the mid-1950s, picked up his trail again. Still referring to him as a "Communist," one agent reported to J. Edgar

Hoover that Zinn had been critical of Robert Kennedy "for his failure to prosecute civil rights violations and to protect the negro against white violence."

From the Bureau's point of view the foremost grievance against Howard was that he'd been denouncing the FBI itself for standing by and not protecting blacks when they were physically attacked. Going still further, Howard pointed out that one of the great problems the Albany Movement faced in getting FBI agents to take action in its behalf was that most of them were Southerners in origin and had been deeply influenced by the mores of their communities of origin. Whatever the reason, the FBI was no friend of the civil rights movement (the Bureau had no black agents). "Every time I saw FBI men in Albany," Howard claimed, "they were with the local police force." Yet in the presence of beatings and mistreatment, the FBI unquestionably had the constitutional right to intervene. But its agents, seemingly indifferent, at most wrote down complaints in a notebook—and then did nothing further about them. "Can you imagine," Howard later said, "the FBI watching a bank robbery and taking notes?"

In February 1963, Judge J. Robert Elliott announced his ruling in Albany against the movement's appeal for desegregation. After the hearing, as if to atone for it, Howard drove out to Lee County, where the night before a number of black homes had been shot into from passing automobiles, and commiserated with the families involved. The Albany struggle sputtered on throughout 1963. Pritchett's police became increasingly violent, and the federal government continued to do little about it. In an article in the *Nation*, Howard put the blame squarely on the Kennedy administration and its timid Department of Justice. "The national government," he wrote, has "failed again and again to defend the constitutional liberties of Negroes. . . . By restricting its activity to a few ineffective court appearances, the Department of Justice left the rights of Albany citizens in the hands of Police Chief Pritchett, who crushed them time after time."

Without giving up its determination to desegregate interstate facilities, SNCC, in coordination with CORE and the NAACP, added an additional goal to its agenda—voter registration—with the state of Mississippi a primary target and with the already-legendary Bob Moses as its lead organizer. Greenwood became the initial hot spot for the voter registration drive, and Howard and Roz were there during the height of the turmoil; he described SNCC headquarters as having "the eerie quality of a field hospital after a battle." The NAACP leader Aaron Henry early on became the racists' victim of choice: an explosive device was thrown into his home, another ripped off part of his drugstore's roof, and bullets were shot directly into his house.

Then, on February 28, 1963, twenty-year-old James Travis, a native Mississippian and a SNCC field secretary, was driving along U.S. 82 about seven miles from Greenwood, along with Bob Moses and Randolph Blackwell (a field director of the Atlanta-based Voter Education Project), when three unidentified white men in a car without a license plate pulled up alongside them and let go with a blast of gunfire. Moses and Blackwell were unhurt, but Travis was hit in his shoulder and neck, where the bullet lodged behind his spine. The doctor who patched him up said that Travis would have died instantly if the bullet had entered his body with slightly more force.

The episode was part of a reign of terror. Eleven voter registration workers, including SNCC's executive secretary, James Forman, were arrested, charged with "inciting to riot," and sentenced to four months in jail. The Greenwood police turned a dog loose on a group of blacks attempting to register. The SNCC office in Greenwood was set on fire, the phones ripped out of the walls, and all office equipment destroyed; the Greenwood police said they could find no evidence of arson. Four black-owned businesses were burnt to the ground just a block away from the SNCC office. And so it went: shootings, beatings, harassment, and burnings became commonplace. The climax came on June 12 with the murder of Medgar Evers in the driveway of his home.

Instead of being intimidated, still more volunteers, remarkably, arrived—many from the NAACP and CORE—to supplement the SNCC workers already on the ground. And Mississippi's own black citizens, long subjected to white violence and humiliation, themselves slowly began to join the activists—among them the sharecropper Fannie Lou Hamer. After trying to register to vote, Hamer was fired from her job, lost her home, and had to take refuge in a friend's bedroom—into which "someone" pumped sixteen bullets. Undaunted, Hamer next tried sitting down in a white waiting room at the bus terminal; she was thrown into jail and beaten all over her body with a blackjack.

When released, Hamer decided never to return to the life of a sharecropper. She became a field secretary for SNCC, joining a number of women—itself an affront to gender norms of the day—in leadership positions. In that, and in stressing maximum input from local black communities (what was beginning to be called "participatory democracy"), SNCC was providing a provocative alternate structure to the traditional one of middle- and upper-class white men monopolizing power and governing through top-down decisions.

When someone later praised Howard (they should have added Roz) for the courage he'd shown in putting himself on the front lines time after time, he responded, "It's not courage to me . . . I'm not going to be executed. I'm not even going to be given a long jail sentence. I may be thrown into jail for a day or two, and that has happened to me eight to nine times. I may be fired, I may get a salary decrease, but these are pitiful things compared to what happens to people in the world."

Howard felt that the newspaper accounts of what conditions were like in Black Belt jails insufficiently conveyed their horror. He decided to tape-record several of the young activists, including Willie Rogers, who'd recently been released: "We stayed in the hot box two nights. It's a cell about six foot square. . . . Long as they don't turn the heat on—with three in there—you can make it. There's no openings for light or air . . . they had a little round hole in the floor which was a commode."

Howard and Roz went with Bob Moses, Stokely Carmichael (a veteran of the sit-ins and Freedom Rides and soon to chair SNCC), and others to one of the more dangerous spots, the town of Itta Bena. "People came out of the cotton fields to meet in a dilapidated little church," Howard wrote, "singing freedom songs with an overpowering spirit." One of them was a fragile, tiny seventy-five-year-old woman who'd just spent two months on the county prison farm for trying to register to vote.

The conditions under which blacks lived in rural Mississippi—the grinding poverty and grisly brutality—could hardly be imagined by outsiders. Terrell County typified those conditions. Blacks were a majority of the population in Terrell in 1960, but only 51 out of 8,209 were registered to vote (in thirteen Mississippi counties no blacks at all were registered). Nothing had changed by 1963, yet forty brave people turned up for a registration meeting in a local Baptist church. Though several were arrested and a nearby black church burnt to the ground, the county's Judge Elliott refused to grant an injunction to prevent further intimidation of prospective voters, giving as his opinion that there was no evidence of any danger to those attempting to register.

It had become increasingly clear by 1963 that court litigation alone would not solve the voting issue as long as segregationist judges like Elliott presided over such litigation. Frustrated at the lack of change, some members of SNCC began to question the tactics of nonviolence. They were tired of passively enduring white violence and of being accused by such "moderate" voices as the *Atlanta Constitution* of being "law-breakers" for engaging in nonviolent sit-ins or voter registration drives. And they were angry after President Kennedy finally got around to passing his modest Civil Rights Bill in 1963 that a number of prominent Southern white "liberals" resisted some of its provisions. Ralph McGill, for one, opposed the public accommodations provision as a violation of white property rights—as did the *Atlanta Constitution*, and on the same grounds. Even a few African American leaders expressed their ambivalence—their caution outraging those in SNCC.

At SNCC's annual conference on April 12 to 14, 1963, in At-lanta, three hundred young people (one-third of them white) gath-ered to plan for the future. Howard appeared as one of the principal speakers. As if to bolster everyone's spirits in the face of an es-sentially stalled voter drive in the Deep South, Howard—whose optimism was nearly always on call, as intrinsic to his person as his warmth—put the best face on it. After all, he declared, the answer to the ongoing problems of discrimination can't be solved by the ballot anyway: "People voting are coming into a basically undemo-cratic political structure. When Negroes vote, they will achieve as much power thereby as the rest of us have—which is very little." The best hope of a solution was to create "centers of power," such as SNCC itself, outside the formal federal structures, and to use those centers as channels for exerting pressure on both local and national governments. There was no guarantee of success of course, not as long as the present administration remained in power; the president had done just enough, Howard felt, "to keep his image from col-lapsing in the eyes of twenty million Negroes." But no more than that.

Even today, one could make the case that racism is still deeply entrenched in the country—though the age cohort eighteen to twenty-five demonstrates far more progressive attitudes than its pre-decessors, and provides the chief grounds for being hopeful about the future. Still, the income distribution of black families hasn't changed much and the asset-ownership gap between blacks and whites is much greater than the income gap (and has become more so since the 2008 recession began). Nearly a third of African Ameri-cans have incomes below the poverty level; the rate hasn't fallen since 1970. Even those blacks who make it into the middle class often have very little financial cushion. For the poor of all colors, the least affluent households—the bottom fifth—no longer receive as much safety net support as they once did, their share of federal benefits falling from 54 percent in 1979 to 36 percent in 2007.

Though many more blacks are in college than previously, more than a quarter of all African Americans still lack even a high school diploma. As Michelle Alexander discusses in *The New Jim Crow*, one out of four black men in their twenties are currently in jail, on probation or parole as a direct corollary of the War on Drugs—often for possession of a small amount of marijuana (and the proportion of blacks and whites who consume drugs is roughly the same).

Residential segregation in the North and West, moreover, remains nearly as powerful as ever, except in metropolitan areas with small black populations—like Tucson. Three-quarters of Americans live under highly segregated conditions: public schools are becoming steadily *re*segregated, and three-quarters of all African Americans are still housed in black *or* white neighborhoods, which in turn leads to segregated schools. Nor has our electoral process seen any marked changes. As of 2011, only two blacks have *ever* been elected governors of their states—and in the current Congress not a single senator is black. Yet liberal "gradualists" continue to argue that electoral politics is the best avenue to social change—though it's nearly impossible for blacks to win a majority of white votes (in 2008, Obama won with only 43 percent of the white electorate supporting him). As *The Economist* summed matters up in its issue of February 11, 2012, "the average black American is more likely to live in poorer neighborhoods, go to weaker schools, [is] less likely to find a job and less likely to own a home than the average white . . ."

Zinn and Vietnam

Howard Zinn, though he had no illusions about Communist rule in Vietnam, became one of the earliest critics of the war, feeling that protest against it was inescapable, and especially when the United States began its deliberate, large-scale bombing of civilians. Nor did he feel that such protest would detract from the black struggle he'd been centrally active in—he thought the two intricately linked. Civil rights workers in the South had long ago learned to distrust the government, local and federal, and they were among the first to resist the draft—unlike the Students for a Democratic Society (SDS) membership.

The older, more conservative black organizations—especially the Urban League, the NAACP, and SCLC—initially tabled all resolutions that condemned American policy in Vietnam. But increasing numbers of young blacks were scornful of those organizations and were outspoken against the war. In 1965, it remained unclear whether the civil rights movement and the protest against the war in Vietnam would become mutually supportive issues or divisive ones.

In the fall of 1964, Howard began to teach at his new academic home, Boston University. He was as conscientious and as devoted to his students as he'd earlier been at Spelman—and no less conscientious about what he viewed as his public obligations. In the spring of 1965, he and Herbert Marcuse were the principal speakers at an antiwar protest on the Boston Common. It drew a disappointingly small crowd of about a hundred people. Still more discouraging, at Howard's own university it was possible to get six thousand signatures on a petition that pledged support for Johnson's Vietnam policy.

In a Gallup poll, only 4 percent of Americans believed there was no communist influence in the antiwar protests—against a full 78 percent convinced that there was "some" or "a lot." At the same time, Johnson began the bombing of North Vietnam and by the end of 1965 had sent 185,000 troops to South Vietnam. It was a difficult, even dangerous time for those openly declaring themselves against the war.

In August 1965, Zinn wrote an article in the *Village Voice* in which he advocated a discussion within SNCC on the question of whether civil rights workers should take a stand on the war in Vietnam. He gave as his own opinion that they should. How would they feel, he asked, if the various peace organizations refused to take a stand on black civil rights on the grounds that it might drain time and energy from protesting the war? Further, Howard likened the Vietcong—originally a small, armed force consisting of various ideologies and committed to land reform, which the autocratic Diem government had labeled "Communistic"—to civil rights workers in the American Deep South, characterizing both as "homemade uprisings against an oppressive system." But it wasn't entirely clear in 1965 who in South Vietnam was oppressing whom, and a number of people protested what they called Howard's "simplistic" analogy.

Yet he started to get a mounting number of requests to talk about the war at this rally or that teach-in. If the date on his calendar was open, he nearly always said yes. He did so primarily out of a sense of moral obligation rather than personal egotism, though being human, he did enjoy the crowds, the give-and-take, and the admiration. In 1966, the peace movement in the United States still wasn't very strong, consisting of roughly 10 to 15 percent of the population; the first large-scale protest march wouldn't take place until the spring of the following year.

In a piece for the *Nation*, Howard argued that our military action in Vietnam could only be justified if it was "helping a determined people to defend itself against an outside attacker." The administration liked to argue that it was acting to counteract the "aggression" of communist North Vietnam against the South. But in fact, guerrilla insurrection in the South was itself a grassroots reaction against the Diem regime's policy of herding villagers into concentration camps called "strategic hamlets" and consistently using torture; the insurgency did not originate in Hanoi and preceded the communist North's decision to take part in it. When the first battalion of some five hundred North Vietnamese—and this is according to U.S. intelligence reports—arrived in the South in late 1964 or early 1965, the United States already had forty thousand troops there and had flown thousands of bombing missions. The first foreign invader of South Vietnam had been the United States.

Central to the argument of Howard's path-breaking 1967 book, *Vietnam: The Logic of Withdrawal*, was the falsity of the Johnson administration's claim that the conflict was due primarily to aggression from the North. The government didn't truly believe in its own argument (it knew that if any cause was "primary," it was the wish to thwart China's domination in Asia) and Johnson had failed to prove his case against North Vietnam. The National Liberation Front (NLF) had inaugurated a civil war in the South as a local rebellion against its own malign government; only several years later, after the United States had entered the war in force, did substantial aid from the North begin to flow (as late as January 1966, when the United States already had 170,000 troops in Vietnam, a senatorial committee under Mike Mansfield visited Vietnam and reported to the Committee on Foreign Relations that there were still only about 14,000 North Vietnamese troops in the South—some 6 percent of the NLF's total strength of 230,000).

The NLF *did* represent a nationalist-communist revolt against Diem's, and, later, General Ky's, brutal puppet administrations— and that alone, given the United States' attitude toward communism (still phobic, though Senator Joseph McCarthy no longer ruled the roost), would probably have mandated intervention. The threat of a unified and communist Vietnam under Ho Chi Minh was quite literally waving a red flag in the face of the United States—though as Howard argued, the chances for social reform and improving the lot of millions of poor Vietnamese would almost certainly be better than under Diem or Ky. But that was hardly the opinion of President Johnson: in the summer of 1965, he said "an Asia so threatened by communist domination would imperil the security of the United States itself."

Howard urged that the United States discard the notion that its withdrawal from Vietnam would—as a result of the often-stated but never proved "domino theory"—lead one Asian nation after another, with the help of China, to succumb to communism. Attempting military solutions for the socioeconomic problems of the underdeveloped world, he argued, tended to "bring about exactly what it is supposed to prevent": the destruction wrought by war made conditions still more miserable and their amelioration more distant. Howard used the earlier Korean War as an analogy. The United States had "won" that war "in the sense that we prevented the North Koreans from forcibly unifying the country. But the cost in human terms was frightful." Estimates of the number of civilians killed ran into the millions, with the landscape turned into a pile of wreckage—to say nothing of the dictatorship brought into power and "the end of political democracy."

Insisting that the United States did not belong in Southeast Asia, Howard broadened his indictment to question whether our numerous bases throughout the world were—despite the national mantra—in any way necessary to our "national security." Why assume, he asked, that various upheavals in Asia resulted from the "domino effect" rather than from a homegrown attempt to topple repressive regimes and to create better living conditions? Howard made the heretical point that Marxist ideals (which he never, unlike most people, confused with communist totalitarianism) appealed to people around the globe—"And why should they not?" he asked. "These ideals include peace, brotherhood, racial equality, the classless society, the withering away of the state."

It can even be argued that some totalitarian governments do improve living conditions. Perhaps Maoist China had done more in this regard than the preceding Chiang Kai-Shek government had, and perhaps Castro's Cuba was preferable in that same regard to Batista's. In any case, Howard was surely on the mark when chastising the U.S. government as tending to see "every rebellion as a result of some plot concocted in Moscow or Peking."

And surely, too, Howard's precocious insistence that withdrawal from Vietnam was the only sensible policy was prophetic. Withdraw we did some five years later, though in the interim causing a vast amount of additional death and destruction. When Howard wrote *Vietnam: The Logic of Withdrawal* in late 1966 (it was published in 1967), he was far ahead of the position nearly all public intellectuals—as well as the population at large—had adopted. Howard believed that "predation"—war and other aggressive manifestations—*was* deeply ingrained in our culture, but was *not* wired into our brains or our evolutionary past.

On April 30, 1970, President Nixon announced on national television that the United States had invaded Cambodia in order to attack North Vietnamese army strongholds there—a decision, he claimed, that he'd previously refrained from making "because we did not wish to violate the territory of a neutral nation." Not quite. For the previous thirteen months, the United States had secretly but steadily been bombing Cambodia. As documents revealed only many, many years later, Nixon had directly told Henry Kissinger, "I want them to hit everything," which Kissinger then relayed to the Pentagon as: "A massive bombing campaign in Cambodia. Anything that flies on anything that moves." In other words, "Let's git us a little mass murder." General William Westmoreland once openly asserted that "Orientals don't value lives."

For three *years* the Nixon administration had been bombing neighboring Laos, escalating by 1970 to the point where the Plain of Jars, previously a prosperous area, was all but obliterated. Now it was Cambodia's turn. Nixon had led the American public to believe that he was turning the war over to the Vietnamese and would be sending American troops home. But his April 30 speech, full of outright lies and overweening arrogance, declared that our "vital interests" were—again—at stake. The speech managed all at once to stun the American public and to give a shot in the arm to the antiwar movement. Nixon, predictably, denounced demonstrators against his ferocious policies as "bums."

One of the hundreds of protests against the invasion of Cambodia took place at Kent State University in Ohio. None of the marchers, who were mostly students, carried weapons or engaged in any violent act. Yet the Ohio National Guard nonetheless fired sixty-seven rounds into the crowd in a mere thirteen seconds, killing four, wounding nine (one of whom suffered permanent paralysis). A huge national response to the frightening event followed, with some four million students leaving their classrooms to protest the National Guard's unwarranted attack. A Gallup poll reported that 61 percent of the country now wanted the United States out of Vietnam no later than the end of 1971.

Howard's own protest activities continued unabated. Political commentators had been widely suggesting that the antiwar movement was in decline, an assessment that proved widely off the mark. Even during the winter months of 1970–71, a hastily planned demonstration in Boston brought hundreds of people out in zero-degree weather to protest in front of the Federal Building and then to march spontaneously through the streets. Only a few days later, fully five thousand turned out on the Common, though the press—unwilling to give the lie to its own analysis of "decline"—barely covered it.

Then, when the weather began to thaw, came the "Mayday" actions in the Capitol. Thousands were arrested on the steps of Congress, Howard included. He'd made the mistake of asking a policeman why he was beating up a long-haired young man—and after being beaten himself, ended up in a one-person cell packed with half a dozen others. They stood for six hours in a pool of water several inches deep, but were comparatively lucky: thousands of protesters were put for some thirty hours into the Coliseum stadium, so crowded and cold that there was no space on the floor to lie down at night, let alone food or blankets.

The following day, May 5, 1971, Howard was back in Boston, speaking on the Common before a crowd of some twenty-five thousand. "People who commit civil disobedience," he said, "are engaging in the most petty of disorders in order to protest against mass murder. These people are violating the most petty of laws, trespass laws and traffic laws, in order to protest against the government's violation of the most holy of laws, 'Thou shalt not kill.' "

—from *Howard Zinn: A Life on the Left* (2012)

Donald Webster Cory:
Father of the Homophile
Movement

Two crucial dates frame this story: 1951 and 1973.

In 1951 a book entitled *The Homosexual in America* appeared as out of nowhere, its author, Donald Webster Cory, entirely unknown. The book was the first full-scale nonfiction account of gay life in the United States, and its author spoke as an insider, an avowed homosexual. In opposition to psychiatric calls for "cure" and religious demands for "repentance," Cory's message to the homosexual was to "turn inward and accept yourself. . . . You are what you are and what I am—a homosexual. You will not outgrow it, will not evolve in another direction, will not change on the couch of an analyst."

We jump to 1973.

The January issue of *Contemporary Sociology* carried a lengthy essay reviewing some dozen books on homosexuality published in the wake of the 1969 Stonewall Riots. The author was Edward Sagarin, professor of sociology and criminology at the City University of New York (CCNY), a specialist in the study of deviance, president-elect of the American Society of Criminology, and the prolific author of a slew of books and articles.

In his acid essay, Sagarin derided the emergent view that homosexuals "are as healthy as anyone else," argued that "cure" was both possible and desirable, and denied that social oppression was the primary cause of such psychopathology as existed in the gay world. Children must continue to be taught, Sagarin insisted, that "it is better to have heterosexual than homosexual patterns."

Donald Webster Cory and Edward Sagarin were the same person.

Edward Sagarin was born in Schenectady in 1913 to Jewish Russian immigrant parents. The youngest of eight children, he lost his mother in the flu pandemic of 1918. After his father remarried, the family relocated to New York City, but Ed got along badly with his stepmother and eventually moved out. He then lived for varying lengths of time with different members of the extended Sagarin clan. His relationship with his father never recovered, and years later Ed had to be talked into showing up for his funeral.

Born with scoliosis, a lateral curvature of the spine, Ed had a noticeable hump on the right side of his back—his "posture problem," he would wryly call it as an adult. Frail, small, unathletic, intense, and very smart, Ed grew up with the taunts of his cookie-cutter schoolmates ringing in his ears. Children thus stigmatized often become sensitive to the pain of others bearing marks of affliction, as well as fascinated with how they cope with the world's mean-spirited assaults. But sensitivity need not automatically manifest as compassion. It can also breed murderous disassociation—or an uneasy mix of empathy and repulsion, affinity for another outsider alternating with oddly erupting, unbidden distaste (the projection of self-hate).

Though money was in scant supply, Ed did go to a good high school, and then managed to spend more than a year in France (where he met Andre Gide and learned French fluently—a skill that would prove important for his future business career). On his return to the United States, Sagarin enrolled at CCNY—in the late twenties and thirties notorious for its political passion and turmoil—and became active in left-wing politics. He felt special concern over the plight of black Americans (the concern would be lifelong), and the militantly left-wing National Student League sent Sagarin and two of its other young members (a second, ironically, the also clos- eted poet Muriel Rukeyser) to observe the 1933 trial in Alabama of the "Scottsboro Boys," nine black youths falsely accused of raping two white women. After the three students were harassed by local sheriffs, Samuel Leibowitz, chief attorney for the Scottsboro boys, appealed to them to leave town—which they agreed to do.

In 1934, approaching his twenty-first birthday, Sagarin met an- other young radical, Gertrude Lipshitz. A shared interest in left- wing politics initially drew the two young people together, and would always be a strong binding force between them; but their involvement deepened beyond politics, and in 1936 they married. Gert came from a warm, caring, orthodox Jewish family—itself a powerful magnet for the love-starved young Sagarin. It was also a family of activists; her father was a staunch union organizer.

Those who *casually* knew the couple during their marriage of nearly fifty years tend to describe Gert as "a Brooklyn Jewish house- wife, pleasant, level-headed, practical," a woman who took care of the home (the couple had one child, Fred), eschewed a career, and devoted her energies to her family. But those who knew the couple *well* shade the relationship quite differently. They agree that Gert assumed a traditional housewife's role, but insist she was far from the shyly hovering background figure described by those who saw the couple rarely and judged them superficially. Gert, her intimates knew, had strong opinions, freely verbalized them, and strenuously argued with Ed over this public issue or that paragraph in something he was writing. An emotionally centered, deeply principled woman, she was powerful ballast for her husband's comparative fragility. She also remained politically involved, and astute, all her life—active in nuclear disarmament groups like Women Strike for Peace, and later participating in protests against the war in Vietnam.

The Sagarins' intimates also uniformly testify to the couple's mutual devotion: "Oh, the marriage hit some rough spots of course," one of their close friends told me, "but what marriage doesn't? The fact is, they adored each other." In his 1951 preface to *The Homo- sexual in America*, Sagarin, writing as "Donald Webster Cory," put his decision to marry in less heated terms: in "later adolescence and early manhood . . . I struggled against my homosexuality. . . . Homosexual love, I told myself, is a myth. . . . At the age of twenty-five, after determining that I was capable of consummating a marriage (In later life, Sagarin/Cory confided to a colleague that "Gertrude is the only woman I had ever had erotic feelings towards. . . ."), I was wedded to a girl . . . who brought deep understanding to our union and who shared many interests with me."

The tone here is decidedly cool, not at all the stuff (or so we have been taught) of a promising union. The standard cultural script calls for the surging rhythms of romance, pressing sexual passion; their absence (we are told) connotes inauthenticity and foretells disaster. Add in the fact that Sagarin, even after marriage, would lead a parallel life as an active homosexual and would keep that secret from most of the world (and for a time from his wife), and we would seem to be looking at a relationship destined to fail.

But the cultural script most sexologists agree on is full of equations too glibly drawn. Sex is not the same as love (though it risks un-Americanism to say so), nor does emotional satisfaction hinge on ecstatic passion, nor "honesty" guarantee a secure peace. Besides, the sexologists contradict themselves. They also tell us that the most reliable bedrock for an *enduring* union is not rapture and frank-heartedness but more prosaic (and scarcer) stuff: being a reliable listener, an enjoyable companion, a caring friend. And all of *that* Gert and Ed had—plus a periodic sex life as well. *They* viewed their marriage as a success. Should we presume to know better?

As for when, and to what extent, Gert became aware of her husband's second—homosexual—life, she's preferred, in our several interviews, to leave the details shrouded. One close friend of the Sagarins believes that Gert went into the marriage knowing, without ever probing for specifics, that Ed had occasional (no more than that) homosexual experiences. But other intimates believe that Gert put the pieces together at some point later in the marriage—after hearing enough rumors, or receiving an anonymous letter, or herself coming upon evidence of a homosexual tryst.

What Gert was willing to tell me was that when Ed was writing *The Homosexual in America* in 1950 (some fourteen years into their marriage), she was well aware of the nature of the project—though not, it would seem from other sources, of the extent of the personal "research" involved. Whenever it was that Gert learned the full truth, she will not discuss (with me, at any rate) the extent, if any, of her turmoil over the knowledge, the shape of the resolutions she made, the exact measure of her accommodation. Perhaps she no longer remembers. Or ever allowed herself to.

With the Great Depression, Sagarin, like many others, had to drop out of college. He held down a variety of jobs to make ends meet, including ghostwriting and editing other people's manuscripts. He also put his fluency in French to good use, handling the European correspondence for a cosmetics firm. Gradually, he branched out into sales and management, and in the process learned a great deal about the chemistry of perfumes and the technology of their production. Born scholar that he was, Sagarin turned that knowledge into the stuff of serious, deliberative inquiry. He published several consequential articles on the sense of smell, and then—characteristically eager to maximize whatever restricted opportunities came his way—managed to persuade Columbia University to let him teach an adjunct course on the chemistry of cosmetics. In the fifties, he produced a massive, three-volume collection (*Cosmetics, Science and Technology*), for which he enlisted contributions from many of the country's leading specialists.

Sagarin stayed active in the perfume industry in various capacities into the sixties (for a while he was involved with a firm in which Lena Horne was a partner) without ever finding in it a true vocation or ever making much more than a decent living at it. Martin Rieger, a Sagarin associate from those years, vividly recalls him "with his old bound briefcase, schlepping through New York City, an intelligent type who didn't fit the business at all."

Neither Ed nor Gert ever cared much about accumulating possessions or money—it was almost a matter of political principle. The woman who edited several of Sagarin's later books, and knew the couple well, put it to me this way: "Ed never knew how to take care of himself," was "hopelessly naive about money" and "an easy mark" for the assorted sharks of the academic and publishing worlds; "Gert was the more practical of the two, but they were both babes in the woods."

Donald Webster Cory believed—and most sexologists would still agree—that Alfred Kinsey's two volumes *Sexual Behavior in the Human Male* (1948) and *Sexual Behavior in the Human Female* (1952) were unmatched for their integrity, scope, and influence. Cory made no claim that *The Homosexual in America* could "stand on the same shelf" with Kinsey's work. But he did claim—and there is no reason to doubt him—that he had "conceptualized [his own book] before I had ever heard of Kinsey." For years, Cory later wrote, "I had been impressed by the gap in the literature of homosexuality"—namely, how homosexuals "themselves felt, how they saw their lives, how they reacted to each other."

Before Kinsey and Cory, penologists and psychiatrists had been the designated experts on the subject, and they'd used their limited clinical samples to declare homosexuality pathological. In the sixties, the professional literature became more majestically moralistic and denunciatory still, as psychiatric "experts" such as Edmund Bergler, Irving Bieber, and Charles Socarides joined journalists like Jess Stern (*The Sixth Man*) in producing a widely accepted portrait of homosexuality as a diseased and dangerous scourge. Hollywood would begin to confirm that image with the 1962 film *Advise and Consent*, followed by a legion of movies with simpering, vicious gay men and murderous or suicidal lesbians.

The only partial exception in the early sixties—there were none in the early fifties—were psychoanalyst Robert Lindner's several books (*Rebel Without a Cause*; *Must You Conform?*). Though Lindner refused automatically to conflate homosexuality with pathology (or nonconformity of any kind with mental illness), he also believed that more needed to be known about homosexuality—"the source of immense quantities of unhappiness and frustration"—so that it could be better "eradicated." For a less tepid and compromised view in those years one had to look to Europe and to the sympathetic works of Magnus Hirshfeld, Edward Carpenter, and Havelock Ellis (all of which, from today's perspective, suffer from too much pseudoscience and too many confident overgeneralizations about "third sexes," and the like).

A good deal of fiction and poetry about lesbians and gay men *had* been published before 1951—from Gertrude Stein's *Tender Buttons* in 1914 to Gore Vidal's *The City and the Pillar* in 1948. But of "insider" nonfiction, there was almost nothing before Cory's 1951 book. The chief exception was *The Intersexes* (1908) by "Xavier Mayne" (the American novelist and scholar Edward I. Prime-Stevenson), a pioneering, underappreciated survey of homosexuality which Cory did not cite in his own book. He did, however, have high praise for Gide's *Corydon*, claiming it stood as a "great" philosophical discussion of homosexuality. It was in honor of Gide that Sagarin chose his pseudonym: Don Cory—a reversal of *Corydon*. He added the Webster to avoid the possibility, given the commonness of the name, of another Donald Cory suing him.

Cory had no team of assistants, no foundation support, no academic legitimization—none of the perks that today are the commonplaces of research in sexology. He did have one volunteer, a footloose, financially independent young man named John Horton, who'd recently gotten his BA in anthropology at Columbia. Cory gave Horton two specific jobs: to look up all the laws in the forty-eight states that applied to homosexuality, and to write to each department of the federal government asking if they had figures on the numbers of homosexuals who worked for them. (The results are printed as appendices to *The Homosexual in America*.)

When I asked Horton why he thought Cory had turned to him for help, he replied, "Maybe because I had a black lover. Cory had had a number of affairs with black men. He used to boast of the frequency with which he was able to pick men up along the benches at Central Park West in the Seventies"—then a major gay male cruising ground. According to Horton, Cory would occasionally invite a sexual partner or friend he'd grown fond of home to dinner, but he, Horton, was "the only one Gertrude thought was homosexual" (so she told her husband, who repeated it to Horton).

In the years Cory spent preparing *The Homosexual in America*, he (as he'd put it in the book) "became more and more struck" by the notion that homosexuals were, like more established ethnic, racial, and subcultural groups, a distinct and legitimate minority. This became the main thesis of *The Homosexual in America*, along with the implied corollary that homosexuals were entitled to the same rights as other citizens, and that majoritarian mistreatment—and not anything inherent in homosexuality itself—was chiefly responsible for whatever "pathology" could be found in the gay world.

Cory may not have been entitled to his claim of absolute originality in applying the minority concept to homosexuals. As early as 1921, Kurt Hiller, the left-wing German homosexual activist, had suggested something similar; and Harry Hay, the pioneering American gay radical, expressed much the same notion at much the same time Cory did. Yet it remains indisputably true that *The Homosexual in America* gave the "minority" concept wide circulation for the first time, thus laying the cornerstone for what has come to be called "identity politics."

Read today, *The Homosexual in America* has its decidedly dated and conventional sections. For starters, its title: the book is not about the homosexual; it's about gay men, and the references in it to lesbian lives are perfunctory and ill-informed. Other offhanded orthodoxies dot the pages: "the sexual instinct . . . is usually stronger in the male"; "a permanent relationship" is the surest guide to happiness; "promiscuity" represents a flight from intimacy; the aging homosexual is a "sad specter"; and so forth. Moreover, even as *The Homosexual in America* tries to demolish many of the reigning stereotypes about the gay world, it corroborates others. Denying the standard (and still current) view that homosexuals are more prone to depression and suicide than other people, Cory nonetheless maintains that "instability and restlessness" are defining features of gay male life. Though he was able—far in advance of his day—to see the iconoclastic stance as central to gay subcultural identity, he also negatively characterized the subculture as "fickle" and "rootless."

Yet the original, even visionary sections of *The Homosexual in America* outweigh the conventional ones and mark its true distinction. Against the current of his day, against the deep-seated tradition of American sex-negativism, Cory insisted that there was nothing dishonorable about sexual pleasure; that the human animal was "basically, instinctually, and naturally" bisexual; that biological theories about homosexuality were mostly bad science; that there existed a well-defined gay subculture, which was all at once unassimilable to mainstream culture and "a banner bearer in the struggle for liberalization of our sexual conventions." Cory urged homosexuals "not [to] fear the group life of the gay world. . . . It is a circle of protection. . . . Alone, you cannot change the world, but the combined efforts of many will surely effect a beneficial change."

Cory also sounded an astute—and astonishingly contemporary—note in insisting that "many homosexuals are, in the totality of their lives, not queer people at all, and many heterosexuals are extremely queer." He emphasized that "hard and fast categories"—homosexual, heterosexual, bisexual—are "rather meaningless oversimplifications." Some sixty years later, such views are at the ideological heart of what is called queer theory—the latest and purportedly new advance in gay self-understanding. Who would believe it? The themes of contingency, change, and fluidity being sounded in 1951 by a frail, gnome-like perfume salesman, trapped in a quixotic body, pulled in the deepest recesses of his being between anarchic Dionysian desires and the ordered virtues of Apollonian civics.

The civics part ("Promiscuity is a flight from intimacy," etc.) might have been less strenuously declared had Cory written in a less fearful and suffocatingly conventional time. In the early fifties, Joe McCarthy was in full, vulturish flight, political and sexual nonconformists were being purged from public and private employment alike, and not even the American Civil Liberties Union (ACLU) would lift a finger on behalf of homosexuals. When Cory, among others, tried to win the ACLU's support in 1952, the organization informed him (as he later described it) that "if we feel our rights have been denied, we should go to the district attorney and to the grand jury and fight without their aid."

Cory decided that "under the circumstances" the individual homosexual had little choice but to "take refuge behind the mask." For himself at least, he couldn't justify "subjecting those close to me to possible embarrassment or injury. . . ." Yet Cory made the decision for pseudonymity ruefully, aware that he was perpetuating a vicious cycle, realizing that "until we are willing . . . to identify ourselves . . . we are unlikely to . . . break down the barriers of shame or to change public attitudes."

But he hoped for the dawn of a different day, and at the close of *The Homosexual in America* he struck a millenarian note: "In the millions who are silent and submerged, I see a potential, a reservoir of protest, a hope for a portion of mankind. And in my knowledge that our number is legion, I raise my head high and proclaim that we, the voiceless millions, are human beings, entitled to breathe the fresh air and enjoy, with all humanity, the pleasures of life and love on God's green earth."

Today such words may sound vacuous and trite, when for decades growing numbers have been coming out and joining up. But in 1951, secrecy and fear were in the saddle, and visionary calls to arms all but unknown. A handful, like Cory, were doing *something*, however locally or anonymously, to change the oppressive climate, but most gay people, having been dutifully socialized in self-disgust, were spending their energies and exercising their willpower in concealing or denying their sexual orientation—or trying to change it through psychotherapy. Even had the needed self-esteem and courage been in greater supply, there was, in 1951, scarcely any organized political movement to come out into.

A handful of gay men, led by Harry Hay, Rudi Gernreich (later famous as a designer), and Chuck Rowland, had just launched the tiny and secret Mattachine Society in Los Angeles—the name taken from a medieval fraternity of unmarried townsmen. That same year of 1951, the owners of a San Francisco gay bar, the Black Cat, won the landmark right from the state Supreme Court *legally* to serve gay customers. Then, in 1953, the homosexual magazine *ONE* (and subsequently its corporate entity, ONE, Inc.) was launched in Los Angeles, followed two years later by the birth in San Francisco of the first lesbian organization in the United States, the Daughters of Bilitis, the name taken from Pierre Louys's erotic poem "Songs of Bilitis." These organizations comprised by the midfifties the minuscule "homophile" movement. The choice of the name "homophile" over "homosexual" itself illustrates the nervous hope of these pioneers that if they emphasized the nonlustful emotions (*philia* = friendship/love) they might better win sympathy and support from the antigay mainstream—not that it was aware, or cared.

When *The Homosexual in America* was published, Sagarin's employer somehow found out about his double identity and fired him. As he lamented in a letter to Kinsey, "I lost my job . . . directly and exclusively due to the book. It is difficult to understand how any progress can be made if economic punishment is inflicted on all who protest." (Kinsey and Cory had met briefly back in 1951 and occasionally corresponded until Kinsey's death in 1956. By mid-1952, Sagarin was using his real name when writing to Kinsey, though the level of intimacy between the two men never proceeded very far.)

Upsetting though the firing was, Sagarin did soon find another job in the cosmetics industry. Besides, the book itself proved a success. It went back to press several times during the fifties, was translated into French and Spanish, and elicited two thousand letters from readers—many of them versions of "Thank you for a ray of hope." Writing to a member of ONE, Cory contentedly summarized his newfound notoriety: "My correspondence is from all over the world, in many languages; people beg me to read a manuscript, leave it on my doorstep, threaten me with a lawsuit for failing to return it, take offense when I tell them how bad it is, and would not dream of paying for the return postage. Oh well, why think of the ungrateful when so many have written me letters that reassured me, if ever I needed it, that my work was worth undertaking?"

The Homosexual in America did indeed prove a landmark for many, including a number of people who went on to play important roles in the pre-Stonewall gay movement. Randy Wicker, active in both the early black and gay civil rights struggles, told me that he considers Cory's book "the most important thing in the early gay movement. . . . I was like a religious fanatic underlining passages of the Bible. . . ." For young Jim Kepner, who joined the fledgling Mattachine Society in 1952 and became an editor of *ONE* magazine, *The Homosexual in America* was "a clarion call in the dark for gays all over the country." Cory's book, Kepner told me, "gave a shot in the arm" to the newly formed Mattachine Society. He leapt with excitement one day when he was passing Pickwick's (the Hollywood bookstore) and saw stacks of *The Homosexual in America* displayed in the front window.

Barbara Gittings was so stirred by the book when she read it a few years after it appeared that she wrote the publisher (Greenberg, a small press that for two decades had been issuing gay novels, bringing down a post office suit on its head) for Cory's address, then went to New York City to meet with him several times. Cory told her about Mattachine and ONE, and in 1956 Gittings managed a trip to the West Coast, where she also hooked up with Daughters of Bilitis; two years later, she helped found its first East Coast chapter in New York City, was elected its first president, and later edited the pioneering lesbian periodical *The Ladder*.

The impact of Cory's book carried beyond gay circles. Kinsey, pressed by Cory for some sort of endorsement, managed (with characteristic Midwestern restraint) to call it "a worthwhile addition to the factual material that is available on the subject." Norman Mailer (with characteristic New York brio) hailed the book as revelatory. He even wrote an article about it for *ONE* magazine, in which he announced that "few books . . . [had ever] cut so radically at my prejudices and altered my ideas so profoundly. . . . I found myself thinking in effect, '*My God, homosexuals are people, too.*' "

In short order, *The Homosexual in America* became the ur-text for the pre-Stonewall homophile movement. And Donald Webster Cory became widely regarded as its "father," an admired, celebrated figure—even if within limited circles. Sagarin slowly began to involve himself further in the embryonic public gay world—always as Cory, not Sagarin. He also—using as a subscription base the large correspondence he'd received in response to *The Homosexual in America*—set up in 1952 the Cory Book Service; it selected for subscribers a gay-themed title each month, usually of high quality (*The Poems of Cavafy*; Angus Wilson's *Hemlock and After*, Roger Peyrefitte's *Special Friendships*).

Further, Cory began to give public lectures as well, most notably a militant speech at the 1952 annual meeting of the International Committee for Sex Equality at the University of Frankfurt in Germany. In it, he excoriated the puritanical view of sex and lauded Kinsey's work. But more, much more, had to be done, Cory argued at Frankfurt. He urged that efforts be made "to enlist friends among the medical, psychological, legal, and other professions," and, as well, to educate homosexuals themselves away from self-condemnation and toward a realization of the necessity of struggling against social oppression—precisely the kind of work that the Mattachine Society would increasingly undertake during the fifties. What had been accomplished thus far, Cory said, might appear "meager." But he stressed "the enormous importance of . . . beginnings. . . . This is a new cycle and a dynamic one. . . ."

When *ONE* magazine made its first appearance in January 1953, Cory agreed to appear on its masthead as contributing editor, a position he held for more than three years. In the most notable of the articles he wrote for *ONE*, he denounced the contempt most homosexual men held for the effeminate among them, labeling the attitude "anti-feminist, anti-woman"—for the day, strikingly phrased. He underscored, too, the irony of homosexuals "pleading for acceptance from the world at large," yet refusing tolerance and understanding to those effeminists within their own ranks who differed from their norm. Once again, Cory was sounding themes rare in that day, ones that continue to resonate.

Cory also distinguished between effeminacy and the "very distinctive [male] homosexual method of speech," with which it was often confused; the latter was a special argot, an "over-distinctive pronunciation of consonants and lengthy pronunciation of vowels." Here Cory was building on his earlier argument that homosexuals constituted a definable subculture—a matter still contested today—itemizing as well what he took to be a distinctive gay walk, stare, and handshake. He viewed these as reflexive, not conscious, and "neither masculine nor feminine, but specifically and peculiarly homosexual."

Back in 1951, after completing the manuscript for *The Homosexual in America*, Cory had asked Kinsey to approach Harry Benjamin, the pioneering transsexual (the term transgendered is now preferred) researcher, about writing an introduction to the book. Benjamin had begged off, but had suggested Albert Ellis as a replacement. Ellis at the time was chief psychologist for New Jersey's Diagnostic Center and had just published an iconoclastic book, *The Folklore of Sex*, in which he had mocked the American need to justify sexual pleasure with an overlay of romantic rhetoric and had made the unorthodox suggestion that "society makes sick people out of 'perverts.'" Meeting Ellis would prove a milestone for Cory—liberatory according to some, disastrous in the eyes of homophile activists.

Ellis had agreed to write the introduction for *The Homosexual in America*—and it had proven a curious one. While applauding the book as "by far the best non-fiction picture of the American homosexual" available and as a "well-warranted indictment of our smug and sadistic heterosexual persecution of homosexuals," Ellis had disputed several of Cory's views—and in particular his "pessimism concerning the possibility of adjusting homosexuals to more heterosexual modes of living."

Cory had argued in his book that homosexuality was "involuntary though not inborn," and therefore not susceptible to "change"—through psychoanalysis or otherwise. Ellis believed that exclusive male homosexuality denoted a neurotic fear of women, and thus could and should be treated. (In these years, almost nobody thought lesbianism was frequent or important enough to be worth much discussion.)

Ellis's treatment goal was not the standard psychoanalytic one of *annihilating* a male homosexual's drive, but rather of adding heterosexual attraction to his repertoire of desire. He claimed a high success rate with his own patients, but never bothered to explore whether those who'd successfully "expanded their options" had actually shifted the focus of their desire or merely their outward behavior—and even in terms of behavior, how many had subsequently "backslid." Similarly, nowhere in Ellis's voluminous writings, then or later, does he satisfactorily define the loaded terminology he casually employs ("neurosis," "disturbance," "inborn," etc.), nor ever question his basic assumption that *some* degree of heterosexuality is a prerequisite for happiness. His logic remained self-enclosed: he simply defined "exclusivity" as "neurotic," without ever offering a cogent discussion of "normalcy" as a concept, or discussing the criteria he used for recognizing it.

Ellis insisted when I talked to him that he'd never argued that *all* exclusively gay men were "disturbed"—merely "most." Yet in tracking his writings through the decades, it becomes clear that he admitted the *possibility* of some exclusively homosexual men being non-neurotic only in the seventies, after the modern gay movement had come into existence. But it needs to be added that as early as 1954 (in his book *The American Sexual Tragedy*), Ellis took the position—remarkable for that day, or this—that "what is scientific sauce for the goose should also be sauce for the gander . . . that exclusive heterosexuality can be just as fetishistic as exclusive homosexuality."

As early as 1951, moreover, Ellis, like Cory, had been arguing that heterosexual prejudice was itself of major importance in accounting for the psychological problems sometimes found in gay people. Moreover, both he and Sagarin were scornful of the monogamous ideal, seeing it as part and parcel of a sex-negative culture, and both argued for a reevaluation of prevailing moral values that disapproved of all sexual activity not (as Sagarin put it in a 1952 article) "romantic in origin and procreative in direction."

But for several years, some distance continued to separate the two men ideologically. Their disagreements centered on the degree to which homosexuality was "curable." Following Kinsey, Sagarin agreed that "people can and do change their patterns of sexual life over a period of years," and he was willing to believe "that certain psychologists can aid certain homosexuals in accepting a bisexual pattern of life." But (doubtless thinking of his own life) Sagarin continued to insist that those able to make a bisexual adjustment nonetheless went right on feeling "a major need for gratification with their own sex"—and therefore "cannot be said to be 'cured.'"

Unlike Ellis, moreover, Sagarin continued to assert in the early fifties that many if not most homosexual men could not—even when they badly wanted to and underwent prolonged psychotherapy—simply "add" heterosexuality to their repertoire of desire. He also insisted that the typical homosexual "can only make a satisfactory adjustment when he is prepared completely to accept himself and his way of life, without regrets, misgivings, shame, or unconscious defense."

By the end of the fifties, however, Ellis and Sagarin had come to hold nearly identical views about male homosexuality, with Ellis standing ideologically pat and Sagarin shifting his views in Ellis's direction. The likely explanation for the shift is that it resulted from Sagarin entering into therapy with Ellis. Ellis denies this ("It was a case of parallel evolution that we came to hold nearly identical attitudes about homosexuality") and even denies that Sagarin was ever in *formal* treatment with him. "The fact is," he told me, "Sagarin and I were never more than moderately close." From time to time, in the course of discussing other matters, Sagarin would talk over some of his problems, "but he was never an actual patient of mine."

But if Ellis wants no credit for either behavioral or ideological persuasiveness, several of Sagarin's intimates insist otherwise. One of his closest friends has strongly hinted to me that Sagarin turned to Ellis as a result of family pressure at a "tumultuous" moment in the marriage—perhaps when his son Fred was born: it was time, Sagarin was told, "to get control over himself." According to this same friend, Ellis's "repression technique"—which insists that one can learn consciously to control disruptive personal "obsessions" (what Ellis would later come to call "rational emotive therapy")— did help Sagarin curtail his homosexual "promiscuity." Sagarin believed enough in Ellis—by Ellis's own testimony—to send him "lots of referrals" throughout the 1950s, mostly "young men who had been his lovers."

On the other hand, we know for certain that Ellis was not Sagarin's first therapist. As he revealed in *The Homosexual in America* back in 1951, Sagarin had earlier realized that marriage had not "reduce[d] the urge for gratification with men," and "to rid" himself of it he had entered a "long analysis." To his surprise, Cory wrote in *The Homosexual in America*, the therapist had focused not on repressing or dissolving Cory's homosexuality but on overcoming his feelings of guilt about it—a goal achieved, Cory claimed in his book. His guilt did diminish and he found himself enjoying homosexual relations more than before, even while feeling fewer "fears and repugnances toward sexual union with a woman." Thereafter, as Cory completes the tale in *The Homosexual in America*, he'd adopted "a temperate and disciplined indulgence in homosexual affairs," and became entirely content with his "successful marriage" and "happy home."

Ellis agrees that Sagarin did have a good marriage, but disputes the rest of Cory's narrative. That first "long analysis," in Ellis's view, "didn't take. . . . When I met Cory he was an exceptionally promiscuous gay man." And remained so—though after *their* "few, informal sessions" together, according to Ellis, "Cory was able to get more pleasure from the sex he had with his wife." By 1959, in any case, after their views had become nearly identical, Ellis described

Cory (in print) as "the best adjusted homosexual, by far, whom I have ever met. . . ."

As part of his gradual involvement in the public gay world, Cory had joined the Veterans Benevolent Association (VBA), a state-chartered New York City gay male organization begun after World War II and serving its seventy-five to one hundred members largely as a social group. The VBA ceased to exist in 1954. (It had "run into a little difficulty," was Cory's oblique reference to a correspondent.) But the very next year saw the founding of a more overtly political organization: the New York City chapter of the Mattachine Society (MSNY). Cory had little involvement with MSNY during its first few years of existence, despite the fact that as early as 1953 he'd praised Mattachine's work on the West Coast as "remarkable." He'd occasionally attend one of MSNY's monthly meetings in its shabby rented loft space on West Forty-Ninth Street, but it wasn't until 1957 that he agreed to be a guest speaker there. Soon after, he brought Ellis along to a meeting and before long Ellis, too, was invited to speak. (This was at a time when most "experts" scornfully turned down Mattachine's invitations.)

Ellis's talk at MSNY raised the hackles of at least a segment of his audience. Many members of Mattachine, though brave and unorthodox enough to join the organization or at least show up at some of its meetings, nonetheless were prone to defer to psychiatric authority and to agree with the profession's then-commonplace equation of homosexuality with pathology. Yet Ellis's overbearing manner and dogmatic assertions that "fixed" homosexuality was a sign of "disturbance" and that psychotherapy should be given "a fair trial" so that "repressed" heterosexual desires could emerge, brought some angry rebuttals.

When he finished speaking, "slings and arrows . . . flew thick and fast" (according to the *Mattachine Newsletter*) with several people in the audience challenging Ellis's view that some degree of heterosexuality was a prerequisite for happiness. Though Ellis, as always, held his ground, he was not only invited back for additional talks but was also asked to write for the *Mattachine Review*. After all, in the context of the psychiatric profession of the day, Ellis was a decided liberal: he called for the decriminalization of homosexuality and was willing to testify in court against the common practice of police entrapment. By the late fifties, moreover, Ellis and Cory had joined forces to compile a comprehensive *Encyclopedia of Homosexual Behavior*—though despite several years of work and the completion of dozens of in-depth interviews, the project, due to lack of funding, was never finished nor published.

After 1957, Cory's own involvement with MSNY quickened. He never took on much of the nitty-gritty organizational work, but he did speak at the fifth annual Mattachine convention in 1958, let himself be listed on the board of advisors, and was then elected to the more hands-on board of directors (where, up through 1965, he compiled the highest attendance record of any director). Yet it wasn't until May 1962 that Cory finally took out formal membership. "After watching your valiant work for many years," he wrote in his application letter to Mattachine, "I have come to the conclusion that the movement for education and social justice deserves my active support. If I can be of some aid in this work, I shall feel gratified and honored."

Cory thereafter served on several committees, spoke before social and religious groups, and initiated dialogues with the YMCA on the treatment of homosexuals and with the New York Board of Health on venereal disease among the homosexual population. Randy Wicker remembers that at Mattachine meetings, he and Cory would, like competing auctioneers, try to outdo each other in exhorting members to increase their donations. By late 1962, Cory, with more than a touch of grandiosity, was writing Dorr Legg of ONE Institute, "There is a danger that the New York group might grow too dependent on me, and I do not want to exercise too much influence."

It was also in 1962 that Cory's real name became known in Mattachine for the first time. When a new book of his, *The Anatomy of Dirty Words*, was published, Randy Wicker remembers someone rushing into the MSNY office one day with a copy—with author

Edward Sagarin's picture prominently displayed on the back. If Sagarin (like so many other members of Mattachine) had tried to conceal his name, he'd never hidden the fact that he was married. As Frank Kameny, the pioneering Washington, D.C., gay activist, told me, "Everyone was aware that Cory was married—[it was] known and accepted, no deal made of it. Almost nobody in Mattachine was out of the closet. People's private lives were considered their own business. Besides, Cory had short-circuited any distrust of him as a married man by having written that book."

Sagarin himself drew firm boundaries, never inviting any discussion of personal matters. Mattachine bigwig Curtis Dewees, who probably got to know Sagarin better than anyone else in the organization, was occasionally invited to the Sagarins' Brooklyn apartment—but not when Gertrude was there. Dewees and his lover, Al de Dion, also active in Mattachine, viewed Cory (in de Dion's words) as "an icon, like a Godfather." Yet even so, they knew not to cross the line. As Dewees recalled, "My conversations with Cory were limited basically to the organization, the direction of the movement—that kind of thing; he *never* discussed his inner feelings with me."

Within Mattachine, Cory was regarded more with awe than affection. Not even Dewees was much drawn to him personally. "I respected the man's intelligence," he told me, "his capabilities, what he had done," but he "wasn't much fun to be around." He was too "dead serious" and when his opinion was challenged he could be "thin-skinned, easily offended, aggressive."

Harry Hay, the founder of Mattachine and *himself* often called "the father of the homophile movement," actively distrusted Cory. Hay first met him (the two had corresponded earlier) when Cory went to the West Coast in 1955 to speak at the new ONE Institute of Homophile Studies. "I did not like him," Hay told me. Having himself been in the Communist Party—and "astounded" when I told him that as an undergraduate Cory had had decidedly left-wing views—Hay had grown accustomed to sniffing the air and avoiding what he sensed might be risky people or places. "I never felt safe with Cory in the room. I had the sense I was dealing with someone shifty. I remember thinking, I wish he wasn't here at ONE. Who is he really?"

Young Barry Sheer felt no such reluctance. When the famed author of *The Homosexual in America* came across the room at an MSNY meeting to introduce himself, Sheer was delighted. He'd read Cory several years earlier when, as an undergraduate at the University of Colorado in Boulder, Sheer had joined the tiny local Mattachine chapter. It was there that he'd been introduced to *The Homosexual in America*. "It was," Sheer told me, "*the* book; we would read it and discuss it all the time." Sheer flunked out of Colorado after two years, returned to the East Coast, enrolled in Fairleigh-Dickinson College in New Jersey, and quickly hooked up with MSNY.

Sheer was a good-looking young man with a muscular body and (in his words) "an excess of testosterone." He discharged it generously into the less-laden bodies of the homophile leadership, gaining a reputation (applauded by some, deplored by others) as a "star fucker." Cory spotted Sheer at a Mattachine meeting one night in 1960 and—never one to play the shrinking violet—invited him out for coffee. "If he hadn't written this book and been a famous person," Sheer told me, "I would have said, 'No,' because he wasn't a heck of a lot to look at. Small, a loud, high-pitched voice, bald, somewhat deformed, and walked with a limp."

Yet Sheer quickly found himself involved in what he now calls "a 'Death in Venice' relationship. . . . Cory would give me a little money and have me help him with some of his research and I would let him have sex with me. . . . I couldn't be especially emotional, but he was quite happy with that, it seemed. . . . He'd come and see me two or three times a week. This went on for about three years." The "comrades" in Mattachine weren't kind about Cory's relationship with Sheer. As one of them told me, "Sheer was generally regarded as predatory," and Cory was privately mocked as a john who had to pay for sex—and who then confused it with affection. Sheer soon learned that Cory's real name was Edward Sagarin, and he even met

Gertrude once. He found her "a right and proper Jewish matron" and, in retrospect anyway, remains a little indignant at the way Sagarin was "two-timing" her.

Sheer enjoyed helping out with Sagarin's research, was attracted to his "powerful intellect," and enjoyed their frequent arguments about homosexuality and "the movement." By 1960 Sagarin's views had not only become indistinguishable from those of Albert Ellis, but were held no less rigidly. "We're a tree that's stunted," he would tell Sheer, "but even if a tree is stunted, does it not grow in its own way and offer shade and beauty? And shouldn't gays be treated that way?"

Sheer rejected that attitude as "condescending tolerance." He was part of a new generation emerging within Mattachine in the early sixties (epitomized by Frank Kameny and the militant Washington, D.C., Mattachine chapter), insistent that there was nothing to apologize for, nothing "stunted" about homosexuals, nothing other than society's irrational prejudice that needed "curing"— much of which, in a more tentative, diluted version, Cory had himself argued in *The Homosexual in America*, way back in 1951, before almost anyone else, before perhaps even *he* was fully prepared for the radical potential in his own message. In the interim had come Albert Ellis, a ton of psychoanalytic books "proving" that homosexuality was "pathological," Cory's growing doubts about the quality of comradeship available in the homophile movement, and his growing ambition to find greater "legitimacy" as an intellectual in the straight world.

At this same time, in the early sixties, the ideological struggle was heating up in MSNY about whether homosexuality was or wasn't a "mental illness," and the emergent forces, forgetting or never knowing what Cory had once stood for, were increasingly targeting him as the epitome of the played-out old guard. Simultaneously, Ellis (and family members as well) was encouraging Sagarin to follow his long-standing scholarly bent and formally pursue an academic career.

In 1958, at age forty-five, Sagarin entered an accelerated BA program for adults at Brooklyn College and completed his undergraduate degree in 1961—graduating in the same class as his son, Fred. He then, at age forty-eight, entered the MA program in sociology and wrote his thesis on "The Anatomy of Dirty Words." Scandalized at so unorthodox a topic, Sagarin's department rejected the thesis, but Sagarin got it published as a book in 1962, thumbed his nose at Brooklyn College, and enrolled in the doctoral program at New York University.

He'd accumulated just enough money to put the perfume business permanently behind him. Against great odds, he'd emerge by 1966, at age fifty-three, with a PhD, an academic job, and a prolific future career as scholar, teacher, and mentor. The orphaned, taunted, physically handicapped youth, the proto-intellectual toiling away uncomplainingly for decades in a business world for which he was temperamentally unsuited, the triply deviant (disabled, homosexual, left-wing) misfit with a double life—these burdensome, knotted earlier selves would never disappear but would recede, soften, inflict less internal pain, less centrally define a life that had refocused in the legitimizing, deeply gratifying new identity of Professor Edward Sagarin. Donald Webster Cory would remain alive in print, and in a corner of Sagarin's heart—but oh, the relief of not having him constantly tugging at the sleeve, demanding to share center stage.

Sagarin's personal transition during the early to midsixties took place at a time when cataclysmic events—the quickening civil rights struggle at home, the escalating war in Vietnam—were pummeling and reshaping American consciousness. The tug-of-war within the tiny homophile movement mirrored in miniature the larger social upheavals: the challenge to "expertise" (like those East Asian "specialists" who'd gotten us into the Vietnam war) and the new value placed on "differentness" (like the heralding of "Black Is Beautiful" and SNCC's rejection of the hallowed goal of assimilation).

Police harassment of gay bars had long been standard, and the clientele of those bars had dutifully cowered under the cop's club. But by the midsixties, knee-jerk deference to authority had weakened, and when the police raided a gay bar in San Francisco in 1964, a new organization instantly sprang up—the Society for Individual Rights—to protest police harassment; by 1966 it had enrolled a thousand members, becoming the largest homophile organization in the country. That same year, a group of progressive heterosexual ministers joined with gay activists in forming the influential Council on Religion and the Homosexual to combat homophobia.

On the East Coast, too, militancy was on the rise. Under Kameny's leadership, Washington, D.C., Mattachine brandished a new "Gay Is Good" slogan that spelled an end to apologetics and prefigured the aggressive confrontational politics of the post-Stonewall period. At MSNY, the conservatives dug in their heels and fought a rear-guard action, but the handwriting was on the wall. The young Turks started to snicker about Cory "the closet queen," Cory "the old auntie," "Auntie Donnie." Where once he'd been almost uniformly hailed for his pioneering role, he was now being ridiculed in *ONE* magazine as a "so-dreary goodykins."

Despite his new legion of detractors, Cory was more active in Mattachine from 1962 to 1965 than ever before, perhaps not least because he was *studying* it: the topic of his NYU doctoral dissertation was "Structure and Ideology in an Association of Deviants"— that is, the Mattachine Society. He sent the manuscript to Dorr Legg of ONE, Inc., who spent considerable time critiquing it and digging out additional source materials for Sagarin's use.

In these same years Sagarin also began his teaching career—on the Baruch campus of the City University of New York, where he offered a course on minority groups. One of his students at Baruch was Phil Goldberg (today a novelist), who was part of the counter-cultural coterie on campus; he and his friends had formed a Human Rights Society, raised money for SNCC, and gone South to help with the voter campaign drive.

According to Goldberg, Sagarin was one of the few faculty members sympathetic to their activities, and they were delighted when he agreed to serve as faculty adviser for the Human Rights Society. Sagarin may have begun his retreat from the homophile movement, but he remained decidedly left-leaning in his politics. Barry Sheer recalls how heatedly Sagarin would insist that "the government should take care of you and give you a good start," and if you then failed, "society should still take care of you."

One of Phil Goldberg's close friends, Eddie Zimmerman, enrolled in Sagarin's "minority groups" course. Sagarin encouraged his students to write in a nonacademic, personal style (he rightly prided himself on the lucidity of his own prose), and so when it came time to do his term paper, Eddie decided to write about what it felt like to be coming out as a gay man. When he got the paper back, he saw that Sagarin had written on it, "This is very remarkable. Please see me." Eddie did drop by the office, and (as he tells the story today) Sagarin expressed "great empathy for what I'd gone through." "I've done a lot of research on this," Sagarin told him, "and I think you would benefit from knowing about a group I'm acquainted with—it's called the Mattachine Society."

Mattachine's monthly meeting, he told Eddie, was coming up, and it promised to be a lively one: the well-known writer Donald Webster Cory was scheduled to speak. Eddie decided to go to the meeting, and when he arrived was delighted to see "so many ordinary-looking, mainstream types who were gay. It was important for me." Then, with considerable fanfare, the speaker of the evening was introduced—and out from the wings strode *his* Professor Sagarin! As Eddie tells it, Sagarin came up to him afterward and simply said, "Look, I took a big chance inviting you here, but I thought I should. But it's our secret." They had little subsequent contact, though Eddie does remember Sagarin introducing him one day to a young, blond-haired man, who he later told Eddie was his lover.

Eddie, of course, told his friend Phil Goldberg the whole story, and the following semester Phil—though not gay—decided he, too, would sign up for Sagarin's course. But he didn't much like the man ("He was strange, troll-like, put people on edge"), and planned a little theatrical coup of his own. For the section in the course on "the homosexual minority," Sagarin assigned reading from *The*

Homosexual in America. Phil carefully rehearsed his plan for how the classroom discussion would begin. Raising his hand, smothering his glee, he boldly asked, "Mr. Cory says such and such. How do you feel about that?" Sagarin momentarily blanched, then said, "Mr. Cory and I are of one mind about it."

Sagarin's ongoing discussions with Barry Sheer had made it clear to him (as Sagarin wrote in 1963) that "I was no longer viewing the new homosexual scene from within. . . . I was not of the generation that grew up after Kinsey (and Cory), the peer-oriented and other-directed youths," whose voices were beginning to be heard. Yet despite the growing disparagement of his views within Mattachine, Sagarin felt no need to adjust them. Instead, he decided to restate them in a new book, *The Homosexual and His Society*, and shrewdly asked young Barry Sheer to be its co-author. (Sheer used the pseudonym "John LeRoy," under which he had earlier written articles for the gay press.)

The book appeared in 1963 and became known as "The Second Cory Report." In it, the authors argued that the homophile movement should primarily concern itself not with trying to get people to join up, but rather with "trying to ease the difficulties" of those already involved and "to enlighten the public on its attitudes." That enlightenment would begin with the acknowledgment that homosexuality was "a disturbance"—but not "antisocial in its nature."

The Homosexual and His Society bravely devoted considerable space to what was widely regarded as "unseemly" topics—like hustling and venereal disease. Moreover, the authors justified their inclusion in words that have a decidedly contemporary ring: "The hustler, the cruiser, the lonely and the distressed, the muscle-flexer, the partner-changer, the effeminate hairdresser, the closet queen who is frightened, and the clothes queen who is courting social ridicule: yes, even the poor disturbed people who are caught up in the sad world of sadomasochism—they are all our brothers, and their cause is ours." This defense, however partial and patronizing, of outsiders of every stripe was complexly at odds with the fact that Sagarin was simultaneously fighting *within* Mattachine to hold homosexuals to a "responsible," nonconfrontational appeasement of the social and psychiatric authorities of the day.

"The Second Cory Report" was immediately and angrily attacked: the reviewer in *ONE* magazine, for example, denounced it as "pseudo-scientific" and a mere "rehash of other people's ideas." Sheer himself, in retrospect, regrets having lent his name to those portions of the book that claimed there was no such thing as a "well-adjusted homosexual" and that homosexuality originated in "a pathological situation based on fear, anxiety, or insecurity. . . ."

Yet in the counterattack, Sheer and Cory published at the time in *ONE*, they gave no ground. Indeed, Cory never thereafter budged from his now formulaic views: homosexuality was not inborn but was a "disturbance"; the homophile movement should "accept therapy for some and adjustment within the framework of homosexuality for others"; the movement should not waste its energy either trying to argue "the utter normalcy of the homosexual" or emulating "a monogamous, romantic concept of sexuality" that derived from the official model of heterosexuality.

Cory left unaddressed most of the troubling questions a new generation of gay activists had begun to raise: By what criteria does one establish "disturbance"? Why, if there was "no such thing as a 'homosexual,' " was there any such thing as a "heterosexual"? Why should an increased capacity to have sex with someone of the opposite gender be taken as the measure of increased health—or, for that matter, an increased capacity to have sex with someone of the same gender? What was a "normal" sex life anyway? And who decided? And on the basis of which fragment of the limited "evidence"? And who had the right to decide?

When Frank Kameny came up from D.C. to speak at MSNY in July 1964, he pulled the plug on the epistemological torture machine. "We owe apologies to no one," Kameny thundered. "Society and its official representatives owe us apologies for what they have done and are doing to us." He insisted that the homophile movement put less effort into trying to educate an indifferent heterosexual mainstream and more into direct demands for civil rights.

He assailed the unproven assumptions behind the psychoanalytic model of homosexuality as a "disorder" and insisted that "the entire movement is going to stand or fall upon the question of whether homosexuality is a sickness, and upon our taking a firm stand on it."

Sagarin was in the audience the night of Kameny's speech and (according to Kameny) expressed his disagreement "courteously." But disagree he did, and proceeded to work hard against Kameny sympathizers taking over MSNY. He even allowed his name to be placed in nomination for president on an opposition slate in the crucial 1965 election. Shortly before, Kameny wrote Sagarin a prophetic letter of warning: "You have gotten yourself associated with bad company . . . you have become no longer the vigorous Father of the Homophile Movement, to be revered, respected, and listened to, but the senile Grandfather of the Homophile Movement, to be humored and tolerated, at best; to be ignored and disregarded, usually; and to be ridiculated [sic], at worst."

The militants won the 1965 election, and most of the Old Guard within MSNY, Sagarin included, left the organization immediately and for good. Sagarin tried to adopt an attitude of resigned inevitability: it is in the very nature of social movements, he counseled his allies, to turn against their founders; but "the politics of rejection would one day lead to the possibilities of rehabilitation." This Olympian abdication concealed considerable indignation and hurt. Sagarin let some of it surface when writing to Dorr Legg the following year: ". . . the homophile movement is a hopeless mess . . . the biggest gang of potential blackmailers against real or alleged or ex-homosexuals in America consists of the leadership of the homophile movement. . . . I should like to state that I regard the homophile movement as inimical to the interests of homosexuals."

During the last twenty years of Sagarin's life, much changed: he ascended the academic ladder, reveled in the interchanges, intrigues, and joustings of scholarly life, and approximated his long-sought dream of working in harness with a group of like-minded comrades. He became an encyclopedic, adept teacher, and for his favored students—mostly male—an admired mentor. And he became the proud paterfamilias: his son Fred, who had chosen to teach handicapped and autistic children as a career, married and had three children of his own, whom Sagarin doted on.

While much changed, nothing changed. Edward Sagarin, his new alias, added volume upon volume to the already lengthy list of writings he'd produced as Donald Webster Cory (none of which he'd any longer formally acknowledge as his). A few of his many books remain in print and toward the end of his life he even got a novel published and a play produced.

Sagarin's nearly two dozen sociological works are (mostly) liberal in content and accessible in style. In his later years he often sounded themes (as he had in 1951) with a strikingly contemporary resonance: the malleability of the self, the need to historicize "expert" opinion and thus limit its claims to universality. ("Part of the changing process," Sagarin wrote in 1977, "is to believe in the possibility of change . . . in the interests of freedom of choice, one must reject identity.") None of his many books, however, can be seen as formative, theoretically innovative, or heretically heart-stopping. (On this, every sociologist I spoke to agreed—and every one requested anonymity.) Sagarin continued to champion outsiders and underdogs of various kinds (blacks, Jews, antiwar protestors, socialists, prostitutes, alcoholics, gamblers, pornographers, schizophrenics, dwarfs). He fought through his writing to rescue them from the categories of enemy, freak, or sinner, stoutly defending their rights against the smug majoritarian morality employed against them.

And yes, he even defended homosexuals—that is, on the limited grounds learned at Albert Ellis's knee: homosexuality should be decriminalized but not normalized. One should work toward alleviating the many injustices that gay people currently suffered, but "without accepting the traits that mark them as different." "In an analogy which I find striking," Sagarin wrote in a 1979 essay, "I have noted that blindness is undesirable but a blind person is not an undesirable." Homosexuality remained to him a "condition," a "pattern of adjustment" (as he put it in 1973) that represented, in essence, "a perversion of the instinctual drives." Sagarin felt no more need in the 1970s than he had in the 1950s to define the loaded, self-enclosed vocabulary that he continued to assert with such unabated confidence.

Yet his own sexuality remained unchanged—argue though he did in theory for the "malleability of the self." Barry Sheer dropped out of his life after some three or four years. Increasingly militant in the post-Stonewall years, Sheer wrote an article in 1970—"The Anti-Homosexual in America: Donald Webster Cory"—in which he cuttingly denounced his old mentor, advising the newly empowered young to forget but *not* forgive him.

Sagarin always scrupulously avoided approaching any of his students sexually. But he would still—the frequency decreasing with age and declining health—do a bit of cruising here or there, have a brief encounter, engage the occasional Times Square hustler. One of his forays to Times Square in the late sixties had particularly dire repercussions. The story centers on "Richard Stein," a young colleague of Sagarin's in the sociology department at CUNY. Stein was part of a group of New Leftist faculty whose politics had proved offensive to some of the older members of the department and who had therefore failed to get tenure. When Stein himself came up for a tenure decision, he felt that Sagarin's sponsorship would produce a positive outcome. But on the day the five-person executive committee of the department met to vote on Stein, Sagarin failed to show up and the vote, by three to two, went against Stein's tenure.

What had happened to Sagarin? The accounts vary. According to one of his colleagues (who feels certain that his version is the accurate one), Sagarin had picked up a hustler in Times Square and gone back with him to one of the fleabag hotels that then catered to trysts and transients. The trick had turned nasty, had mugged Sagarin, and then fled. Sagarin had had a heart attack in the hotel bathroom and been taken to the hospital. His wallet gone, he could not be identified for a full day. Stein himself doubts the accuracy of this account, primarily because he "saw no bruises of any kind" on his mentor when he visited him in the hospital.

In any case, Sagarin felt terrible about missing the crucial tenure meeting, and after he got back on his feet, he took Stein to lunch to express his deep regret. During the lunch Sagarin spoke openly—as he almost never did and had not before to Stein—of the fact that he was gay. That he did so—since the heart attack would itself have been sufficient explanation for missing the meeting—suggests intense guilt and remorse, giving added credence to the tale of the Times Square hustler. As for Stein, his career never truly got back on track.

By the early seventies, the "secret" of Sagarin's double identity had become known to a number of his colleagues and even to some of his students and friends. But those who were aware of Sagarin's other life, both sexual and authorial, mostly ignored it. As one of his most admiring graduate students told me, "There's a distinction between knowing and acknowledging. I felt it was impolite, not fair, nasty, to acknowledge Sagarin's homosexuality if he preferred not to discuss it."

But far from everybody knew. Robert Bierstedt, for example, who'd been chair of Sagarin's doctoral committee in 1966, was astonished when I revealed to him that Sagarin and Cory had been one and the same person; Bierstedt had never, in the intervening thirty years, heard any rumor or gossip to that effect.

Sagarin himself was still not publicly owning up to the double identity. The sociologist Vern Bullough told me that after Sagarin saw galley proofs in 1975 of Bullough's forthcoming *Sexual Variance*—in which he'd said something like, "Donald Webster Cory is also known as Edward Sagarin"—Sagarin contacted the publisher, Wiley, and threatened to sue. Before Wiley would agree to go to press, they made Bullough get depositions from various individuals who'd been active in the homophile movement affirming that Sagarin and Cory were one and the same person.

When the January 1973 issue of *Contemporary Sociology* appeared with Sagarin's denunciatory essay-review of a dozen recent gay liberationist books, Laud Humphreys, a professor of sociology at Pitzer College in California, hit the roof. Humphreys's own (by then notorious) 1970 book *Tearoom Trade: Impersonal Sex in Public*

Places wasn't among those damned in the review, but Sagarin had managed glancingly to refer to Humphreys's "unconvincing" work.

The two men had some startling commonalities in their histories: both had come late to academia and sociology, both were left-wing in their politics—and both were gay men who'd married and fathered children. The parallels may have fueled Humphreys's anger; he was feeling suffocated by his own half-opened closet door and enraged at the homophobic hypocrisy of his own university, which had tried to delay his degree and also the publication of *Tearoom Trade*.

After reading Sagarin's essay, Humphreys's first reaction was to send off a rip-snorting letter of protest to the editors of *Contemporary Sociology*. He accused them of having "ordered this mass slaughter . . . as a sort of 'protective reaction' strike to rid us of the troublesome 'homosexual researchers' and that embarrassing gay question all in one operation . . . a whole genre of contemporary sociology, not to mention a movement for human freedom, is scheduled for clever annihilation."

When Humphreys failed to get a response that satisfied him, he decided on a second line of attack: he would speak out publicly at the 1974 annual sociology convention in Montreal. Humphreys was scheduled to appear as a discussant on a panel ("Theoretical Perspectives on Homosexuality") where Sagarin was due to give a paper surveying the recent literature. In the paper, distributed to the panelists in advance of the session, Sagarin denounced those fellow sociologists who encouraged or supported homosexuals in "coming out." In particular, he denounced the respected "pro-gay" researchers Evelyn Hooker and John Gagnon as special pleaders who'd falsified or misread their own data.

After reading Sagarin's paper, Humphreys contacted a number of sociologists who he knew to be gay and urged them to attend the panel on the following day. He then stayed up all night preparing his rebuttal. Humphreys would ever after refer to the next day's events as "Bloody Monday." Sagarin read his paper exactly as he'd prepared it; he attacked recent "liberationist" scholarship and for good measure appealed to homosexuals to seek therapeutic counseling. According to *The Body Politic*, a leading gay publication of the day, Sagarin's remarks "were greeted with disbelief and laughter from attending delegates."

Humphreys then rose to respond. He began by fully coming out himself for the first time as "a gay man," and then—as he'd rehearsed the night before—periodically inserted "fake slippage" into his responding remarks; that is, he'd refer one minute to "Professor Sagarin," the next to "Mr. Cory"; at one point he addressed Sagarin directly as "Mr. Cory." In all likelihood, most of the audience had never heard of Donald Webster Cory—just as today almost everyone I've mentioned the name to responds with a blank stare (my favorite: "Don Cory? Was he the Mafia owner of the Stonewall bar?"). But Sagarin himself got decidedly rattled. When Humphreys moved in for the kill and sardonically asked, "And where did you get *your* data?" Sagarin's hands clenched and his voice choked up. "I am my data," he finally said. Tears fell from the corners of his eyes. To no one's surprise, Sagarin was not one of the participants when, soon after the 1974 convention and in part to protest it, the Sociologists' Gay Caucus was formed. Humphreys served on the original steering committee.

Edward Sagarin/Donald Webster Cory died of a heart attack in 1986 at age seventy-three.

—Harvard Gay and Lesbian Review, Fall 1997

Kinsey's Urethra

Beware the facts; they can lead you away from the truth. James H. Jones has unearthed an enormous amount of new information in his biography, *Albert C. Kinsey*. Let no one underestimate the achievement. But let no one confuse it with an understanding of Kinsey's life and work. Diligence is the beginning of scholarship, not the end point. Through research, scholars discover what material exists. Then they must decide what it *means*. Jones gets high marks for industry, low ones for insight.

The most myopic moment comes near the beginning of his book and is repeated throughout: Alfred C. Kinsey was "a homosexual." Oh, really? By what definition? Jones presents evidence—full, incontrovertible, and previously known only to a small circle of insiders—that Kinsey often had sex and occasionally fell in love with people of his own gender. Yet Jones also tells us that Kinsey was lovingly married for some forty-five years to Clara McMillen, and that their relationship was in no sense perfunctory, certainly not sexually. A decade into their marriage, Alfred and Clara were "eagerly" exploring various coital positions newly recommended by a friend, and they maintained a sexual relationship until Kinsey became ill near the end of his life. With Clara's knowledge, Kinsey also slept with other women during their marriage—as did Clara with other men.

Isn't it obvious that if Kinsey must be labeled, then bisexual or

pansexual is more appropriate than homosexual? For some unfath-
omable reason, Jones has chosen to ignore Kinsey's own famous 0–6
scale (0 = exclusive heterosexuality; 6 = exclusive homosexuality). By
using that scale, the simplistic category "*a* homosexual" would be
reserved for individuals whose sexual behavior was exclusively confined to their own gender. Or if not their behavior, then their fantasy
life. Perhaps Jones meant to argue that Kinsey *self*-identified as a homosexual on the basis of his erotic fantasies, discarding as irrelevant
his ability (and desire) to perform bisexually. *If* that's what Jones
means, he's forgotten to provide the evidence or make the argument.

Insiders at the Kinsey Institute place Kinsey between a 1 and
a 2—more "straight" than "gay"—when younger, then shifting increasingly to the "gay" side of the scale as he aged, but never becoming an exclusive 6. In other words, whether the yardstick be
behavior, fantasy, or self-definition, Kinsey considered his sexuality
malleable (and long before queer theory reified fluidity as the signi-
fier of sexual, indeed personal, authenticity).

Astonishingly, Jones doesn't get it. He not only persists throughout in referring to Kinsey as "a homosexual," but he tries to force
Alfred and Clara's relationship into the canned mold of "homosexual man seeks cover in a heterosexual marriage." Along with
vitiating all that was special and brave about the couple, Jones can't
even manage a complicated version of the gay man/straight woman
arrangement, presenting instead a tired stereotype of lost souls
(which he bases on a few outdated articles from twenty to twenty-
five years ago that he nervily refers to as "recent studies").

The other slot Jones drops Kinsey into is "masochist." It is one
of many terms—"voyeurism," "exhibitionism," "prurience," "pathology," "perversion"—Jones slings around, never pausing for
close definition. Judging from his footnotes, Jones's guiding experts
on "masochism" have been Havelock Ellis, Richard von Krafft-
Ebing, and Theodor Reik, now partly or wholly superseded by recent scholarship. None of the vast literature on sadomasochism that
has accumulated over the past two decades is cited, let alone argued
with or theorized.

Still, *Alfred C. Kinsey* does contain a considerable amount of new information. Thanks to Jones's prodigious labors, we are now privy to aspects of Kinsey's sexual life previously known only to his family and a closed circle of associates and co-experimenters. Kinsey, it seems, found that tugging on his testicles provided pleasurable/painful sensations; later in life, the stimulus had to be increased to maintain the desired effect and he took to tugging on them with a length of rope. Kinsey also discovered that the urethra was, for him, an erogenous zone, and over time he teased and plied it with various instruments, culminating in the use of a toothbrush. Later in life, he was also drawn to watching various S/M performances, but he preferred looking to participating.

These were occasional practices, not exclusive, narrowly focused fetishes. Kinsey utilized many other more conventional outlets for sexual pleasure. How we evaluate his more "extreme" (unconventional) practices will very much depend on our own sexual histories and our willingness to explore our own fantasies. In the process, we would do well to remain modest about our inevitable subjectivity and our limited imaginations.

James Jones is limited, but not modest. He is very sure what Kinsey's behavior means, and is very quick to characterize and denigrate it—usually with heavy-handed psychologizing. Kinsey's "inner demons" are given vast explanatory powers; catchall references to his "confusion," "anger," and "guilt" are made to substitute for any sustained, persuasive analysis of the inner man. A few samples: "By late adolescence, if not before, Kinsey's behavior was clearly pathological, satisfying every criterion of sexual perversion" (the "criteria" are not provided); he was "an exhibitionist extraordinaire"; an "aloof loner"; headstrong, stubborn, highly opinionated, gruff and arrogant; a man of "iron will," whom few liked; an unpopular teacher (who somehow attracted droves of students), a thin-skinned, manipulative elitist; a self-styled martyr and would-be messiah.

This kind of crude psychologizing (which is really moralizing) is far too formulaic to inspire confidence. Indeed, several of Kinsey's surviving colleagues guffaw at such a reductive view of the complicated man Kinsey was. "It's nonsense," says C.A. Tripp (author of *The Homosexual Matrix* and, in my view, the most rigorous and fearless disciple of Kinsey's sexual iconoclasm). "All that guilt and anger Jones keeps talking about—well, you could say that about anybody. Kinsey can't even get interested in gardening without Jones ascribing it to 'deep tensions' or explaining his scanty clothing while working the soil as a need to 'shock' people. And how naughty of Kinsey to stand nude in his own bathroom as he shaved!"

Where another biographer might, with justice, have emphasized Kinsey's remarkable capacity for open-minded exploration, Jones persists in negatively labeling nonconventional sexual behavior as "skating on the edge," or "compulsive" and "addictive" risk taking. He can manage to credit the homophobic sexologist Richard von Krafft-Ebing as having been prompted "by deeply moral concerns," but pansexual Kinsey is merely "sex-obsessed." This is like calling Albert Einstein "physics-obsessed." And it leaves us wondering what to think about James Jones, who has devoted twenty-seven years to researching Alfred Kinsey's "perverted" life.

Where all this becomes serious is when Jones uses his defamatory portrait of Kinsey, the man, to discredit his work as a sexologist. He does so through a morally slippery ploy: he generously quotes from Kinsey's antagonists (often mistaken), letting them do Jones's talking for him. Now and then, however, Jones's own indignant voice breaks through: "Despite his claim of coolly being disinterested," Jones hisses, "Kinsey was nothing of the sort . . . enthusiasm for sex was a fundamental tenet of Kinsey's thought, and it rang out loud and clear in his writing." Enthusiasm for sex? For shame!

Elsewhere, Jones refers to Kinsey's "facade of objectivity"—as if value-free social science has ever existed or been more than approximated as an ideal. *Of course* Kinsey's "personal needs and motivations" influenced his findings; this is primer stuff in social science. Besides, subjectivity cuts both ways: what it often means is that the sensitized investigator is able to see and reveal much that had previously been closed off to less personally engaged scholars.

The bottom-line question is whether Kinsey's personality, and personal engagement with his material, led to serious distortions in his findings. The two most common accusations against his *Sexual Behavior in the Human Male* (1948) and *Sexual Behavior in the Human Female* (1953) relate to the statistical methodology he employed in arriving at his conclusions, and especially at the finding that 37 percent of the adult male population has had at least one homosexual experience to orgasm and that 4 percent of the male population is exclusively homosexual. (Kinsey is often misquoted as saying that 10 percent of males are homosexual, a rating he reserved to males who score 5–6 on his scale *for three years* between ages sixteen and fifty-five.)

Jones repeats most of the long-standing critiques of Kinsey: "For all his posturing and bluster, Kinsey was chronically unsure of himself as a statistician . . . his sample was far from random," etc. But we are not told that Paul Gebhard (one of Kinsey's co-authors and his successor as director of the Institute for Sex Research), himself reacting to criticism leveled against the two volumes, spent years "cleaning" the Kinsey data of their purported contaminants— removing, for example, all material derived from prison populations.

In 1979, Gebhard, along with Alan Johnson, published *The Kinsey Data*, and—to his own surprise—found that Kinsey's original estimates held: instead of Kinsey's 37 percent, Gebhard and Johnson came up with 36.3 percent; the 10 percent figure (with prison inmates *excluded*) came to 9.9 percent for white college-educated males and 12.7 percent for those with less education. And as for the call for a "random sample," a team of statisticians studying Kinsey's procedures had concluded as far back as 1953 that the unique problems inherent in sex research precluded the possibility of obtaining a true random sample, and that Kinsey's interviewing technique had been "extraordinarily skillful." They characterized Kinsey's work overall as "a monumental endeavor."

In his shrewd way, Jones sprinkles his text with periodic praise for Kinsey the master researcher, the brilliant interviewer, the daring pioneer, the debunker of conventional morality. No heavy-handed conservative frontal assault for Jones. We learn that Kinsey was an active, loving parent (perhaps that's why we hear so little about his four children), a concerned mentor who stayed in touch with many of his students for years, a man of childlike wonder, and one capable of great warmth, gentleness, and generosity. How does this Kinsey fit together with the near-monstrous one Jones more frequently portrays? It doesn't. Jones never manages a coherent portrait (and personality contradictions *can* intelligibly cohere); the pejorative assertions that dominate the book simply overwhelm occasional references to Kinsey's positive qualities.

Why this insistent pathologizing of Kinsey the man and, by implication, the devaluing of his work? The moral values that have guided Jones's choice of emphasis come into sharpest focus in the contrasting way he treats two of Kinsey's closest associates, Paul Gebhard and Wardell Pomeroy. Gebhard, who gave Jones four interviews and whose testimony is crucially enlisted against Kinsey at various points, appears to have been the only male staff member unwilling or unable to sleep with men; he is pronounced "a free spirit," "a very likable man" with "a terrific sense of humor." Wardell Pomeroy, who distrusted Jones and refused to see him (now, with Alzheimer's, he is unable to defend himself), loved all kinds of sex with all kinds of people; he is dismissed as a "sexual athlete or superstud . . . a randy boy in a man's body," with "a character of little substance."

Get it? The exclusively heterosexual Gebhard wins the kudos. (Jones even dares to claim that among his associates "Kinsey probably respected Gebhard the most professionally.") Pomeroy, a man *by other accounts* of great charm, intelligence, and warmth, is dismissed as a vain creature, "whose taste in partners could be described only as broad, if not indiscriminate." "He fucks just everybody and it's really disgusting," says one of Jones's informants, who clearly speaks for Jones.

James Jones has not understood, or does not approve, Kinsey's foundational message: erotic desire is anarchic and will necessarily break free of and engulf all simplistic efforts (like Jones's) to categorize, and thus confine it.

Kinsey's work will survive this book.

—from the *Nation*, November 1997

Masters and Johnson

It's been clear for some time now that William H. Masters and Virginia E. Johnson aren't noted for their conceptual clarity or sophistication. In their first two books, *Human Sexual Response* and *Human Sexual Inadequacy*, their boldly modernist findings on physiology (the multiorgasmic and clitoral nature of female sexuality) were presented in jarring tandem with their highly traditional psychosocial assumptions (monogamous lifetime pair-bonding as the optimal condition for human happiness). But sympathy for the overall daring of their enterprise disarmed some critics, and their Olympian tone and forbidding technical vocabulary intimidated others. Besides, many hoped that Masters and Johnson's reluctance to speculate signaled the kind of stringent self-denial that might one day result in a carefully constructed theoretical synthesis that would subsume the earlier contradictions in their work.

With the publication of Masters and Johnson's *Homosexuality in Perspective*, that hope must be foresworn. If anything, the conceptual fog has thickened, the intellectual evasions and simplicities multiplied. One now fears the problem is less presumption than obtuseness, for the most astonishing aspect of Masters and Johnson's altogether astonishing new study is their inability to distinguish the banal from the noteworthy. They overvalue their more obvious findings and negate or misconstrue their most original ones.

Just as Masters and Johnson are overemphatic in declaiming the importance of their most obvious findings, they fail to recognize and underscore their most genuinely startling ones. Though its significance seems to have escaped them, they do offer data of immense importance in helping to advance debate on a number of long-standing (and long-stalemated) issues—and particularly the question of bisexuality.

Masters and Johnson present data on sexual fantasies gathered over a twenty-year period, even as they try to muffle the materials' subversive impact. To give but a few samples: homosexuals, according to Masters and Johnson, show "greater psychosexual security" than heterosexuals; all four groups studied—homosexual men and women, heterosexual men and women—express a high level of interest in "forced sexual encounters"; the fantasies of homosexual men contain a greater amount of violence than those of heterosexual men (who envision themselves more frequently as rapees than rapists—as victims of "groups of unidentified women"); lesbian women record the highest incidence of fantasy, and are the only group that includes current partners in their fantasies to any significant degree; the most common fantasy pattern for both heterosexual men and women involves the replacement of their established partners with somebody else.

Masters and Johnson's single most intriguing finding is the high incidence they report in all groups of "cross-preference" fantasies. Among gay men and lesbians, overt heterosexual interaction was the third highest fantasy; to an only slightly lesser degree, straight men and women fantasized about overt homosexual interaction. The last finding is especially remarkable, and for two reasons: the heterosexual subjects were overwhelmingly Kinsey 0 (that is, exclusively heterosexual); during face-to-face discussions and interviews, moreover, they described same-gender sex as "revolting" and "unthinkable." Yet the same men and women who vitriolically condemned homosexuality showed in their fantasies "a significant curiosity, a sense of sexual anticipation, or even fears for effectiveness of sexual performance."

If Masters and Johnson fully recognize the explosive nature of these findings, you'd never know it from their brief and bland discussion of them. On the high incidence of fantasies involving force, their sole comment is to caution against "necessarily" assuming any desire exists to act on such fantasies in "real life"—a statement that exudes less the air of scientific scrupulosity than personal repugnance. Masters and Johnson have never shown—unlike Alex Comfort, say, or Kinsey—much tolerance or understanding of "perverse" variations on the missionary theme. For them to acknowledge the appeal of "force" would be tantamount to admitting that the household staples (coitus, partner manipulation, fellatio/cunnilingus) do not exhaust the imaginations or appetites of even the sexually proficient. It would also mean opening the Pandora's box of sadomasochism, exploring the rising incidence in our society of sexual scenarios involving domination and submission, retrieving the S/M phenomenon from the scummy fringe to which traditional moralists (like Masters and Johnson) have comfortably consigned it.

Their reaction to the "cross-preference" data they present is cut from the same tweedy cloth. They simply warn against assuming that such fantasies indicate "latent or unrealized" attractions. And no more said. Yet it takes no great insight to deduce other plausible readings. It strains neither the evidence nor the imagination to see in the high incidence of cross-preference fantasies confirmation of Freud's hoary suggestion that all human beings are potentially receptive to bisexual stimulation, that even when we have grown up in a homophobic culture and have long since declared ourselves gay or straight, the wish to be both retains a strong subterranean hold.

Masters and Johnson keep to the same adamantly bland posture in the face of their remarkable finding that for both heterosexual men and women, the single most common fantasy is the displacement of their established partner. Five years ago [1975] in *The Pleasure Bond*, their only book aimed at a popular audience (an aim that required the services of a co-author to translate hieroglyphics into basic English), Masters and Johnson sternly equated infidelity with immaturity. That same animus, in more muted form, pervades *Homosexuality in Perspective*—indeed pervades all of their work. Though enamored of their self-image as "objective scientists" and tireless in referring to their "neutral," "value-free" approach, their books have always been drenched in ideology. In choosing to deny this, they've merely ensured that their own personal values would contaminate their data more, not less; for when the subjective component isn't acknowledged, its distorting effect is less easy to measure and contain.

Masters and Johnson's therapeutic concern firmly centers on the couple, with the needs of the individual subordinated to those of the marital unit. To maintain or salvage a committed relationship, the individual is expected to sacrifice a certain amount of freedom—especially in pursuing sexual pleasure. Pleasure and union, in this view, are apparently seen as at odds: the sexual drive inherently strong, the marital unit inherently fragile. What then justifies the heroic effort to curtail the one in the name of saving the other? According to Masters and Johnson, the marital unit is the only context in which something called "growth" can proceed. Does that mean "growth" and "pleasure" are discrete, even antagonistic entities? Unlike their Puritan forebears, Masters and Johnson seem never to have posed that question consciously, or thought through an argument for asserting the paramount claims of "growth," or that "pleasure" can't produce it. All that's clear is that on a subliminal level, they link growth with safety—the kind associated with the security of lifetime pair-bonding. But in substituting muddy hints for a reasoned exposition, they prove unconvincing advocates—especially for those who associate growth with the ability to remain open and take risks, with a willingness to explore the manifold, hidden recesses of desire.

Given Masters and Johnson's theoretical opacity and evasion, it comes as no surprise to find them unwilling to face the subversive implications of their own data. To do so might shake loose some foundation stones in their own wobbly value structure. To absorb the fact that heterosexual men and women involved in long-standing relationships frequently—almost obsessively, it seems—fantasize about displacing their established partners, might raise the feared specter that familiarity really does breed contempt (or, minimally, loss of erotic interest). For Masters and Johnson to digest their further finding that among the previously unattached couples they studied, "fewer functional failures" turned up during sex than among committed couples, might lead to speculation that people find excitement in the unfamiliar—that outside "spice" provides respite from the familiarity and boredom and dysfunction that commonly assail long-term lovers. Rather than explore such implications. Masters and Johnson simply reiterate their belief in the prime importance of maintaining the marital unit—that "port-in-the-storm," that "retreat from social pressures." Security remains their supreme value, the ultimate benefaction, the essence and sum of human needs. We are in the landscape of the 1950s.

—from the *New Republic*, June 16, 1979

MEMOIR

Calgary

We arrived at the Calgary Stampede—Canada's "legendary yearly event, the World's Greatest Rodeo"—in July 1948, just before my eighteenth birthday. I was on a Youth Hostel trip with a group of some twenty other teenagers, and we had already put in a month of grueling but happy cross-country biking and backpacking. Calgary was a rest stop. We had heard great tales of its spectacular fairgrounds and rodeo events, and rushed to take it all in. We watched the opening-day parade of high school bands, covered wagons, cows and cowhands, dashed to the arena to see the chuck wagon races, thrilled to the feats of daredevil Dick Griffith as he jumped over a Buick car while straddling two horses.

Come evening, we headed out for the midway and amusement park, a vast stretch of dirt road that included (as I gushed in a letter home to my parents) "roller coasters, ice cream and soda stands, circus barkers, gyp joints, international exhibits such as the Ford Company, freak shows, girlie reviews, even Sally Rand herself doing the one and only fan dance!" What I didn't tell my parents was that as the evening grew late and the rest of our group went off to bed, I stayed on alone.

The midway was still feverish with activity, packed with carousers, most of them men, most of them (from my vantage point) middle-aged, clustered in groups of three or four, noisily drunk, vaguely frightening, and exciting me with their self-confident swagger, their unpredictable shouts, the sudden way they halted at a duck-shoot booth to challenge each other's prowess or to grab a kiss from any woman within reach. The booth owners egged them on, yelling out encouragement even as they scurried to nail down a scuffed tent peg, run test spins on a roulette wheel, line up rows of oversized dolls to tempt the contestants.

Every fourth or fifth booth advertised a fortune-teller. Why so many? I wondered. Didn't everybody know that fortune-tellers were a pack of thieves and liars? Most of them weren't even real gypsies—just renegade Spaniards from Brooklyn. Plus they had every known disease, since they never bathed or washed their hair. Boy, people were gullible! You had to be a dope to hand over real dough to some filthy hag, just to watch her shuffle a deck of cards and spout prepackaged mumbo-jumbo at you. I guess it *could* be fun, if you took it in that spirit, maybe worth a laugh or two, something to write home to the folks about—that is, if it only cost a few bucks, and you kept one eye over your shoulder in case somebody tried to bop you over the head. Yeah, maybe as a joke, a kind of lark, it might be worth trying . . .

She was sitting on a small camp stool in front of a tent. She must have been watching me because when I glanced over I had the feeling she'd already been staring at me. I didn't like that. It felt creepy, like she'd picked *me* out. If I was going to waste money on a parlor trick, *I'd* pick the parlor. She smiled at me. That made me feel really stupid, like I was some scared kid who had to be reassured. So I smiled back. I didn't want to be rude, after all; this was a carnival, where people were supposed to be friendly. Besides, she looked pretty decent; clean, too; and sort of young.

"How are you tonight?" she called over. "Are you having a good time?" I was surprised at her neutral, quiet voice, and that she spoke English. Didn't gypsies speak their own language, called something like "Romanoff"? I told her I'd only been in Calgary a few hours, but it looked fine so far. She asked where I was from. I said New

York and explained that I was with a group of other kids biking across the country for the summer. Before I knew it, we were having a regular chat. She wanted to know about the group, what places we'd been, where we were headed next. She seemed so ordinary, I soon felt at ease. She told me her family were *real* gypsies, that they traveled from fair to fair making a living telling fortunes. She said real fortune-tellers, like real gypsies, were rare, and gestured with disdain toward the other booths nearby: "Fakers, liars! Fortune-telling is an art"—her eyes blazed—"a *heritage* passed down from generation to generation."

The more we chatted on, the more pleased I felt with myself. I could hardly wait to write my parents about my gutsy encounter with the exotic Gemma (for that turned out to be her name). After we'd talked for some fifteen minutes, Gemma asked me if I "had any interest in learning about what the future held for me"—whether I was "brave enough" to live with such knowledge. I started to feel nervous again.

"Do you mean do I want to have my fortune told?"

"Yes." She stared hard at me.

I stammered something like, "Gosh, I don't know . . . I mean I've never thought about it."

"That is untrue. You must never say anything to me that is not true."

Now I felt really nervous—because she was right. I did want my fortune told, even though I thought it was a lot of hocus-pocus. How did she know I wanted to?

"That is why you came to the midway tonight. That is why you came to me." Her eyes stayed on me.

"Well, I guess the idea . . . did . . . well, kinda cross my mind."

"Why are you so afraid?" Her voice was warm again.

"I don't know . . . but I am." Then to my surprise, I blurted out, "I really don't believe in . . . in anyone being able to . . . in fortune-telling."

"Only a very few are able. I am one of the few. You showed excellent judgment in seeking me out."

"I did? I mean . . . did I?"

She smiled at me. "You answer that question."

"Well, I . . . I did come over to say . . . hello."

"There is no reason to be afraid." She was now very calm, dignified.

"But I am afraid."

"I can tell you why. If you will let me. It doesn't matter whether you believe in my powers. I can still help you. Particularly with the one problem that most troubles you."

"What problem?" I asked, already knowing what she meant, even if she didn't.

"One question above all others is on your mind. Constantly on your mind. It troubles you far, far more than any other question. Should I tell you what it is?"

"No—NO!" I could feel my panic rising. "Not *here*. Not here, for God's sakes—anybody could overhear us!"

Gemma rose and moved toward the flap opening into her tent.

"I agree," she said. "It is better said inside."

"You dumb schmuck!" I silently yelled at myself as I hesitantly followed her into the tent. How can you fall for such an obvious sales pitch? You didn't even ask her how much it would cost!

"Ten dollars is my usual fee," she said as soon as we were inside. "But I will only charge you five. Money is not important when weighed against pain. You are full of pain. Deep pain. It moves and saddens me. A fine young man like you should not be carrying so heavy a load of pain. I can relieve it. Pay me only what you can afford."

I fought back tears as Gemma closed the tent flap behind us and secured it with a peg. I put down the five dollars, and she motioned for me to sit on one of the two chairs drawn up to a table in the middle of the room. Above the table was a dim light, and in the center of it sat a large, square-shaped piece of glass.

"What's *that*?" I said, the quaver in my voice compromising my attempt at mockery. "Don't tell me that's a *crystal ball*, for God's sake!"

"It is a piece of crystal. Why does it bother you?"

"It's so corny! I thought you were . . . the 'real thing.' " I was pleased at the bravado in my voice.

"The crystal can be a useful tool. But not a necessary one. I can remove it if it bothers you."

I felt foolish again. "Why should it bother me?" I managed to mumble.

"Good. Then we can begin. I want you to write down"— seemingly from nowhere she produced a pad and pencil—"the one question that most preys on your mind. Do you understand?"

"I thought you already knew the question."

Gemma smiled enigmatically. "I feel I need to provide you with proof."

"One question?"

"Keep it brief. As short as possible. After writing down the question, fold the paper once, and then place it under the piece of crystal. Be sure to fold the paper over, so that the writing is not visible. After you have done that, I want you to sit back, close your eyes, and concentrate as deeply as possible on the question you have written down. I, too, shall close my eyes. I will empty my mind to receive your message. But you must concentrate very hard or you will not succeed in transmitting the message to me. Is that clear?"

"Wouldn't it be simpler if I just asked you the question?"

Again the enigmatic smile. "But then you would not believe that I have the power to read what is inside you without being told."

I wrote on the piece of paper, "Will I always be a homosexual?" Then, following her instructions, I folded the paper and put it under the crystal. But my skeptical side simply refused to sit back and concentrate. Not for the last time in encounters with my saviors, my rebellious streak abruptly took over. I peeked. I saw Gemma take the piece of paper out through some opening in the bottom of the table, read it, then put it back.

"Open your eyes now," she said. "You are indeed a very troubled young man. Just as I had thought. But there is hope. Your particular trouble can be cured. But you must want to be cured"—a phrase I would hear often in the years ahead.

"What do you mean?"

"I mean, you must give yourself up wholly to the cure. You must leave your old life, at once, and join our gypsy family so that I can be constantly by your side."

"Join your gypsy family?" The full absurdity of what Gemma was suggesting was clear. And yet, I *was* tempted—though I'd seen her trick with the paper, though my skepticism was entirely to the fore. I can still feel the powerful impulse within me to do exactly as she suggested. *Anything* to relieve the burden.

At least I was able to delay the decision. Fumbling toward the tent opening, I told Gemma I would have to think about it overnight, that in all likelihood I would do as she said, but that I first had to make "certain arrangements." As I walked out of her tent back on to the midway, she whispered gently, "It is your one chance for happiness"—another prediction I would hear often in the years ahead.

In the upshot I did not appear at Gemma's tent at dawn carrying my worldly goods. I went to Yale instead.

—from *Cures: A Gay Man's Odyssey* (1991)

Education

The year I entered Yale as a freshman, 1948, also saw the publication of Alfred Kinsey's *Sexual Behavior in the Human Male*. The book proved a bombshell on many counts, but particularly for what it said about homosexuality. According to Kinsey, 37 percent of adult American men had had at least one orgasm with another man, the experiences co-existing in many lives with heterosexuality. The incidence might be higher still, Kinsey suggested, were it not for social constraints.

Others before Kinsey—notably Edward Carpenter, Havelock Ellis, and Magnus Hirschfeld—had argued that homosexuality was a normal variant of human sexuality. But their views had long since been eclipsed by the consensus within the American psychiatric establishment that, contrary to Freud, homosexual behavior *always* connoted pathology (a consensus reinforced by popular culture and exemplified by the negative images of gays in films). It was in the nature of heresy for Kinsey to suggest in 1948 that erotic feelings for people of the same gender might be a garden-variety human impulse—rather than, as psychiatry insisted, the pathological response of a small group of clinically disturbed Others.

Kinsey went still further. He argued that heterosexuality did not represent a biological imperative and that in insisting it did, psychotherapists were functioning as cultural police rather than as physicians or scientists. The psychiatrists, predictably, responded with a mix of scorn and fury. Lawrence S. Kubie, a prominent therapist and author, commended Kinsey and his associates for the diligence of their research, but then loftily declared that only those experienced in clinical psychopathology (namely psychiatrists) could provide a reliable interpretation of "normality." And their judgment, Kubie made clear, had long since been rendered: homosexuality did not qualify.

Adding his voice, Dr. Robert P. Knight—of Yale, my new home—declared that although the cold was also common in the American population, no one would be foolish enough to describe *it* as "normal." Another Yale professor, the zoologist George A. Baitsell, wrote plainly in the *Yale Daily News*, "I don't like Kinsey! I don't like his report; I don't like anything about it." Welcome to college.

I in fact arrived at Mother Yale's portals oblivious of the Kinsey controversy—though like most middle-class, white Americans, I'd ingested psychiatric assumptions with my baby food and was reflexively on Gemma's side of the argument, not Kinsey's. I was also very nearly innocent of sex. At age eighteen I was still a virgin, though with women, not for want of trying. I had gone the whorehouse route while still in high school. It happened in Florida over one spring vacation. Three of us, with standard teenage bluster, had managed to badger each other into a local brothel. The madam, with the trace of a smile and a manner just a bit too gracious, ushered us into a small sitting room, where four or five scantily dressed women were rocking slowly in their chairs; apparently they were enjoying their own kind of game. We sat down, covered with embarrassment, in the empty chairs. No one spoke. The women kept rocking, rocking. Finally, just as I felt I would bolt for the door, one of them broke into a laugh and said, "Okay, boys, time to choose. We can't spend all day."

I jumped up first (let's get this *over* with!), awkwardly grabbed the woman nearest me, and headed with her into a back room. She dropped her robe as soon as we got there and asked me what I had in mind. Everything, it seemed, had a different price tag, with "around the world" costing the most, a whopping twenty dollars. I told her I only had seven dollars, and showed her my wallet as proof; nobody was taking me around the world! She said for seven dollars she could only screw me ("Only!" I thought).

She called me over to the bed, where I dutifully got on top of her and, as instructed, rubbed up and down against her body. My cock stayed resolutely limp. Sensing my rising panic, she put aside the rules of the price scale—though I wasn't to tell the madam or she'd catch hell—and blew me a little. To no avail. She said not to worry, that married men often came into the house and they couldn't get it up either. She promised not to tell my friends and, to aid in the deception, kindly put some ointment in the urethral opening of my cock, wrapped it in gauze, and snapped on a rubber band (could this really have been standard preventive treatment in the forties for VD?). With this outward proof of heterosexual grace, I later bragged to my friends about how great the fuck had been. One of the two, off guard at seeing the gauze and rubber band concoction that I triumphantly displayed, confessed that he had no bandage on *his* cock; suspicion promptly deflected onto him as the "chicken."

The night of the senior prom in high school, I realized that sex with women wasn't my thing. Seventeen, I'd been dating a "wild" girl, Rachel, for some time. We were known as an "item" and had promised ourselves—and announced to our friends—that we would "consummate our love" on the night of the prom. When the school dance was over, our crowd continued the revelries at Al's apartment (his parents were away). It was a fancy one, fit setting for the Big Event. Everyone sprawled out on the living room floor drinking and making out—and waiting for the moment when Rachel and I would go into the back bedroom; the whole group was vicariously losing its virginity through us.

Once in the bedroom, Rachel and I got undressed and lay together on the huge bed. Again, I was impotent—but this time more desperate, a little crazed:

"The doctor warned me," I told her, "that this might happen—

I've been making out too much lately. He warned me to cut down on the sex or I'd get impotent." Pure invention, of course, and obviously a little nuts, but Rachel took it in stride, neither questioning nor accusing me.

Again, I lied to my friends. This time the excuse (agreed to by Rachel—I was lucky in my choice of women) was that we hadn't been able to do it because she was having a period.

As far back as I could remember, I'd been attracted erotically only to men, and my masturbation fantasies had always focused exclusively on them. Even as a preteen in summer camp I'd had a "special friend." In the camp yearbook for 1940, my write-up described me as "one of Bunk 6B's twins. Many a night his counselor came in to find Dubie [my nickname] sleeping beside his pal, Katz." And the last line of Katz's write-up poignantly posed the question, "What will you do if they ever separate you from Duberman?"

Two years later, the beloved Katz no longer sharing my pillow and, at the onset of my twelfth year, advancing rapidly on puberty, I organized my current bunkmates into a ritual we called "fussing." We would put a mattress at the bottom of the closet in our bunk and, through trial and error, developed a code question: "You feel like fussing?" If yes, we'd go into the closet, two at a time, and body-rub ourselves into pleasure. There was a definite hierarchy as to who got to go into the closet with whom (my first lesson in the tyranny of beauty, which the gay bars of later years would greatly reinforce). Teddy and I, pretty blonds both, were much in demand, and on the occasions when we would haughtily disappear into the closet *together*, the bunk would be ablaze with sexual tension.

Psychiatry in those days dismissed such boyish antics as altogether natural, an expected, even necessary, prelude to achieving "adult" (heterosexual) identity. But in my own case, the psychiatric prediction had not come true: my attraction to men hadn't disappeared over time. I nonetheless refused, tenaciously, to put the obvious label on myself. That would have been tantamount, given the current definitions of the day, to thinking of myself as a stunted human being, one whose libidinal impulses had been "arrested" at the stage of early adolescence. I still remember the overwhelming shame I felt when I came across a *LIFE* magazine picture gallery of "criminal types" and saw that the one labeled "the homosexual"—a sweet, pretty blond—looked exactly like me.

All through my undergraduate years at Yale I steeled myself against looking for sex, sensing that the only kind of experiences I would be drawn to would force on me a self-definition I wasn't ready to accept. I was protected by the notion, standard for isolated, young homosexuals in those years, that there were so few of us and we were so desperate to guard our secret that no places existed where we could meet. But then one day an undergraduate friend offhandedly warned me to stay away at night from the Green (the large park abutting the Yale campus): "It's a hangout for fairies." I was shocked—and thrilled.

That very same night, having gotten myself so drunk I felt conveniently muddled, I headed toward the Green. It was dark and looked empty, but as my eyeballs focused, I saw a very fat, middle-aged black man sitting quietly on a bench. I sat down on the empty bench opposite him. After a minute or two, he started whistling softly, tantalizingly, in my direction. Fueled by liquor, I got up, reeled my way over, and stood boldly in front of him. He started playing with my cock, then took it out of my pants. Wildly excited, I started to fondle him.

"Do you have any place we can go?" I whispered importunately.

"Nope. No place."

Suddenly I heard laughter and noise coming in our direction. I was sure it was some undergraduates—and equally sure we'd been seen. Zipping up my fly, I ran out of the park, ran without stopping, panicked, hysterical, ran for my life back to my dorm room. I stayed in the shower for hours, cleaning, cleaning. I actually washed my mouth out with soap, though I hadn't used my mouth—other than to make a prayerful pact with God that if He let me off this time, I'd never, never go near the Green again.

The panic lasted for days. By the end of the week I was back on the Green, drunk again. This time I let myself get picked up by one of the cars cruising the area—and let the driver give me a blow job in the backseat. He was expert and it felt delicious. But perhaps because I let myself actually touch his penis, I went back to the Green only two or three times after that, when the urge for contact overwhelmed my controls; and only once after that did I let myself get another blow job. Then, in my junior year, drunk and desperate, I groped another equally drunk twenty-year-old outside a fraternity house—and barely escaped a nasty fight. Except for a single clouded experience in New York City—where I met someone in Grand Central Station, but then, in the hotel where we went, felt too uneasy to go through with it—that was about the sum of my sex life until age twenty-one. Two blow jobs, two panic attacks.

I graduated Phi Beta Kappa from Yale and near the top of my class. It was clear where I was going to find applause and the self-esteem that purportedly follows in train. I had all the important traits for a successful life in scholarship: a huge capacity for isolation (to endure all those mandated hours alone in the archives), a deeply perfectionist nature (to persevere in tracking down every last fact), and a well-developed sense of fairness (to prevent me from reducing complex evidence to cartoon heroes and villains).

The particular appeal of history as my chosen field for scholarship hinged somewhat on my relish for having the last word but was more centrally related to the need (which I couldn't have articulated at the time) to find some balance for a life heavily tipped toward the present and almost devoid of personal memory. It was as if, in my own life, I had an enormous blackboard eraser suspended down my back to the floor, which, as I walked, instantly erased all trace of my footsteps. To compensate for that blank, I could turn to the comparatively painless collective memory we call history.

In blocking out my own past, I was following the example of my parents. Both of them, but especially my mother, seemed to regard any lingering on yesterday as an encumbrance to getting on with today, the source of useless anguish rather than useful experience. My mother was second-generation Austrian American, but neither she nor her parents ever passed on to me family tales they may have heard about life in the old country, and certainly no one made reference to upholding a Jewish religious tradition, in which they themselves had been barely schooled. My mother's family, with their determined lack of interest in all that had preceded, seemed hell-bent on outdoing the citizens of their adopted country in the national trait of present-mindedness. It was part and parcel of their conformity to mainstream values. But whereas my father, a Russian emigrant, submitted with gratitude, my mother did so with an underlay of resentment.

Like her two sisters, she was urged to go straight from high school into secretarial and sales jobs—to "go to business," to meet eligible men, to assimilate as fully as possible into the American Way. That driving passion to become just like everybody else predestined my mother to a traditional life as wife and mother, although her striking beauty, high spirits, and intelligence might, in a later generation, have led to a life far more vivid and satisfying. She passed the goal of fitting in down to her son, along with the high spirits that would keep us both in a state of repressed rebellion, and this side of total capitulation. My athletic carriage would help me conceal my sexuality as successfully as my mother's feigned ordinariness had masked her own instinctive strength.

My father, more than ten years older than my mother and mad about her when they first married ("Marry him, Josie," her mother had urged, "he'll be a good provider"), was far more obviously foreign. One of seventeen children born to peasant parents who worked on a large farm in the Ukraine, his had been the only Jewish family in the area. The epidemic of anti-Jewish pogroms in Russia in the early years of the twentieth century made survival, not assimilation, the paramount issue. Passing reference was once or twice made by my father's sister to narrow escapes from the Cossacks, but no elaboration was ever forthcoming.

Though my father had little formal education, he'd risen, while still a teenager, to the rank of foreman on the farm. In his early twenties, he'd been drafted into the Russian army, decided to desert, somehow made his way to Hamburg, and in April 1913, aged twenty-two, came steerage to the United States. I know that much only because I have his boarding pass and his naturalization papers. All that I ever heard from my father himself about his early life as an immigrant in New York—single, without money, contacts, skills, or English—amounted to an occasional passing reference: that he'd lived in a furnished room with the elevated subway screeching by outside his window; that he'd somehow learned the cutter's trade in the garment industry; that he'd gotten his first job in a factory at a salary of seven dollars a week; that he'd quickly learned English and risen, again, to a foreman's job. My family was as apolitical as it was areligious. The watchwords were the standard immigrant ones: making a good living and protecting the family from a hostile outside world. No energy or inclination remained for civic involvement of any kind—beyond considering Franklin Delano Roosevelt a god ("He's good for the Jews," my father would say).

In the fall of 1952, I headed up to Harvard to get a doctorate in history. From the first I prospered. Unlike most of my fellow graduate students, who within months were lamenting their fate (my youth! my beauty!—squandered over musty texts!), I was serenity itself. Nothing pleased me more than *not* having to squander my youth in pursuit of wine, women, and song. I'd found scant pleasure in the touted joys of the flesh—and a plethora of it in the praise I'd won for the quality of my mind. Solace lay in the library, not the bedroom.

The more secure I became in my status as an intellectual, the less gloom I felt about being—as the psychiatric establishment then insisted—a disabled human being. I did implicitly accept the culture's verdict that I was defective, but could now somewhat circumscribe the indictment; I no longer felt wholly unworthy—merely crippled in my affective life.

Now and then I even had an inkling that the psychiatric depiction of homosexuals as disordered and diseased people might be suspect. After all, unless one was prepared to argue (as I sometimes was) that pathology is itself the enabling ingredient in human ac-

complishment, then something seemed wrong with the character-
ization; how could a "sick" young man like me be functioning with
as much clarity and insight as my Harvard professors assured me
I was? My psychic confusion hardly lifted as the decade of the 1950s
proceeded and the country's blanket and vehement (one might now
say pathological) rejection of political and personal nonconformity
deepened in tandem.

If anything resembling self-acceptance was still light-years off,
my academic achievements had begun to provide me with a base
of self-esteem from which I could begin to venture out. It became
possible to explore my sexuality, however tentatively, without the
overwhelming fear that failure with women (or success with men)
would entirely obliterate me.

I've forgotten how I picked up the information, but I wasn't at
Harvard more than a few months when I heard that there were two
gay bars in Boston, the Napoleon ("a collegiate crowd") and the
Punch Bowl ("down and dirty"), as well as one or two more that, on
the right evening, could be interestingly ambiguous. Slim pickings
by today's standards, but for me, having lived so long in isolation, it
sounded like a cornucopia. Later on, as my contacts and confidence
grew, I would explore the two spots available in Cambridge itself:
the riverbank in front of the residential colleges, where I once spotted one of my professors in the bushes and discreetly moved off; and
the Common, less appealing because townies looking for trouble
rather than sex hung out there, and because whenever I did loiter
under one of the historic elms, I couldn't shake my mother's ancient
injunction never to walk through a park alone for fear of the sick
people who lingered within; I had become the person my mother
had warned me about.

During my first year in graduate school, I went almost exclusively to the comparative safety of the Napoleon. It was located in
the then-derelict Back Bay area, down an obscure side street where
few people wandered. There was no sign (if my memory holds) on
the door of a rundown brownstone that seemed indistinguishable
from its seedy neighbors; even after one knocked, discreet inquiries,

along with a full visual assessment, took place (the point was to screen for plainclothesmen, not beauty) before entry was granted. Once you were inside, the range of amenities was surprising: two floors, with hatcheck, piano bar (*de rigueur* in the show-tune fifties), and a mostly jacket-and-tie crowd content to conform to the management's efforts at upscale elegance.

On my very first foray, I met a fellow graduate student and, unwilling to jeopardize my miraculous good fortune, agreed to go home with him that same night. Since my roommate was out of town for the weekend, Leo and I had sex in my dorm room. Perhaps because it was so pleasurable, I thereafter avoided him like the plague, rushing in the opposite direction whenever I caught sight of him on campus. Finally he cornered me one day: "Look—can't we be friends at least?" Caught somewhere between hysteria and relief, I managed to mumble yes.

It was the beginning of a long friendship and the beginning, too, of allowing myself to socialize with other gay people. Through Leo [Bersani], I gradually developed a circle of friends, almost all of them graduate students like myself, and entered a subculture that blessedly brought me from individual isolation to collective secrecy—a considerable advance if one can understand, in this day where all furtiveness is decried, the quantum leap in happiness from private to shared anguish.

And anguish we did, though with saving interstices of campy hilarity and genuine camaraderie. Howard, loyal and thoughtful, taught us much about the possibilities of gay friendship, even as Billy, with his malicious tongue, schooled us to be wary of its limitations. Charles, a languid Southerner, provided much of the hilarity. He took every opportunity to refer to, and sometimes display, his enormous cock, which he assured us in dulcet tones, eyes lifted dreamily toward heaven, had become legendary south of Mason-Dixon. Nearing thirty, Charles took advantage of his seniority to lecture us twenty-two-year-olds regularly about the dire perils of the gay life and the need *at once* to bind ourselves to a lover with hoops of steel as the only possible stay against despair.

Sharing Charles's view, in the couple-oriented fifties, that a lifetime partner was indeed essential for human happiness, we pressed him for an explanation of his own single state, offering the needling suggestion that perhaps an overdependence on astonished praise for his remarkable member might have kept him from settling down with one, perhaps jaded, fan. Charles would sigh loudly, call on heaven to forgive our youthful philistinism, and regale us with gothic tales about how the treacheries of Good Old Boys had turned him into a crumpled rose (an invaluable asset, he added, in his chosen field, the study of literature).

Leo and I were the specialists in anguish. Being Jewish—which is to say, inclined to feeling guilty about being alive and at the same time to feeling superior in suffering—predisposed us to the psychiatric notion of homosexuality as curse and apartness. (It was preferable, perhaps, to feel guilty rather than powerless.) As the most earnest and ambitious of our group, we were tormented by the notion that life's deepest emotions and highest prizes might be forever outside our grasp. We seemed to have but two choices: to conclude that psychiatry was wrong about us or, that failing, to accept our fate as diminished creatures.

We could do neither. Though the culture had taught us to think badly of ourselves, our families (not yet aware we were gay) had raised us as princes of the realm, entitled to all we surveyed. This flawed upbringing, which ordinarily would have doomed the little princes to lives of presumptuous arrogance, in our cases provided needed ballast; having been valued at home, we could never *entirely* succumb (though we leaned) to the cultural view of us as disfigured and depraved. But the only integration of two such disparate self-images that we could manage in the fifties hardly made us candidates for serenity: we were pieces of shit around whom the world revolved.

It might have been easier had I *not* been intellectual. Priding myself on being the kind of rational person who based his opinions on so-called objective evidence (rather than popular superstitions or slogans), I put my faith in social science, hardly doubting that its products were "value-free." And in the fifties, the evidence generated by the social sciences continued overwhelmingly to corroborate the orthodox view of homosexuality as pathology.

Kinsey's work had, to be sure, provided a notable, if disputed, challenge to that orthodoxy. But most of the data that would later confirm Kinsey—the work, especially, of Evelyn Hooker, Thomas Szasz, and Judd Marmor—lay in the future. Only one significant book emerged in the early fifties to bolster Kinsey's minority views on homosexuality: *Patterns of Sexual Behavior* by the anthropologists Cleland Ford and Frank Beach. Using data from the Yale Human Relations Area Files on seventy-six cultures, Ford and Beach concluded that nearly two-thirds of those cultures sanctioned, and in some cases mandated, some variant of homosexual activity. But Ford and Beach also concluded that in most cultures homosexuality was considered inappropriate for *every* stage of life, and in no culture was it the sole form of sexual activity for adults.

Since Leo and I were, and had always been, Kinsey 6s (exclusively gay), and since we had trouble seeing the bright side of anything, we looked on the Ford and Beach data as mostly negative confirmation of our benighted status. We even managed to twist it into a new instrument of self-torture; in portraying homosexuality as a "stage"—of adolescence, that is, not adulthood—the anthropological evidence (we decided) seemed to confirm the psychiatric view that "fixation" at one stage of development precluded progress to the otherwise natural culminating point of human maturation: heterosexuality. We would never, it seemed, have "complete" lives; we would always be some ungrown, truncated version of humanity.

That the conclusion did not overwhelm us was attributable partly to our upbringing (which had stored in us an irreducible amount of self-regard that transcended intellectual debate); partly to our confidence in our intellectual abilities (perhaps all great minds, or talents, we would argue, were housed—nature's way of balancing out traits—in otherwise deformed personality structures); and partly to the fact that we had found solace in a community of like-minded souls and, in the shadow of the hangman, were managing to have a fair amount of fun with our lives.

My trips to the Napoleon had quickly given me some much needed sexual experience (though my inhibitions remained multiple) and then, within mere months, an introduction to the still more threatening world of romance. One night in the Napoleon, I ran into a classmate from Yale. We had barely known each other as undergraduates, since I was an ardent student and "Rob," as befitted his society lineage, had ardently steered clear of scholarly associations. But in Boston, where Rob had returned after graduation to his family, he and I were on a somewhat more equal footing. He was far more sexually experienced than I and also far more determined, from the first, on a love affair. To my skittish hesitations and withdrawals, he counterposed vigorous courting and glamorizing visits to family estates. The most memorable was a trip to Grandmama's Manhattan triplex.

A formidable dowager well into her eighties, she was—Rob was quick to tell me—Herbert Hoover's long-standing bridge partner (expecting him to say paramour, I was puzzled at the triumph in his voice). She received us in her library, seated unmoving in an armchair, dressed in a full-length black gown, a mass of snow-white hair framing a still beautiful face. After allowing the exchange of a few rigorous pleasantries, she had the butler show us into an upstairs bedroom so we could change into "appropriate" clothes for dinner.

Properly dazzled, I told Rob I "probably" loved him. He responded expansively by letting me fuck him for the first time—in the shower, itself a new experience. But I resisted his badgering insistence that I pronounce it the "best fuck" I'd ever had, though I'd had precious few. I had stretched my limits far enough for one day. My father's peasant stubbornness asserted itself; bristling at the hint of *droit de seigneur*, I told Rob the fuck had been "okay."

Rob and I called ourselves "lovers," but the affair was a good deal less profound than that, and the actual lovemaking was sharply circumscribed. It wasn't simply that I was a novice. I was also deeply bound by sex role conventions and by the determination—if I *had* to be gay—that I was going to be a manly (that is, "acceptable") version. None of this, of course, was consciously worked out; I simply performed according to the cultural script then dominant—though finally, of course, it's mostly a mystery as to who adopts which social cues and why.

A "real man," as we all knew in those years (and as many continue to affirm), was unyieldingly dominant, the penetrator, the aggressor, someone who took *only* the so-called active role in bed. To help reinforce this neat paradigm, all sexual acts were conveniently labeled "active" or "passive," and those qualities were presumed intrinsic to the acts themselves. Thus, giving blow jobs and getting fucked were innately passive, female activities; getting blow jobs and giving fucks were active and male. There seemed no understanding at the time—and precious little since—that the muscular contractions of the throat, anus, or vagina could, by several definitions, be considered "active" agents in producing any cohabitation worthy of the name—to say nothing of the psychological truth that s/he who sets and controls the scenario is, regardless of the nature of the scenario, the true "actor." I was somebody who got blow jobs and gave fucks.

For most of the few months I was with Rob, I was "trade"—I let him blow me. The boundaries suited us both; they assuaged my guilt by reinforcing my "masculine" image, and they fed his preferred view of himself as seducer and guide to the uninitiated. It wasn't until several years later that I could even begin, at first in fantasy, to acknowledge a desired role reversal; only rarely could I put the fantasy into action.

—from *Cures: A Gay Man's Odyssey* (1991)

Life in the Theater

As a teenager I had toured in summer stock as "George Gibbs" in Thornton Wilder's *Our Town*, and the director had strongly urged me to think about a professional career in acting. But college—and caution—had intervened.

By the early sixties, though, I'd begun to write plays, and I'd found a (deceptively) early success with *In White America*, the story of being black "in white America" as told through documents, diaries, newspaper accounts, and the like. The play had opened off-Broadway in 1963, run for a year and a half, won a prestigious prize, had two national tours, and a large number of productions.

Edward Albee and Richard Barr produced an evening of my one-acters at the John Drew Theater in Easthampton, and two years later they were done at the Manhattan Theater Club, with two of the three chosen for the annual *Best Short Plays* volumes. PBS commissioned me to write *Mother Earth*, the life of the radical anarchist Emma Goldman; Warner Brothers sounded me out about writing the book for a new Broadway musical and CBS asked me to script the inaugural special "The Presidency," for their thirteen-part series *The American Parade*.

To add still more encouragement, I was told by a producer friend that the eminent theater critic Harold Clurman had confided to her that he was "putting his money on Duberman and [John] Guare as this generation's best bets." Jules Irving and Alan Mandell, who were then running Lincoln Center, used nearly the same words in telling me they hoped I would let them have first crack at any new play I wrote.

I was flying. Briefly, that is. *Mother Earth* was ultimately turned down as "too radical and too ambitious"; Clurman got over his purported admiration and gave my one-acters a decidedly middling review in *The Nation;* and when I submitted a new play to Irving and Mandell for Lincoln Center's "Explorations" series, I was told it was "too good—too mature and authoritative" for that particular venue. I learned privately that they had been "dismayed" to see the homosexual subtext in my work becoming increasingly explicit; they regarded that as "the wrong choice."

Magically, a timely new offer refurbished my fantasies of theatrical apotheosis. It came from the Francis Thompson Company, the firm commissioned to prepare a film to celebrate Philadelphia's 1976 Bicentennial. Thompson himself called to offer me the job of scriptwriter, and our early meetings were intoxicating. The project, I was told, had been budgeted at twelve million dollars (*very* big money in the midseventies). Ten million of that would go to putting up a building (to be designed by Max Abramovitz, the architect of Avery Fisher Hall) suitable for IMAX, the special process that required, among other things, a hundred-foot-wide screen. Now here were gargantuan appetites to match my own.

For the script, the Thompson people had in mind some fairly standard, benign thematic material like the signing of the Declaration of Independence, the Constitutional Convention, and so on. I argued from the first against settling for such patriotic clichés; they would do little more than reinforce a long-standing and misguided emphasis on the supreme importance of a few heroic personalities. Francis Thompson, a kindly, courtly man, warned me that the project did have a "commercial component"—meaning, I later learned, that the underwriters, a collection of wealthy Philadelphia businessmen, had to be satisfied. But he did suggest I come up with a specific counter-suggestion for the historical narrative. This seemed to me tantamount to a green light. I have an optimistic temperament.

I dug out all my old colonial history books from graduate school days, and ransacked them for a resonant political theme and time frame. I finally decided to focus on the story of the Pennsylvania Quakers during the 1750s, when six Quaker members of the colony's assembly had resigned rather than comply with a call for military action against the Delaware Indians, thus ending Quaker control of the legislative body after a rule of some seventy-five years.

I went back to the Thompson people and passionately defended the centrality of what might, I realized, appear to be a peripheral story. Quaker beliefs, I argued, were in fact at the ideal heart of the American story. It was among the radical Pennsylvania Quakers, like John Woolman and the younger William Penn—not the merchant grandees—that "liberty of conscience" had been more consistently stressed than elsewhere in the colonies, God's "Truth" declared directly, equally, to all (with no need for priestly intervention), the profit motive held subordinate to the public interest, war and violence eschewed as instruments of social policy, the Delaware Indians asked for their "love and consent," and black slavery denounced and abandoned. This egalitarian emphasis was, I argued, the ideal spirit in which to celebrate the *ongoing* Revolution—especially since that spirit seemed notably absent from the countless other Bicentennial projects that had already been announced.

Francis Thompson raised his eyebrows and cleared his throat. "I've *got* him!" I thought, ignoring the assorted frowns on some of the other faces in the room. For the next month, I put all other writing projects on hold and, working twelve-hour days, completed a fifty-page draft film treatment. I entitled it "The Independent Spirit" and euphorically mailed it off to Thompson.

The night before I was due to go back down to Philadelphia to discuss the draft at a meeting that would also be attended by several of the wealthy businessmen being solicited as sponsors, Francis Thompson called me at home. To my dismay, he talked vaguely of the need somehow to reintroduce the signing of the Declaration of Independence and so on into the script. I reminded him that I thought we'd earlier agreed to eschew such tired clichés, to which he mumbled something like "That wasn't *my* understanding." In retrospect, I think Thompson was trying to prepare me, in his muted but honorable way, for what I was likely to encounter in Philly the next day.

If so, he failed. I arrived to find that my script had been completely reworked by unknown hands, with no more than five of my original fifty pages intact. Among other things, the rewritten draft now had the Delaware Indians carrying out an unmotivated massacre of settlers and Ben Franklin explaining *to* the Quaker legislators why they had to resign from the Assembly! As I fumed about the misrepresentations, and as several of the bigwig backers smiled contentedly, one of Thompson's people took me aside to hint that once the sponsors had signed on, a good portion of my original material would "probably" be restored.

That wasn't good enough. Unless they would *guarantee* such a restoration—and in full—I threatened to quit the project. They refused, and I resigned. I told them I would sue if my name appeared anywhere on the credits.

Oh, swell—another moral triumph! The accumulation of credits in heaven was not the way to get my handprints in cement at Grauman's Chinese Theater. I counseled myself to stay calm: it all ended up with a concrete slab of one sort or another anyway. Film and theater—it was all one, I grumbled; the mission of the entertainment industry was to sell tickets, and that, irreducibly, meant catering to the lowest common denominator in public taste. Print was my medium, and I had damned well better get back to it. At least for a while. At least until my unaccountably delayed passport to the entertainment industry finally got stamped.

The Bicentennial was not yet finished with me. I was asked by the Kennedy Center for the Performing Arts in Washington, D.C., to be part of an ambitious season-long celebration in honor of the nation's 200th birthday. The Center said it planned to produce ten

American plays, six of them revivals (including William Gillette's 1894 comedy *Too Much Johnson*, and Percy MacKaye's 1909 drama *The Scarecrow*), and four of them new plays to be chosen from a batch of six that the Kennedy Center intended to commission. The six playwrights they'd decided on were John Guare, Romulus Linney, Preston Jones (*The Texas Trilogy*), Joseph Walker (*The River Niger*), Ruth Wolff (*The Abdication*), and—me!

To say I was stunned, after my recent string of near—and far—theatrical misses is to understate the case. I was delirious. And when I was further told that I'd have free choice of topic (so long as I dealt with "some phase of the American experience") and that after the engagement at the Kennedy Center the plays would tour nationally, I thought I might quite possibly be dreaming. A front-page article in *Variety* and a long piece in *Time* on the Center's planned season of plays confirmed that I was not.

I gave euphoria free rein, even after some alarm bells went off in my head during my first face-to-face meeting (in a Manhattan restaurant) with Richmond Crinkley, who, with Roger L. Stevens, director of the Kennedy Center, was going to co-produce the Bicentennial season. Crinkley was a Southern good old boy—charming, smooth, manipulative, unreliable—who *just happened to be* gay. Aside from an occasional dropped hairpin during our first meeting, *that* topic never became explicit between us, not even when we were joined at dinner by his demonstratively affectionate young actor boyfriend. Richmond wasn't *that* kind of gay man. Art and politics were in his view of the world separate realms; art was what the talented few did, politics was the poor substitute resorted to by the benighted many. Richmond was far too urbane ever to caution me directly against introducing gay-themed material into my pending play. But he nonetheless managed to convey the message that "free choice of topic" shouldn't be taken too literally.

In pondering what to write about, I played for some time with the notion of an evening to be called "Unofficial Heroes": the story of America as seen through the eyes of its radical outsiders—people like William Lloyd Garrison, Frederick Douglass, and Emma

Goldman. I thought, too, about returning to the documentary form that had served me well with *In White America*. But when I tried my hand at it, the form felt played out for me, and I couldn't come up with an appropriate alternate format.

Then—somehow—I got on to the Beats. The "how" in these matters always seems to me more than a little mysterious: I'd never been much interested in the Beats, or been much of a fan of their writings. It was only gradually that I came to see the actual locus of my newfound interest: the relationship between Jack Kerouac and Neal Cassady. Each had been the most important person in the other's life, but neither (and especially not Kerouac) could find ways to express it apart from the acceptable buddy-buddy ones: tough-guy heroics, all-night Benzedrine sessions, screwing together in whorehouses, sharing women, treating women like shit.

That, writ large, was the destructive tragedy of growing up macho male in America (or anywhere else, for that matter). Through the Kerouac-Cassady relationship, I wanted to write a play about the horrors of "manliness"—which so many heterosexual men seemed to believe accrued in direct proportion to the *absence* of tenderness. The tragedy, as I saw it, was that Kerouac as a young man was palpably tender. Yet the sweet person inside could never get out, or stay out. With liquor in him, he could be a brute and a bully. And the older he got, the more he drank, until finally he did little but drink, along with cursing the radical young he'd once inspired. Had Kerouac been able to connect profoundly with *anyone*, had he and Cassady been able to acknowledge the depth of their passion for each other—and I meant much more than sexual passion, and perhaps not *even* that—Kerouac might not have succumbed in his forties to alcoholism, and Cassady to a drug overdose.

Once that story grabbed hold of me I couldn't let it go. I knew it was likely to make Richmond apprehensive (to say the least), but I managed to persuade myself that the power and poignancy of the theme would somehow capture him—after all, I told myself, he *was* a gay man.

I began by reading through all of Kerouac's published work—

some twenty volumes of the stuff. And "stuff" is how I felt about much of it; a lot of Kerouac's "spontaneous writing" came across to me as just that, the work of someone high on bennies, unable (as Truman Capote once put it) to stop typing. I admired many sections of *On the Road*, *The Subterraneans*, and *The Dharma Bums*, but my real fascination was with the life, not the work.

The play became an amalgam of Kerouac's words and mine. I sometimes directly incorporated lines or phrases from Kerouac's own work (with permission from his estate); more often a sentence of his would trigger a continuation of my own, spark off a page of dialogue from me or, once in a while, a scene. Some of the events in the play I wholly imagined; some of the characters became composites that I created from several real-life figures. In the end, the amalgamation became so complete that within a short time of finishing the play I could no longer identify the constituent parts, disentangle the two voices.

I finished the first draft, a whopping 250 pages, in June 1975. Actor friends did a reading of it in my apartment to help me discover what sections needed reworking, and as a result I trimmed away sixty pages. It was now ready, I thought (doesn't one always?), to be seen. I gave it the title *Visions of Kerouac*—meaning to convey that it was a subjective meditation on Kerouac's life in much the way his own book *Visions of Cody* had been a meditation on Neal Cassady's. And off the play went to Richmond Crinkley.

One week turned into two, two into four. No word. My agent phoned Crinkley's office repeatedly, but got not a single return call. "Doubtless." she said with feigned cheerfulness, "they're awaiting the arrival of the other five commissioned scripts before offering any comments. Why not use the time to do some of the those additional revisions you've been talking about?" So I did. By August, I'd completed another, still trimmer version. Off it, too, went to Richmond's office.

Now I started calling him myself. After a dozen tries, I was finally put through. He suggested a meeting, and my eager little heart soared. It shouldn't have. The meeting lasted half an hour.

Richmond nervously admitted that he had not yet "finished" the new version (it was clear from his comments that he'd never started it). But both he and Roger Stevens *had* read the original, and Richmond wanted me to know (his voice ominous) that "Roger thinks your play is too long."

"Was that his *only* comment?" I asked, nonplussed.

"Mmm, yes."

"That's reassuring."

Richmond giggled, but said nothing.

"The script *was* too long," I continued. "That's why I did a revision sixty pages shorter. I urge you to read it," I added pointedly.

Richmond responded airily that of course he would, then confounded my gloom by declaring Arvin Brown's prestigious Long Wharf Theater his first choice as the tryout site for *Kerouac*. Before I could catch my breath, he was waving good-bye, off to another "urgent meeting."

I didn't know what to make of it all. *Would* Richmond ever read the new version? Or had a negative decision already been reached on the basis of the subject matter alone, with the "excessive length" being merely a convenient excuse for turning the play down? If so, why had Richmond tossed off the prospect of a tryout at Long Wharf? Was it just to get me out of his hair?

Via Crinkley's assistant, Jack Hofsiss, word soon filtered in that the main office was sharply divided. Hofsiss himself was high on the play, Crinkley unwilling to commit, and the big boss Roger Stevens decidedly negative. That was bad news indeed, since it was Stevens who ultimately called the shots. There had probably never been much chance that he would take to *Kerouac*. This was the man, after all, who during a recent interview with the *Washington Post* had referred to the language in the film he called "The Cuckoo Flew Over the Roof" with "Jack Nichols" as "disgusting." This was the same Roger Stevens who had rejected the Tony Award-winning play *Equus* for the Kennedy Center because he'd been offended by "its four-letter language and nudity." Could I really expect him to embrace a play about male love filled with raunchy Beat language and behavior? No, I could not.

Neither Stevens nor Crinkley was under any obligation to like my play simply because I wanted them to. But I did think writers—*commissioned* ones, no less—were entitled to less rude, evasive treatment. I told my agent to withdraw the script from the Kennedy Center and to start sending it out to other managements.

She did, but the reactions were hardly what I'd hoped for. "Too long," said Circle Rep. "Too literary," said the Chelsea Theater Center. The American Conservatory Theater in San Francisco liked the play but decided the cost of mounting it would be "prohibitive." The producer Stuart Ostrow sent my agent a note that made me laugh—grimly—out loud: "Duberman has done a wonderful job. Wish it was a musical. But of course it shouldn't be." The veteran producers Diana and Herman Shumlin took me to dinner at the Plaza Hotel to express their "enormous admiration" for the writing *and* their distaste for the contents. Sylvia Hersher, another long-established pro, told the agent she thought the play "not good—but *great*," yet couldn't imagine who might actually be willing to stage it.

In the end, the Kennedy Center produced not one of the six commissioned plays—but I didn't know that in time to stanch the worst of the bleeding. Nor did the failure to carry off the Bicentennial season prevent Richmond Crinkley from being chosen in 1979 to head the theater at Lincoln Center (disastrously, in the opinion of many). That same year, Jack Hofsiss—the good guy in my Kennedy Center melodrama—had a notable triumph directing the stage version of *The Elephant Man*.

In 1978, *Kerouac* was produced to excellent reviews in L.A. But audiences proved thin and after about seventy performances it closed.

—compiled from *Partisan Review* no. 3, 1968 and no. 3, 1969; *SHOW*, January 1969 and February 1969; *Harper's*, May 1978 and December 1978

Bioenergetics

My friend Pete, he of the endless faith in alternative therapies, soon came up with another suggestion for me. He'd become involved recently in one of the new "body" therapies called "bioenergetics." Pete claimed it had helped him enormously (but then he always said that) and recommended I give it a try. "What is bioenergetics?" I asked impatiently, my tone implying that I already knew it was a form of charlatanry.

Pete was patience itself, explaining that bioenergetics was an eclectic combination of body therapies "deriving from the work of Alexander Lowen," and its chief practitioner in New York was a man named John Pierrakos. "Oh, Pete," I moaned. "Give it up! We're talking about a body and psyche that've been pummeled and (purportedly) reshaped time and again, only to snap right back to their original form. It's time you accepted the reality of imprinting. I am what I am—and probably have been since age three."

Pete nodded sagely. "Ummm . . . I hear you . . . except you do have a greater capacity for change than you like to admit, and have shown it over the years. You're not as fortified as you prefer to think. And despite your advanced years"—he smiled sweetly—"you could go right on changing." (Thank God he didn't say "growing"! That would have scotched the deal right there.) "Why not try it?"

he added. "It's not like you've got anything better to do at the moment." That was true enough. And so with a shrug, I agreed on impulse to go for a consultation.

When I arrived at John Pierrakos's office, it turned out he was an hour behind schedule. While waiting, I thumbed through the reading material on his end table, and found that most of it consisted of reprints of his own articles. Just another blowhard, I thought resentfully. *Why the hell did I let Pete talk me into this?* Picking up one of the articles, my eye lingered lovingly on every bloated abstraction—of which there were many: "We must create new concepts, new processes, and new leadership models for a New Age of Mankind"; "We must open to the benign nature of the universe, to the amplitude of life." *Oh swell*, I thought; *Dr. Pangloss tacked on to a regimen of push-ups. Just what I don't need.* Yet I didn't bolt on the spot. Maybe because of the one line in the article that *did* impress me: "The more we feel the pain, the more we accept it, the less we feel it . . . when we accept the hurt we feel deeply, it gives us a sense of dignity."

When Pierrakos called me into his inner office, it was immediately apparent that this was not a traditionally antiseptic psychotherapeutic setting. On the wall were a photomural of Egyptian pictographs and a large anatomical diagram of the human torso with lines pointing to what were regarded (I later learned) as key "energy meridians." Certain objects in the room seemed startlingly anomalous: a large wooden sawhorse, several oversized plastic baseball bats, three or four huge beanbags doubling as oversized pillows. The desk and two chairs were standard issue.

Pierrakos was a trim, handsome man with graying hair and a classically chiseled face. I guessed him to be in his early fifties. He motioned me to one of the chairs and we began to talk, along the standard lines I had long since grown accustomed to in traditional psychotherapy. He asked what had brought me to his office. I explained my connection to Pete, my ambivalence about therapy of any kind, my conviction that it was "too late" for me to hope for any major personality transformation.

Until recently, I said, I'd viewed my life as successful and stable.

I had few overt fears, enjoyed my work, had a surfeit of acquaintances (and even a few friends), had given up on the "adolescent" notion of a "lifetime partner," was content with occasional (sometimes paid) sexual adventures with mostly younger men, and had told myself (and everyone else, including Pete) that I was no longer interested in any basic reorientation of my life, and certainly not of my sexuality. I wanted to focus my energies on becoming more of what I already was: I wanted to deepen, not spread.

I paused, thinking Pierrakos might make some comment, give some clue about his reaction thus far. But he simply sat there quietly, waiting for me to continue. The events of the past two years, I went on, had shaken my complacency. I had, despite expectations, gotten deeply, romantically, involved with a man, and had been left by him. The shock of that, in combination with my mother's illness, had left me feeling disconsolate. Such hope as I could muster—and what had brought me to his office—came from Pete's conviction, more than mine, that the non-traditional therapy of bioenergetics might be a way of dynamiting my fortified defenses, even though I wasn't at all sure what bioenergetics was or whether I wanted my defenses breached.

On a deeper level, I said, I suspected that I'd come to him because I was, by nature, an "impossibilist": a man who continues to seek what cannot be had, whose tenacious will refuses to capitulate to the preordained, who insists he can still be "happy" when all the evidence suggests he can't.

Pierrakos listened attentively. So attentively that I felt unnerved, and in a distancing gesture I suddenly started complaining about his article. "This business of a 'benign universe,' " I heard myself say. "I have to tell you that it makes me uncomfortable."

"Why is that?" Pierrakos asked amiably.

"Well, how can I put it without sounding rude?"

"Don't worry about that," he interjected.

"You see, I've never thought of the universe as exactly 'benign.' I don't see how anyone can, given the misery everywhere around us."

"When I speak of the 'benign nature of the universe,' I am referring to its amplitude. The rhythmic renewal of all things. Nature's continuing ebb and flow."

That's just what I was afraid you meant, I thought uneasily, putting him down as an utter lightweight. I nodded in vague assent, but said nothing. Pierrakos allowed the pause to lengthen. Then he said, "I suspect it is precisely this universality that you are out of touch with."

Then, without waiting for a reply, he went on: "It has been a difficult time for you. Not knowing what to do to feel better, you have come here. But you keep asking yourself *why*. What I suggest is that too much of your life has been 'Why, why?' With no answers coming back, eh? You are here. That is enough." He stood up and gestured toward the adjoining bathroom. "Please go into the bathroom and strip down to your underwear."

"Strip down to my underwear?" I echoed in disbelief.

When I remained rooted to the chair, he added, "To offer a full diagnosis, I must see your body."

Still in shock, I headed toward the bathroom. Watching me, Pierrakos suddenly said, "There is surprising strength in your movement. Even as you equivocate."

"I don't understand. . . ." I mumbled.

"Excellent! For you, not understanding is already an advance. The value will be precisely in the foreignness. If I may quote St. Augustine, 'Believe *so that* you may understand.' "

St. Augustine, eh? That adds a little weight to the proceedings, I thought sardonically, trying to neutralize the compelling feel of what he'd said. I proceeded dutifully to strip down to my underwear. When I reappeared, I nervously asked if I could keep my socks on. "It's chilly in here."

"Socks off," Pierrakos peremptorily replied. "It is essential to see the way your foot grasps the ground."

Off came the socks. He then placed me in front of a large mirror, and walked slowly around me, stroking his chin and grunting inaudibly.

"It is very much as I thought," he finally said. "Except for the legs." He let out a small groan. "Ai, the legs. The legs are *much* worse even than I expected."

I flushed with embarrassment. I had had polio as a teenager and had long felt self-conscious about my thin legs. I resented attention being called to them.

"There's nothing wrong with my legs," I said defensively. "I happen to be in very good shape for a man my age. So I've often been told, anyway."

"Yes, no question about it," he said without enthusiasm. Then he added enigmatically, "Even as a young child you were treated as a Greek god, no?"

"I don't think I'd put it quite that way—"

"—and as an adult much attention, much applause still comes your way, eh? But now it does not please you so much. Now you are more the melancholy god. Perhaps no god at all, eh? Perhaps now too much the opposite, in fact."

I felt acutely uncomfortable and reached for the familiar as an anchor: "You mean what my ex-therapist used to call my God/shit syndrome."

Pierrakos seemed not to have heard. "Now there is a dry, hopeless quality," he went on. "Great sadness. A sadness you often enjoy."

" 'Enjoy'!" I snorted in protest.

"You take great pride in suffering, in the assumption you feel more pain than others. It is your badge of superiority, no?"

As I began to mouth a protest, Pierrakos sailed right on. "You are also a man of deep feeling." (Now *that* was decidedly better!) "Feelings that are now largely immobilized. Allow me to demonstrate what I mean." With that, he directed my gaze into the mirror. I reflexively flinched, never having liked staring at myself. Pierrakos immediately picked up on that.

"I expected you to flinch. You are an intellectual. Intellectuals dislike paying attention to their bodies."

"Isn't that something of a cliché?"

"You are right. Perhaps I should have said, they do not like to touch the ground. Look at your feet. Look at how your feet curl away from the floor—as if you were touching hot coals. You are so badly grounded!" He let out a yelp of distress.

"Walk!" he ordered. "Walk!" When I did, he barked, "See, see? Your feet barely grasp the ground. Your walk is gingerly—like a pussycat. Now, come and see the difference." He pulled me back in front of the mirror. "Look! Look here!" he said, poking my upper torso, his voice exuberant. "Look at the difference! Look at how easily the energy flows through your chest and shoulders! The vibrations are full, steady—really quite wonderful! And sitting solidly in the center: a great head, *alive* with energy. *Pulsating* energy!"

As I proudly stole a glance at the mirror, Pierrakos shifted his gaze back to my lower torso, sighed, and scowled. "You are like two halves of two different people. The top is a giant. But connected to what? To nothing. A Greek god with no pedestal, no base."

"Is it as bad as all that?" I asked, not sure whether to laugh at the dramatics or cry at my plight.

"We will *build* a base!" Pierrakos nearly shouted. "We will bring the energy bunched on top down . . . down into those melancholy legs. We will ground you to the earth!" He grabbed my hand and moved me over to the wooden sawhorse in the middle of the room. "Come! I will show you more."

He positioned me on my back on top of the sawhorse, with my arms hanging loosely over the sides. Then he told me to start slowly kicking my legs into the air, gradually increasing the tempo. As I kicked away, he watched me intently, occasionally encouraging me with a "Good, good." After a while my legs began to ache, but he cheerfully told me to "keep going—keep going!" As I started to pant, and then groan, he unexpectedly said, "Your great sadness comes from your inability to find love. You have a large capacity for love. But it is thwarted."

Tears welled up in my eyes. "This is really beginning to hurt," I said, with no metaphor in mind.

"Yes. Faster now, faster."

"Faster? This is killing me!"

"The opposite, I assure you."

"It hurts like hell!"

"*What* does?" Pierrakos asked eagerly.

"My legs are *killing* me! I can't keep this up!"

"You can, you can. Your legs are shriveled.... Stretch them out.... Stretch them! Climb into the sky, Martin. Climb! Higher, higher. Reach into the sky. Reach up to your mother.... The more you feel the pain, the less its hold on you...."

That did it. I was sobbing uncontrollably. But when I abruptly stopped kicking, Pierrakos grabbed my legs and set them back in motion.

"I can't!" I groaned. "I *can't!*"

"A little longer ... just a little longer.... Feel the pain, you must feel the pain...."

My whole body started to shake, my legs spastically shooting into the air. "You are very brave ... very brave," Pierrakos said encouragingly. "You are going straight into the abyss...." (*Hadn't I heard that during LSD therapy? Probably came from the same New Age workbook*.) Then—just as I thought I would pass out—Pierrakos suddenly grabbed hold of my legs to stop them and wrapped me gently in his arms. "It will be all right, Martin ... it will be all right..." he whispered soothingly. "So much pain ... so much pain...."

My body shook with sobs, but Pierrakos held me tight, softly rocking me back and forth. The warmth from his powerful, encompassing arms entered directly into my body. By comparison, my embrace of him felt constricted, lame. I suddenly knew that I trusted him—trusted the feel of him; my suspicions dissolved.

It took a good five minutes to calm down enough to begin to breathe normally. Pierrakos gently released me and suggested I get dressed.

Afterward, we sat and talked again. He repeated his conviction that whereas I had no trouble "activating" my intelligence, I had great trouble "finding a focus" for my emotions, getting them to work for me. He repeated, too, that my pain was "enormous" *and* that I "took considerable pride in it."

I said I was amazed that so much had come out of me just by kicking my feet in the air.

"And you lived through it," Pierrakos replied, smiling.

We both laughed, which prompted another homily—"You see, after pain comes laughter"—that I liked less. The follow-up made me still more uncomfortable: "And your aura has changed—from muddy gray to pale blue."

"Aura?"

"The color around a person's head."

"I'm afraid I don't believe in that sort of thing."

"It's a well-established scientific fact," Pierrakos said nonchalantly. "But it doesn't matter. We don't want you becoming adversarial. Combativeness is how you have always dissipated strong feelings—feelings better put to other use."

That sounded right. But I wasn't prepared to have all strong feelings reduced to a single status. I needed to know more about *what* he and I disagreed over, before deciding which part of it I could "put aside." Especially since Pete had warned me that Pierrakos "tended to be traditional in sexual matters." And so I asked him directly what he felt about my homosexuality.

"I have no bias against homosexuality. I pass no judgment on it."

Too flat, I thought; the first part sounds rehearsed, the second part a polite way of being negative. I wanted to know more.

"Would changing my sexual orientation be any part of the therapeutic agenda?"

"I have no interest in changing your orientation. If I questioned anything, it would be the way you separate love and sex—not who you have sex with. And I will not disguise from you my belief that anonymous sex, or sex with comparative strangers, is not in your own best interest. It works against wholeness."

That sounded less judgmental about homosexuality than anything I'd heard in psychotherapy in the sixties, but the part about "sex with strangers" was traditional enough to leave me uneasy. Contrasting "promiscuity" with "wholeness"—even should the contrast be, in some ultimate epistemological handbook, "true"—was a time-hallowed code for portraying homosexuals as sick.

What I said was, "In my view love and lust *can* coincide—at least in the early years of a relationship, when erotic zest is at its peak—but love and lust don't automatically, or maybe even frequently, come in tandem. And there is nothing dishonorable about lust when disconnected from love."

"I am talking about *acting* on disconnected lust," Pierrakos countered, but then sighed. "Look, Martin, it can't be a coincidence that immediately after an emotional experience such as you have just had, you embark on an intellectual argument. I would like to suggest that you are doing your best to dissipate the experience."

"That could well be," I admitted. "It does sound right. So let's drop it. At least for now. But it is unfinished business. I want to make it clear," I added, mustering up a final dollop of defiance, "that I have a serious problem with some of your attitudes about sex."

"It is clear. Can we now move on?"

"What do you suggest?"

"I want to return to the current situation. You are in crisis. You need a lot of help, and as soon as possible. A crisis *faced* can prove of great benefit. I believe I can help you."

I let out an almost involuntary yelp—and to my absolute astonishment, started to cry again. I could hardly believe it. And the shock was redoubled when I felt Pierrakos's arms instantaneously around me.

"You know," he said, "You're a very tough man in argument. But you are not exactly encased in concrete." That made me smile. "You're all dammed up inside, but the dam is *very* leaky. That is a good sign."

I dried my tears and started to laugh.

"Why have you stored up so much, I wonder," Pierrakos said. "For what use? When?"

"I didn't know how much was in there. All I knew was that I felt stale, arid, unhappy. If anything, I felt dried up."

"Parched would be closer."

"Right now I feel completely drained."

"I will tell you what I recommend." Pierrakos shifted from an intimate to a professional tone. "For the moment, I cannot see you myself; my schedule is entirely booked. But I would like you to work for now with André Cossen, one of my associates. He is very good. I know you will like him. Think about it. I will write down his number for you, and when you feel ready you can call him for an appointment."

"Are you sure you can't see me yourself?" My disappointment was palpable. *Same old story*, I thought bitterly. *I open myself up—and it turns out the person isn't available.*

"Hopefully, there may be an opening in my schedule later on. I assure you that you will like André very much."

There was a pause. Then Pierrakos took my hand and, his voice earnest, urged me not to use my disappointment that we could not work together as an excuse for retreating into isolation. "You need help. You need it *now*. There is no reason for you to suffer like this."

As my tears welled up again, we hugged good-bye. And I thanked him.

I did call André. And I did like him immediately—he was sweet and warm—just as Pierrakos had predicted.

We worked together once a week for more than three months. The sessions continued to be powerful: floods of rage, tears, tenderness. It was enough to know that the physical techniques of bioenergetics were capable of unlocking an astonishing swell of feelings—whatever I might then be able to do with them—and was surely unlocking more than the "talking cure" had ever been able to.

Two months into bioenergetics, André told me I was "moving at a great clip" and in his opinion was ready to undertake a ten-day "intensive." I had no idea what that meant, and he explained that it was simply a way of accelerating the therapeutic process. The Pierrakos group had a commune in the mountains at Phoenicia,

New York, called the Center for the Living Force (the name alone made rational me a little queasy) and that was where "intensives" took place. They involved concentrated "self-exploration." "With the "guidance and support" of a five-person team, an "intensive" consisted of a variety of practices, from physical exercises to meditation to periods of isolation—all in the context of "the community's healing and love energy."

On arriving at the Center for the Living Force—an attractive collection of unpretentious cottages and community buildings set on three hundred acres in a wooded valley surrounded by hills and crossed by streams—I was introduced to my five-person "team," all of whom seemed pleasant and one of whom, Alex, I felt an instant, urgent attraction to.

Gradually, in an unpressured way—at meals, at a stream, in the rustic building where I had been assigned a room—I met various members of the community. Some of them were East Coast bio-energetic therapists who spent weekends at the Center; others were occasional visitors like myself. There was also a small number of year-round residents—the Center was only five years old—from whose ranks came most of the staff, including part-time farmers, dieticians, bookkeepers.

It soon became apparent to me that, as Pete had warned, the community was traditional in its views on sexuality and relationships. At dinner one night, a woman stared disapprovingly at me when, in answer to her question about my marital status, I said "I'm not married. I'm in fact gay." She quickly disclaimed any disapproval—too quickly, I thought, as if eager to avert possible discussion.

Later on, I did meet one man in the community—and only one—who openly described himself as gay. But he was skittish around me from the beginning. And when, one day, I brought up politics, asking if he might be interested, back in the city, in attending one of our "Gays for Bella Abzug" meetings, he stammered, "Maybe—doubt it though," and thereafter was always hurrying off on some urgent business whenever I ran into him.

Another night at dinner, Larry, one of the year-round residents, made an offhand comment about not liking the ice cream parlor in town because it was "so gay." I didn't say anything at the time, but the remark rankled, and I told him so when I saw him the next day. He used the word "gay," he said, to mean "super-refined" rather than specifically homosexual, and claimed "not to be in touch with any negative feelings within myself toward homosexuals."

But then—more believably, and with impressive frankness— Larry told me that he felt "a strong feminine component" in his nature, and that it frightened him. He, too, was a writer, and had been going through a period of "blocked creativity" that he ascribed to his inability to accept "the feminine within." He confessed to having deliberately avoided me since my arrival in the community, and thanked me for approaching him so openly; it had helped him acknowledge more directly the inner struggle he was going through. Since I'd expected bland denial or a belligerent "What's it to you?"—the usual responses when a homophobic remark is challenged—Larry's attempt at self-scrutiny threw me happily off guard.

I told myself, the community wasn't that conventional. Though it adhered to a traditional model of coupledom, it deviated significantly from a traditional view of sex roles. Men were encouraged to develop their warm, gentle, nurturing side, and women spoke out decisively at community meetings, seemed to share equally in decision-making, and, on spiritual matters especially, usually took the lead. (That, to be sure, could be viewed as the most traditionally hallowed female role: woman as the repository of piety—whoops! I was at it again.)

Bursting with vigor, I sampled all the community's offerings, determined to do everything possible (to quote from the Center brochure) "to bring to consciousness, energize and dissolve the barriers we have created against the spontaneous flow of life." To steam open my pores, I sat in a Native American–style hut filled with glowing coals—and then plunged into the ice-cold stream nearby. I had my aura read, my body massaged, my biorhythm chart diagnosed, my numerological prospects analyzed.

Then came the contraction: for a whole day, I felt barely able to move. My team told me that was to be expected; up to now, I had gone at "such a rapid clip, that a pause was inevitable." They urged me to sink—for once—into apathy, to experience fully my need for inactivity and rest. I lay around, nearly catatonic, feeling I should force myself back into engagement. "That's what you've always done," Alex said (insightfully, I thought), "forced yourself to maintain a constant level of intensity, even if that means an unnatural exertion of will, or a reliance on pills. Part of you doesn't believe in your own creativity, so you constantly, artificially, keep the flame up full blast. You lack faith in the natural ebb and flow of life. You must learn to accept an alternation of rhythms, of intense activity being followed by deep rest."

To help me better experience my body's need for quiescence—and the natural springing back to life that would follow—the team prescribed a deep massage, all five of them working on my body simultaneously. They dimmed the lights, put on a background tape of Indian music, and began to massage me with some kind of oil—ten hands at once working every part of my body. (But avoiding my penis, I groggily noted; I wondered if that was standard policy or a precaution adopted when working on gay men, a class notoriously prone to arousal).

A sense of deep peacefulness alternated with tears and joyful laughter. After twenty minutes or so, I turned on my back. It was then that I abruptly flipped over into another reality, tripped out, entered an earlier time frame—the team's later words for it; I didn't have any.

I was back at Camp Idylwold, where, as a preteen, I'd spent every summer for some six to eight years. I was with my bunkmate and best friend, Billy Katz, with whom I often crawled into bed at night. I saw myself in my gray woolen sweater with "C.I." sewn on the front. I saw the bumpy dirt road leading into camp. I saw—Morty Offit! And now the tears really flowed. Beloved Morty, whom I'd adored, the senior (age eighteen? seventeen?) who had taken me (age ten? eleven?) under his wing. I saw—I was back in the middle of—our last, painful good-bye. Morty was leaving camp midway through the summer to join the army (Was it 1941?). As the taxi pulled up to take him to the railroad station, I hid behind a bush, too overcome to face him. But just as he was getting into the car, he spotted me, got back out, came over, and put his arm around me. "It's going to be all right, Marty. It's going to be all right. . . ." Then he was gone in a blur, the last time I ever saw him. . . . I was blinded by tears. . . .

As I groggily came to, one of the team members gently suggested that I could "redo" that "crushing departure," transform it into a positive memory. I had been loved and blessed; Morty had cared deeply for me. That was what I should try to remember—not the obliterating sense of loss. It wasn't a matter of reinventing my history, the team explained, but rather relocating its essence so that I could experience it differently. I was entitled to my grief over Morty's departure, but the grief could be recalled within the original context of his love for me; to remember the caring was to soften the pain.

I felt hugely comforted, cried some more, and then started to sink back into other memories. . . .

On my last night at the Center, I had dinner by candlelight with my team, joined by a few other members of the community with whom I'd gotten friendly, and by André, who'd come up from New York for the occasion.

The next morning we met at seven for our final session. We went into the woods and sat on the rocks next to a mountain stream, at a spot where the water fell with special fullness. We held hands, meditated together, spoke from our hearts. I realized, and said, that for the past few days I had felt the occasional urge to walk farther upstream, to get closer to the source. Something had held me back. I now realized what it was: I wanted to go there with these people. It was through them that I had gotten in touch with deeper resources of strength within myself than I'd ever known. . . . As we said good-bye, I was swept by waves of sadness.

The next day, back in New York, I was desolate: punchy,

frightened, unable to stop crying. Then, toward nightfall, I started to get angry. Had I been conned? Had I yet again allowed others to pass judgment on my life, accepted those judgments as valid, put myself through needless spasms of self-doubt? Wasn't bioenergetics a greater instrument of self-torture than any of the more obvious ones I'd begun the therapy to alleviate? The anger astounded me— and the swiftness with which it replaced my sadness. Wasn't that itself a clue?

During my session with André the following day, I continued to rail against the "smug," formulaic words I'd heard at the Center. I dismissed their "Aimee Semple McPherson certitudes," their authoritative charts and credos, as "stone engravings on air." I raged at the assumption that one could—at any age—radically alter one's core perspective or personality. Haven't they heard about imprinting? Couldn't they see that the path of wisdom was to accept the basic parameters of one's personality after a certain point in life and to stop pursuing the chimera of "fixing" it, making it different or better or perfect?

At the end of the session, my fury vented, I heard myself say that "at bottom" what might well be going on with me was simply desolation; after ten days of closeness, I was again alone. I recorded the session in my diary:

> Stupefied. Trouble moving my body around. Hopeless, stuck. But haven't hit the depth of my hopelessness—that it's all a repeat, another game in the void.

I made an appointment to see Pierrakos. In essence he told me, "Forget the spiritual dimension! Concentrate on *your* process."

"Which is tantamount to saying, 'Put aside your intelligence.'"

"Not at all," Pierrakos shot back, exasperation in his voice. "What you need to put aside are the categorical judgments your intelligence creates in order to distance yourself from available love and support."

That sounded devastatingly plausible. And the stalemate might have been broken then and there. But in response to my further accusation that he and the Center were homophobic, Pierrakos insisted that he was not, and then added—fatally—that he did regard male homosexuality as "a flight from woman," did find it "regrettable" that I had chosen to "block out half the human race."

To which I replied, anger mounting, "I don't—other than genitally." Why, I asked, didn't he also lament the way heterosexuals "block out half the human race"?

"I do regret," he answered in a measured voice, "that men, men much more than women, do not relate to each other on a deeper emotional level. But I do not regret their failure to relate sexually."

"You're applying different standards for gays and straights," I said angrily. "I've always had strong emotional connections, though not sexual ones, with women. Why do you equate the absence of sexual desire with 'flight'? Or if you do, why don't you say the same thing about men who refuse to acknowledge feelings of erotic desire for other men? I'm capable of emotional intimacy with men and women, and most straight men are capable of neither. Yet somehow in your view I and other homosexuals don't qualify for full admission to the human race. What does qualify one, if not the capacity for intimacy? Merely the ability to have sex with a member of the opposite gender?"

Pierrakos sighed deeply and then, a note of finality in his voice, quietly said that I was "inventing" disagreement between us in order to create needless distance. He added—to my astonishment—that he thought "overall" I was "in a very good place," and he hoped that henceforth I'd concentrate on the physical work and continue to move ahead.

The stalemate had not been broken. I never went back. To this day, I don't fully understand why. Part of me thinks that I "came to my senses," saw through the ersatz heart of the whole ridiculous cosmology. Another part of me thinks that I fled out of fear, that I'd opened up too quickly to too much pain—to say nothing of hope—and needed to clamp the lid back on. Probably both explanations contain some truth—and which the greater part, I still could not say with assurance.

—from *Midlife Queer* (1996)

Feminism and the
Gay Academic Union (GAU)

As a founding member in 1973 of the Gay Academic Union (GAU), we took as our tripartite mission protecting the rights of openly lesbian and gay students and faculty on campuses, pinpointing needed areas of research on homosexuality, and originating pilot courses in gay and lesbian studies. We worked for months putting together a two-day inaugural conference, "The Universities and the Gay Experience," sometimes frantically stitching together the mundane pieces, from workshop titles to registration forms, that go into creating a conference of any kind.

But this was no run-of-the-mill event, and until the day of the conference itself we were never sure we could pull it off. Most lesbian and gay academics had previously stayed firmly bolted in their closets, understandably fearful of the consequences of coming out in a university setting that despite its purported liberalism was likely to be nearly as pervasively homophobic as society at large. With the modern gay movement still only a few years old, and with lesbian and gay academics never having previously made any effort to band together, we were afraid few would actually risk showing up for the conference.

To our stunned delight, more than three hundred people ended up registering (and another hundred or so milled skittishly about);

the atmosphere was abuzz with excitement and enthusiasm and the plenary sessions and workshops alike proved vividly alive. Barbara Gittings and I were chosen as the two keynote speakers. I labored long and hard over my speech, eager to strike a chord of cautious utopianism. What I hadn't foreseen at the 1973 GAU conference was that infighting within our own ranks would take as large a toll as would the struggle against homophobia in the outside world. GAU's second conference, in 1974, drew some six hundred people, and by 1975 the organization had broadened from its New York City base to additional chapters in Boston, Philadelphia, and Ann Arbor (as well as, subsequently, Chicago, Los Angeles, and San Francisco). All the standard signs of success were present. Yet within a year of GAU's founding, I'd developed a queasy feeling that the victory might be pyrrhic. From the beginning, the organization drew many more men than women, and the women, early on and frequently, expressed disappointment in the lack of feminist consciousness among most of the men.

Some of the GAU men, myself included, self-identified as radical; we not only agreed with feminist analysis, but also with the criticism already being sounded by radicals outside the university that the middle-class white-male mentality dominant in GAU meant the organization was in danger of replicating rather than challenging the academic world's patriarchal attitudes, hierarchies, and rituals—right down to constructing its conferences around "panels," a format likely to perpetuate suspect divisions between "experts" and audience, teachers and students, haves and have-nots. Instead of working to broaden standard definitions of what intellectual work was, and to break the connections between academic research and established bastions of power, GAU was, so the critique went, in danger of becoming such a bastion itself (or at least it seemed to be earnestly trying to).

Sympathetic to these warnings and complaints, I decided, when asked to give the concluding speech at the second GAU conference in 1974, to use the occasion as a vehicle for talking openly about my own fear that the organization was moving in dubious directions. I expressed disappointment, first of all, that while GAU was largely male, few tenured male faculty had affiliated. I suggested that we probably needed to face the fact "that in a very real sense a generation of gay men has largely been lost to us—that they've been superbly, probably irretrievably, indoctrinated and cowed by the patriarchal culture. If community is to come, the work and rewards alike are going to belong to the young."

What I didn't point out, and probably should have, was that there weren't enough nontenured faculty involved with GAU either. Anyone who wanted to attend a GAU function was welcome—there was no other way to build the organization—so as time went on, GAU became increasingly attractive to well-educated gay white men looking for a congenial environment in which to come out and to find partners and friends. After the first year, these men probably outnumbered the graduate students and junior faculty who actually had university affiliations. Which meant that GAU was handicapped nearly from the outset in its specific mission to change the climate on the country's campuses.

In my closing speech in 1974, I also expressed discomfort over how much of the organization's energy during the previous year had gone into social events and consciousness-raising sessions. I realized how necessary such activities were: "For most people consciousness-raising is a needed prelude to active political commitment. And continuing social contact is a valuable device for keeping that commitment humane—oriented to the needs of people rather than to the dictates of ideology."

But the *amount* of time invested in social events and consciousness-raising sessions, I argued, had been excessive to the point of self-indulgence. True, much of the consciousness-raising work had come about in response to criticism from GAU women that many of the gay men were sexist; yet sexism hadn't been consistently addressed during most of the consciousness-raising sessions. And beyond the issue of sexism, I wasn't convinced that we needed as much consciousness-raising as we were lavishing upon ourselves.

Most of us were college-educated, middle-class, and white—in other words, as I pointed out, "already overprivileged when compared with the majority of our gay brothers and sisters." And most of us, I added (probably overstating the matter) "are in better shape psychologically than we sometimes care to admit to ourselves. The argument that we 'have to get our heads together before we can do any political work' can become a standing rationale for doing nothing: our psyches are somehow never quite ready, our motors never quite tuned up. I think a lot of this has to do with American perfectionism, and even more to do with male selfishness."

We were in danger of talking too much and doing too little. And talking, moreover, about a limited set of issues. We'd heard almost nothing during the second conference—indeed, during the whole second year—about the class and race divisions that characterized the gay community no less than the society at large. It was time to face those divisions, I argued, and to do something about their root causes. As matters currently stood, we were in danger of becoming an organization that gave a conference about middle-class white male issues once a year. "And at that, a conference modeled rather closely on those genteel gatherings we're already familiar with in our respective professional caucuses."

I also voiced concern over the contempt I'd heard expressed for those whose style differed from that of the gay mainstream—for bisexuals and the transgendered, and for those involved in S/M. That intolerance, I said, was to me tantamount to playing "a version of the same game the larger society plays with us. Namely: 'either do it *our* way or be prepared to find yourself ostracized.' It smacks of the same contempt for individual differences that we deplore in the culture as a whole. If we castigate those who deviate from our norms, how do we protest when those who adhere to the heterosexual norm choose to hound and humiliate us? To my mind, we have to oppose *any* prescription for how consenting adults may or must make love."

I strained to conclude the speech on a more upbeat note, praising us for coming together and staying together, for at least beginning the work of combating homophobia and sexism in society at large, in a college setting—and within ourselves. Using my own experience as an example, I spoke about how I'd learned more about myself through involvement in political work than I'd ever had through formal, obsessive psychoanalysis. I'd also gotten to like myself better. The still-common psychoanalytical view of me, of all homosexuals, as truncated human beings had come to feel stale and mistaken when measured against the competence I'd displayed and the respect I'd earned from my work in the movement.

I then went on to discuss the shifting political climate within the country as a whole and within GAU in particular. I myself still held, I said, to the vision of a broad-gauged movement devoted to substantive social change that had been forged during the radical optimism of the sixties. Globally, *the* issue for the vast majority of the world's population was still the one that had engaged socialists for generations: how to ensure freedom from material want, how to improve the terrible conditions of daily life endured by most people. Richard Nixon may have been forced from power but, as I saw it, his arrogant assumption of American entitlement to dictate the affairs of the globe remained alive and well in national councils, accompanied, as it had long been, by a firm commitment to the "traditional" values of male power, black inferiority, and homosexual pathology.

Mean-spirited, vindictive bigotry was flourishing anew in the land by the midseventies. Los Angeles police chief Ed Davis showed neither embarrassment nor hesitation when he spoke out against law reforms that would extend rights to those "predatory creatures" called "gays." And *Chicago Daily News* columnist Mike Royko seemed equally assured when, in a 1974 column entitled "Banana Lib," he described how "men in love with monkeys" were winning acceptance by "coming out of the cage."

The picture wasn't all bleak. Even as L.A.'s Davis spewed his antigay bile, San Francisco's police chief signed an order prohibiting his officers from using the words "fruit," "queer," "faggot," or "fairy." Even as Royko mocked homosexuals, the American Bar Association adopted a resolution urging states to repeal their antigay sex laws, Governor Milton Shapp of Pennsylvania issued the first state executive order banning employment discrimination against gays, and a national Council of Churches of Christ conference concluded that antigay discrimination was "immoral."

Despite these seesaw political developments, overall the conservative trend had become ever more pronounced by the mid-seventies. And GAU wasn't immune to that trend. A growing number of men with less than progressive views became more visible and active in the New York chapter of GAU, with the result that most of the men (myself included) who self-defined as radical and who'd founded the organization began to drift away. Almost all the women—who from the first had thrown in their lot with GAU uneasily and tentatively—became disaffected (as, with the growth of lesbian separatism, they were simultaneously withdrawing from other co-gender gay organizations as well).

As early as the second GAU conference in 1974, one conservative gay male professor locked horns with Charlotte Bunch, a leading lesbian-feminist writer and organizer (she was a founder of D.C. Women's Liberation, of the Furies Collective, and of *Quest: A Feminist Quarterly*). In her speech to the conference that year, Charlotte had expressed the view that gay men insufficiently acknowledged the rights and needs of women, and she spoke movingly of the value of the burgeoning separatist movement in providing lesbians with respite from being constantly on the offensive and with the needed time and space to build a community congenial to their needs. To end separatism, Bunch said, we had to end the reasons that had made separatism necessary: the failure of the gay movement to fight male supremacy.

The conservative professor indignantly replied that Charlotte's speech was nothing more or less than an invitation to male self-flagellation. He was tired of being told what was wrong with him, he said, tired of "obligatory therapy" that at bottom undermined the self-esteem of gay men; and, he added ominously, he rejected any purported self-examination that came at the "expense of mind"—whatever that meant. He insisted that GAU's proper mission was simple and straightforward: to pursue cases of antigay discrimination in academia and to increase the amount of reliable scholarship on gay lives.

Barbara Gittings, the longtime lesbian activist, also took issue at the conference with Charlotte, though the cordial tone of her criticism and her underlying wish to build bridges were light-years away from sardonic divisiveness. Gittings deplored the growing mystique about "vast differences" between gay men and lesbians, fearing it would minimize our very real commonalities and thereby our ability to join forces against shared oppression. "Nothing would suit antihomosexual bigots more," Gittings said, "than that we fragment." Separatism, she added, "seems to me uncomfortably close to the notion that anatomy is destiny."

Though I basically agreed with Charlotte, I shared some of Barbara's fears. In particular, I felt that Charlotte had failed to acknowledge that some gay men—not enough, certainly—had been trying to incorporate feminist values in their lives and work; almost certainly more gay men than straight men. Yet basically I believed, with Charlotte, that fighting sexism had to become central to our movement work. Gay men and all women *were*, I'd become convinced, natural allies in the struggle against a politically powerful—and emotionally constricted—machismo that the culture had long enthroned as the noblest form of humanity. Only an infusion of radical feminist insights, I believed, could keep the gay male movement from edging ever closer to a narrowly gauged agenda that would simply allow gay white men to take their place beside straight white men at the apex of privilege.

The gulf between many of the men and women continued to widen. In a letter to me in 1975, a gay man characterized feminism as "a rickety ideology . . . playing a parasitic and negative role in the gay movement," and he characterized Charlotte as "virulently homophobic and man-hating," insisting that she had a "considerable history of antimale thinking," and even suggesting that "her activities would make a good subject for investigation."

This seemed to me beyond cranky and I decided to respond in

a letter. I suggested that instead of "investigating" Charlotte, he might try investigating her writings. If he could "get beyond his own pre-judgments," I wrote, he'd find a wise and humane attempt "to point out how much *all* of us still adhere, at some semi-conscious level (to put it in the most favorable light), to patriarchal and hierarchical values—the very values that stand in the way of the psychosexual 'revolution' we call for out of the other side of our mouths."

Vitriol has always, it seems, been a staple of movement politics (gay and otherwise). How to account for the endemic cut-and-slash style of movement work, the penchant for converting *each other* into the Enemy, is an ongoing puzzle, even as it takes an ongoing toll on oppositional strength. Does it reflect accumulated anger (and even psychic damage) resulting from entrenched oppression and from frustration over the failure to win long-overdue substantive change? And is the anger more "safely" (if inappropriately) discharged against one's own, much as an abused child's rage will often turn not against the offending relative directly but toward some infinitely more benign adult authority figure in their lives?

I've never been sure what is at the root of the penchant for movement infighting and invective. Nor have I (or apparently anyone else) figured out how constructively to rechannel such vehemence. Though I see myself as a skilled conciliator in some situations, I know perfectly well that in others I can be thin-skinned and defensive—which usually surprises those who confuse a controlled exterior with internal serenity. If someone comes at me with what I take to be an unfair accusation, I go right back at them, punch for punch. It wasn't always that way. Earlier in my life, I "made nice" when assaulted. But that, I painfully learned, only incites the bullies of the world to pummel you more. Yet if I've found self-assertion to be necessary self-protection, it can sometimes get triggered too quickly or expressed too fiercely, bringing it regrettably close to that very machismo I theoretically deplore. My defenses, alas, were developed long before my ideology—and have proven far more intractable.

* * *

Although intensively involved in the first two formative years of GAU, by the time the third annual conference came around in 1975, I moved myself to the sidelines. Indeed, along with almost all the women and radical-minded men, I was more than halfway out the door, distressed at the increasingly mainstream (male) tone and goals of the organization. Perhaps those of us who dissented from that trend should have stayed and fought the good fight longer. But the odds seemed poor, our energy limited, and the need to get on with other work compelling.

—from *Midlife Queer* (1996)

The National Gay Task Force

My primary movement work shifted from GAU to helping establish the National Gay Task Force. It should be kept in mind that in the midseventies the gay movement in the United States may have been the strongest in the world but involved only a small fraction of the LGBT population as a whole. The vast majority of gay men and lesbians, if visible at all, were struggling primarily with issues relating to their individual decisions about how best to come out—or how successfully to cover their tracks and remain in the closet; they had scant remaining energy for or interest in political activism. The few who did participate in the fledgling gay movement were sharply divided over agendas and strategies.

Additionally, gay men and lesbians found it increasingly difficult to work together politically during the seventies. The reasons were multiple: the waning of gay male militancy, as characterized by the decline of the Gay Liberation Front in the immediate post-Stonewall years, 1969–1972; the indifference of even many activist gay men to feminist politics and values; and the emergence instead of a gay male style that aped machismo (even if it marginally and, for most, unconsciously, simultaneously parodied that style). To many lesbians, the lives of gay men seemed chiefly devoted to rampaging sexual consumption in bathhouses and backroom bars, to sex disconnected from intimacy—suggesting that their values were closer to those of straight men than to women. Though subsequent studies have shown that only a small minority—no more than 20 percent—of gay men ever frequented bathhouses and backroom bars, the perception of some lesbians, especially those committed to a more traditional set of values centering on nurturance, sharing, and community building, led them to feel increasingly alienated from their purported "brothers" and to turn to creating a separatist movement. Yet others continued to feel that they shared a common enemy with gay men—homophobia—and remained willing to work with them politically.

These were the women who proved available for joining the National Gay Task Force. The organization—its name subsequently changed to National Lesbian and Gay Task Force (NLGTF)—emerged as an offshoot of the growing dissatisfaction some of the leading figures in the Gay Activists Alliance (GAA) felt with that organization. GAA had become the dominant gay political group in New York City in the early seventies (superseding the Gay Liberation Front); its creative "zaps"—militant street confrontations—on behalf of gay civil rights, fair housing, and job equity had managed to draw considerable media attention and even some public policy changes. Despite these achievements, GAA's practical-minded emphasis on "changing laws" had drawn fire as "mere reformism," especially from those who measured the organization's "limited" agenda against the earlier attempt by the Gay Liberation Front (GLF) to treat gay issues in conjunction with those relating to racism and sexism. From the radical GLF perspective, the goal of getting sodomy statutes off the books, or putting antidiscrimination laws on them, could never end the oppression of gay people; homophobia was embedded in the minds and hearts of mainstream Americans, and antigay statutes and court opinions merely reflected the negative national bias. What had to be ended, the radicals argued, was the mind-set that equated heterosexuality with "normalcy," the nuclear family with optimal human happiness, and dichotomous gender roles with divine intention.

But the radical-minded had a limited constituency and no clear-cut strategy of their own for ending the institutionalized heterosexism to which they rightly called attention. And even less apparent in those years—to radicals and reformers alike—was the understanding that there might not be one strategy, one path, one kind of politics or temperament that would put an end to what we now call heterosexism, let alone general inequalities of opportunity and wealth.

Even today not enough people (in my view) seem willing to acknowledge that our movement needs to make room for—and applaud—diverse contributions on a variety of fronts. Social transformation requires a range of efforts and a plethora of skills: lawyers, lobbyists, media experts, scholars, cultural workers, youth advocates, sexual liberationists, community organizers, mainstream politicians, and so on. "Let each contribute according to his or her abilities" rings like stale Marxism; yet the sentiment serves a goal at the opposite pole from sectarian rigidity. A bit less insistence on the absolute rightness of this path, and a bit more openness to the possibilities of that one, might cushion (although it could not obliterate, since diversity does require expression) some of the more bruising divisions, past and present, that have diluted the strength of the gay movement.

None of the three principal figures who put NLGTF together—Nathalie Rockhill, Ronald Gold, and Bruce Voeller—were radical ideologues; they prided themselves on being (in Gold's words), "incremental pragmatists." Which is not to say that they were devoid of strong convictions, or had feather-duster personalities. Hardly—of the three, only Rockhill was able to hold firmly to a position without becoming abrasive. Indeed, her even-tempered good sense, her ability really to listen to opposing views without defensively flaring up, made her, in the eyes of many, something of a movement saint.

Bruce Voeller, a handsome thirty-eight-year-old once-married father of three, had a doctorate in biochemistry and until recently had been on the staff of Rockefeller University. He thought of

himself as a tough-minded, efficient professional with enough accumulated experience in a variety of worlds to play a leading role
in the burgeoning gay movement. Articulate, smooth-tongued,
and shrewd, he knew how to cut through, co-opt—or, if need be,
circumvent—opposition, though when it persisted, he could become testy and authoritarian.

Ronald Gold, roughly the same age as Voeller, had been an antiwar protester and a member of CORE, the civil rights organization.
A Brooklyn native of independent means who'd also been a reporter
for *Variety* and a longtime editor at *TV Guide*, the outspoken, opinionated Gold was both admired and feared for his sharp intelligence, his rapid-fire speech, and his caustic, sometimes overbearing
manner. But he was also a modest man with a capacity for hard work
matched by a willingness to let others take credit for it.

Gold, Voeller, and Rockhill had all been active in GAA but
had become increasingly fed up with what they characterized as
its self-indulgent, sophomoric talkathons, endless countercultural
chatter about peace and love, and tedious "consensus building"—all
of which in Voeller's view had turned GAA into an obstacle course
impeding the ability to get concrete tasks successfully completed.
Yet none of the three could be accurately characterized as establishment squares or over-the-hill spoilsports. Voeller insisted that "we
gays have some unique contributions to make to the world *from
our experience of being gay*." And among those contributions, Voeller
gave high priority to the way gays and lesbians had pioneered non-
traditional families, and egalitarian, nonmonogamous relationships.
This was not the standard we're-just-folks argument favored by gay
establishmentarians.

Gold saved some of his strongest views for his private correspondence. "Let's not be afraid to be angry at the immorality of the 'establishment' we face," he wrote in one memo. "I think we ought to
be saying it is a moral question. . . . We must push the parallels with
Jews . . . and with blacks, who said, 'We demand your acceptance,
but we don't need your approval. . . .'"

During the 1976 campaign, Jimmy Carter had said that he

opposed discrimination based on sexual orientation and would support and sign a federal civil rights bill to that effect, but had then withdrawn his support for a gay rights plank in the 1976 Democratic party platform (the plank was adopted at the 1980 convention) and admitted on television that homosexuality "puzzled" and "troubled" him. Not a bad state of mind, to be sure, when measured against the overt, unapologetic homophobia of the Republican party's leaders. But not exactly a clarion call to end antigay discrimination, either.

Not the least of the Task Force's accomplishments during the seventies was the mere fact of its survival. A national gay and lesbian political organization with a paid professional staff demonstrated, by virtue of continuing to stay the course, that a certain level of visibility had been achieved and could be built on—and that gay people could no longer be *entirely* ignored. By 1978, five years after its inception, the Task Force could boast eight thousand members (though not even a third were women) scattered in all fifty states, a steady rise in revenues (though still not sufficient to establish hoped-for regional offices, let alone to provide the staff a decent wage), and a board, initially reliant on East Coasters, that by the end of the decade included representatives from around the country. And throughout the seventies, the Task Force worked hard to exert pressure on large corporations to examine their antigay bias in hiring—and succeeded in getting such giants as IBM, American Airlines, and Citicorp to put antidiscrimination policies into writing. The Task Force also created a Gay Media Alert Network (a listing of local gay organizations paired with local television stations in more than a hundred cities) to protest negative media representations of gay life; the Network won an especially notable victory in pressuring ABC to soften an episode in the popular *Marcus Welby* television series that stereotypically portrayed gay men as child molesters.

Which isn't to say that the initial doubts I and others had had about the Task Force had been laid to rest. We'd still involuntarily twitch at the periodic charge that NLGTF was an "elitist" organization out of touch with the needs of ordinary lesbians and gays and their grassroots communities, and unwilling or unable to embrace nonwhite or working-class cultures. In this regard, nothing made us more uneasy than the favorable opinion West Coast millionaire David Goodstein (who had purchased the *Advocate* in 1974) expressed about the Task Force. Middle-class respectability was his totem; he wanted those of us who might qualify (namely affluent white men) to take their place on the assembly line of the American Dream, and those of us who couldn't qualify, to get out of the (his) way. By 1979 Goodstein was claiming that "moderates" were responsible for all the movement's successes to date, and the "left-wing radicals" responsible for nothing but "noise . . . an enormous amount of friction in the gay community and a lot of unhappiness."

Friction within the Task Force was a constant—friction between Voeller and certain staff members, between the staff (which often felt underappreciated) and the board (which usually felt underconsulted). The Task Force's real accomplishments always seemed to be accompanied by serious personality conflicts, turf wars, and angry divisions based on gender, race, and—less, or less visibly—on class. (After all, most of us were squarely—in both senses—"middle.")

The Task Force had been barely three months old when board member Frank Kameny—who in the pre-Stonewall years had played a heroic, militant role—shot off a furious letter to the staff and board declaring himself "dismayed and, in fact, appalled" at the lack of leadership and systematic planning thus far apparent. Frank wanted a formal constitution, a firm statement of purpose, and a clear-cut demarcation of lines of authority between board, staff, and executive director. He wanted the board to govern NLGTF "rather closely and in considerable detail," and believed the role of the membership, no matter how large it eventually became, "should be close to, if not actually, nil."

Frank's view that the board should set policy and priorities and not be, as some boards are, simply a high-profile, fund-raising body was shared by most of us (but not his view of the membership) and, after considerable debate, this was established as a guiding principle. But in practice, policy decisions during most of the seventies were primarily made by the staff; and to maintain that control, the executive director usually presented the board with only a carefully limited set of agenda items to debate. The board, however, had more than its fair share of tough and independent-minded characters; it frequently rebelled against playing a secondary role and insisted on reasserting its policy-making power, even as the executive director tried, with minimal success, to get the board to take on more fundraising responsibilities instead.

All of which produced frequently fractious board debate, with Frank usually the most fractious of the lot. Anyone who had known Frank earlier in the movement had grown familiar with his penchant for emphatic, and sometimes throbbingly self-righteous, *diktats*. In the face of one of his repetitive tirades, most of us on the board would try to keep our eyes on the floor and our tempers cool, repeating over and over a silent mantra: that only someone with Frank's truculent personality could have had the guts to take on the federal government and the psychiatric profession in the sixties, at a time when the gay movement was little more than a gleam in the eye. And so we tended to let Frank vent, to think of ourselves as high-minded for doing so, and to resign ourselves to the interminable discussions of structure that made us almost as irritable as they did him.

It became apparent early on that others besides myself on the board were uneasy about the Task Force's (mostly) reformist orientation. Several resignations hinged on racial issues. The first African American member of the Task Force board, Jon L. Clayborne, stayed but a short time, making clear his view that the elimination of racism in the gay world "should be as much a consideration" as the elimination of sexism. And Clayborne was certainly right that to date it hadn't been.

Just as in the early feminist movement, the gay movement could not seem to focus its attention on issues relating to race and class. Its inattention kept most nonwhites (and most nonurban working-class whites as well) unwilling to set aside their own agendas and their sense of multiple identities and loyalties, in favor of a single-issue political movement. Besides Clayborne, who stayed briefly, the only other African American on a Task Force board that by 1976 had thirty members was Betty Powell, an instructor at the Brooklyn College school of education; she was soon elected co-chair. And before the end of the decade, the board had implemented as formal goals that a minimum of 20 percent of the body should consist of minority members and that the ratio between men and women should be fifty-fifty. But the awareness that such goals were desirable was not tantamount to meeting them; as regards minority inclusion, especially, the accomplishment was (and in most gay organizations remains) woefully incomplete.

I had myself formed friendships and a loose political alliance with several of the women on the board, especially Betty Powell and Charlotte Bunch. Our alliance was based on the shared perception that NLGTF's continuing focus on winning powerful mainstream allies in order to foster a civil rights agenda was insufficient. We felt (as I wrote in my diary) that "a radical commitment should underlie our reformist activities"—and felt that most of the male board members disagreed.

But as I was told at the time (and since), I have a way—a deplorably "essentialist" way—of overcategorizing and overcriticizing "middle-class white men" (that is, people like myself) and, in contrast, overgeneralizing about the superior political insight and all-around wisdom of lesbians. I persist in this, I'm told, even while well aware that the lesbian community has itself been racked with factionalism and ideological warfare through time. And so I try, like a good analysand, to work on my bias about the superior virtue of lesbians—of women in general. Yet it stubbornly holds.

By the midseventies, the women on the Task Force board had formed a women's caucus and had made it clear that the organization would henceforth function on a coalition ("women *plus* men") not a unity ("people") model. That might not represent the optimal hopes some—including some of the women—had, but it did represent the current reality of how gay men and lesbians could best work together. Though not separatists, the Task Force women understandably concluded that they couldn't sanction a male-dominated political movement. Too many male members of the board had from time to time made it clear that they lacked sympathy for a feminist perspective and held centrist political views. Also, this was a time period when cultural feminism, with its insistence on the fundamental differences between women and men, had eclipsed radical feminism, and its adherents considered the "lurid" gay male lifestyle as at odds with their own values. This didn't mean that the lesbian-feminists of the midseventies were antisex prudes. But it is true that they defined lesbianism less as a *sexual* identity (in contrast to the way most gay men regarded themselves) and more as one centered on their gender interests as women. The women who participated in NLGTF in the midseventies were somewhat unusual in their continued willingness to work with gay men, but they weren't willing to keep letting lesbian-feminist issues take a backseat to gay male ones.

This outraged Frank Kameny above all others. By the time of our weekend-long retreat in June 1976, Frank had already exploded several times in board meetings over the "intrusion" of feminist values. At the retreat, the heat went up several notches. As I wrote in my diary afterward, "Every time one of the women talked of the need to end lesbian invisibility or insisted upon the semantic propriety of 'gay men and lesbians,' Frank, leaping to apoplectic cue, would either shake his head with vigorous displeasure, mumble something about the 'fanaticism of revolutionaries,' or do some of his furious (and infuriating) speechifying about the need to maintain a clear separation between the feminist and gay movements."

In any case, the hoped-for transformation of the Task Force proved tough sledding. And probably because, at bottom, transformation, personal or social, wasn't what most gay Americans (any more than most straight ones) have in mind. Voeller's we-want-in politics were [and still are] far closer to what the majority of gays and lesbians desire than are the policies of us self-styled radicals. Most gays, after all, see themselves—and want others to see them— as good mainstream Americans, and Voeller's strategy of working through established channels for piecemeal change was, and is, entirely consonant with their own views. Thus it was in the seventies that tens of thousands read David Goodstein's *Advocate* and far fewer the radical *Gay Community News*.

Beset on the one side by lesbian separatism and on the other by the mounting gay male conviction that discoing till dawn was certainly more fun and infinitely more chic than politics, the organized gay movement seemed badly positioned for the onslaught from the religious right that swiftly gathered momentum in the midseventies. The bell in the night sounded in 1976, when the Supreme Court, refusing even to hear oral argument, voted six to three in *Doe v. Commonwealth* to let stand a Virginia statute (and by implication laws on the books in thirty-four other states) punishing sodomy *between consenting adults*; that law, the Court declared, was not an unconstitutional invasion of privacy.

Signs of a backlash had been evident for at least a year: the New York City Council had again defeated a gay civil rights bill, with the Archdiocese of New York proudly leading the fight against what it liked to call the "sexually disoriented." City Council member Matt Troy had, during a television show, scornfully referred to gay people as "lepers." William F. Buckley Jr. had written a vicious "let's face it, they're *sick*" column (in the eighties, during the AIDS epidemic, he seriously advocated tattooing HIV-positive gay men on the buttocks). And the psychiatrist Charles Socarides had been pressing hard for the American Psychiatric Association to repudiate its 1973 vote dropping homosexuality from the category of illness.

The sweeping 1976 Supreme Court *Doe* decision felt (as I put it in my diary) "like a snake breaking suddenly, hungrily, through the crust of the earth." And what could we do about it? Should we try to organize a mass rally in protest? That would at least provide an outlet for anger, but low attendance could prove an embarrassment.

Should we have a teach-in on homophobia? But wouldn't we end up preaching to the converted? How about tax refusal, like that practiced by a segment of the opposition to the Vietnam War on the grounds we wouldn't support a government that denied basic rights? Would even a handful mobilize behind a measure so unorthodox? Should we put our energy into lobbying for the gay civil rights bill recently introduced into Congress? But was there even the remotest chance we could collect the needed votes to enact such legislation when the Court had just announced that it was constitutional to discriminate? In fact every tactic we could think of, from militant zap to quiet plea, had already been tried, and none seemed able to touch the country's entrenched—and seemingly deepening—homophobia.

I tried remembering two things: that movements for social change are always subject to fluctuating fortunes; the graph never traces linear upward progress but rather peaks and valleys of varying, maddeningly unpredictable duration. And that for all the "one step forward, one step back" nature of the gay (or any) advance in the United States, progress here seemed infinitely greater than elsewhere in the world. In Barcelona in 1977, the police fired rubber bullets into a gay pride march; in London that same year, the editor of *Gay News* was convicted on charges of blasphemy. In 1978, when Australia finally managed to field a gay rights march of two thousand people (more than a quarter million turned out that year in San Francisco), the police moved in and made arrests for "indecent behavior." And in Iran in 1978, six men were executed by firing squad for the crime of homosexuality—with thousands of additional executions to follow under the Khomeini regime.

In 1977 Anita Bryant announced her Save Our Children campaign to repeal the recently passed Dade County, Florida, law that forbade discrimination in jobs and housing based on sexual orientation. The Dade County law was one of some three dozen such ordinances that the outraged singer (and Florida citrus pitchwoman) characterized as protecting the rights of "human garbage." By the following year, California legislator John Briggs had introduced a state bill—for which he'd collected some half-million signatures—calling for the expulsion from the classroom of not only gay and lesbian teachers but also any other teacher who presented homosexuality in a positive light.

The hard-fought Briggs amendment ultimately went down to defeat by the considerable (and unexpected) margin of 59 to 41 percent. But Anita Bryant's forces, after a vicious campaign that portrayed gays as recruiting and molesting children—and aided by a pro-Bryant letter from Archbishop Coleman Carroll, read aloud in Catholic churches on the Sunday preceding the referendum—succeeded in rescinding the Dade County ordinance by a vote of more than two to one. The readers of *Good Housekeeping* that year named Bryant "The Most Admired Woman in America."

The rising tide of social conservatism in the late seventies saw the defeat of the Equal Rights Amendment, attacks on affirmative-action programs and social welfare legislation, and the popularity of "right-to-work" laws aimed at diluting the strength of labor unions. Not surprisingly, gay rights—the newest kid on the block—suffered its own share of setbacks. In 1978 alone, gay civil rights ordinances went down to crushing defeat in St. Paul, Minnesota; Eugene, Oregon; and (by a three-to-one margin) Wichita, Kansas.

To build a movement of larger numbers and impact, we needed to demonstrate to a diverse and mostly still closeted gay population that the movement was concerned enough with the difficult realities of their daily lives to be worth joining. And beyond all that was *the* problem: how to build and sustain a collective struggle in a country that emphasizes radical individualism. We (especially the already privileged) are constantly reinforced in the notion that the cultivation of one's own precious personality is more important than binding oneself in common cause to others.

It's true that political involvement requires some detachment from self-obsession. But the process is paradoxical. Participation in a common struggle with others opens up opportunities that feed the self in unexpected ways. Though political work *does* demand that we concentrate on the common purpose at hand, it simultaneously provides the individual with the comfort of community and new-found security and confidence. That, in turn, can lead those long suffering from the corrosive effects of oppression to self-discoveries and assertions that previously felt too "dangerous" to experience or express. And these discoveries often, for the individual, transcend in value any of the public gains won by the political struggle itself.

In any case, when I received early in 1977 a bulky packet of materials to read through for yet another upcoming, talk-laden meeting of the NLGTF board, I knew I had come to a divide. As I wrote Betty Powell, then serving as co-chair, the planned agenda "seems to me so top-heavy with organizational matters and so little concerned with substantive issues that I simply can't face sitting through the meetings anymore." This wasn't to say, I added, "that I no longer value the work of NLGTF. It *is* to say that my own association with it feels increasingly lifeless, perfunctory." It was, I wrote Betty, time for me to resign.

Perhaps, at bottom, my perfectionist temperament gave a certain inevitability to that resignation. I had a lifelong malcontent's way of overemphasizing what was wrong, and losing sight of or under-valuing what was right. Perhaps that's what "burnout" comes down to: that not all expectations have been met; not all old wounds magi-cally healed; not all hopes—such as complete transformation of the world—realized; not all secondary gains—like finding a bevy of intimate new friends or one mate—secured.

For a few months I tried to fill the void by sitting in on meetings of the tiny Committee of Lesbian and Gay Male Socialists, but its protracted and fractious doctrinal debates very quickly grated on my activist nerves. I considered myself a socialist in the sense that I believed that the amount of suffering in the world could and must be reduced, that neither "human nature," as conservatives claimed, nor the "mysterious intentions of the Deity" mandated its continu-ance. I was a socialist of ends, not means: priority had to be given to the needs of the *least* fortunate; how we established that priority was unclear, though I didn't view state monopoly of the means of production and distribution as *necessary* preconditions to a classless—or at least more just—society.

As my politics waffled uncertainly and remained unaffiliated, the jaws of Reaganism—and AIDS—were closing down hard and fast.

—from *Midlife Queer* (1996)

AIDS

Digging on my terrace one day, happily debating whether impatiens or dahlias would look better in the planters, I was interrupted by a phone call from a friend. Had I heard the strange news? The Centers for Disease Control and Prevention had announced that a handful of young, previously healthy gay men in Los Angeles had been diagnosed with an unusual form of pneumonia called pneumocystis.

No, I hadn't heard. But soon other reports came filtering in. An equally rare form of cancer, Kaposi's sarcoma—which usually attacked only older men of Mediterranean ancestry—was being seen among homosexual men in their twenties and thirties in several large cities.

By the end of 1981, the reports were no longer a handful, and it had become abundantly clear that a devastating new illness was upon us. The *New York Times* didn't think the news worthy of a feature article—though it put a story about the outbreak of a viral illness among the much-beloved Lippizaner horses on the front page.

But pastor Jerry Falwell immediately saw the significance of what came to be called AIDS—and its usefulness in whipping up antigay hysteria. He heralded the new disease as "the judgment of

God," insisted that gay men deserved no sympathy for a plight their own "sick" lifestyle had brought down on them, publicly rejoiced that the sickness seemed incurable and "hopeless," and warned all good Americans to stay away from these foul creatures, these "disease carriers" called gay men.

DIARY

JANUARY 22, 1985:

The moral bigots are constantly citing "God's will"—i.e., punishment—to explain the AIDS scourge and its concentrated incidence (in this country) among the gay male population,

Is the famine in Ethiopia, then, God's will?

The chemical explosion in Bhopal?

The Holocaust?

If so, God has a penchant for using savage weaponry to heap pain among those already heavily afflicted. If this is the definition of a "just God," it's time to topple divinity and redefine justice. If inclined to assist the moralists in this ethical dilemma of their own making, one might suggest a variant theology—the one ministers cite at the funeral of an angelic five-year-old. To whit, "We cannot know His inscrutable purposes." But to risk a guess—He strikes down the most innocent and promising among us in order to underscore His displeasure with the rest of us. By that variant interpretation, gay people would be elevated from the status of moral lepers to that of the Chosen—doomed saints of physical beauty, supernal gifts, psychic precocity.

FEBRUARY 28:

The *Wall Street Journal* (Feb. 8, 1985) has raised a "bemused" question about the "curious" lack of public debate over possible quarantine measures—thereby helping to provoke such measures. All gay aliens are being detained, not merely deported, on the West Coast. The cry to force gay men to submit to the new blood test mounts.

The vote in Houston is 4–1 *against* a gay civil rights bill. The disease and the citizenry seem to be descending in tandem over the gay population.

APRIL 20:

Bruce [Voeller, founding executive director of the National Gay Task Force; he later died of AIDS] called on his way home from the AIDS conference. He reports continuing horror— and indifference. Says Margaret Heckler [Secretary of Health and Human Services] gave a speech so overtly homophobic that the three hundred (out of two thousand five hundred) openly gay participants caucused and submitted a formal protest. Bruce says no money is being made available for testing new drugs of *possibly* therapeutic value, and the Centers for Disease Control is secretly sending (limited) funds to France in order to support the needed scientific work.

NOVEMBER 10:

Discussing AIDS in my class on Thursday, the students split over the issue of whether to close down gay bars and baths, with some shocking venom expressed about the danger of gay people contaminating the general population. Then Friday [the writer/ psychologist] Helen Singer Kaplan's letter to the *Times* rang a change on that theme: gay people somehow *owed* it to the general population to submit themselves for blood tests—with no awareness shown of the moral hypocrisy inherent in treating gay people like scum for generations and then demanding that they behave like saints, of the victims being told they should sacrifice themselves for the greater peace of mind of their oppressors.

If any doubt remained of the malignity of the heterosexist vision of us, the last few issues [1985] of the *Post* have laid it to rest. Their inflammatory defamation sickened me. One article reported the trouble nurses are having in preventing AIDS patients in the hospitals from having sex. Another excoriated the gay bars for evading taxes. A third gleefully detailed the "sick" sex rituals of the Mine Shaft's [the famed gay male orgy bar] "animal" habitués. The last time the media felt entitled to use the term "animal" was in justifying the lynchings of blacks. . . .

AUGUST 11, 1986:

I read of Davey C.'s death from AIDS at 28. . . . He had so many qualities—was so physically beautiful, smart, *and* politically hip. Plus he was a sweet and generous man; soon after I came out of the hospital following my heart attack [in 1979], he came to visit me. We talked a while, he then offered me a blow job— thought I "needed" it. I did, psychologically—some connection with the possibility of getting pleasure out of my body, out of life, again. He sucked me off on the couch, a gesture of generosity, not lust. To my surprise, I came. We were both pleased. What is there left to say about this gruesome, senseless killer AIDS? Except that the wrong people are dying, those who gave themselves incautiously to experience, to life; the risk takers, the inventive ones. The fearful ones who literally sat on their asses still sit.

OCTOBER 14, 1987:

Epidemics always lay bare the rudimentary attitudes of the culture in which the epidemic occurs. The government and the public alike used the syphilis scourge of the early twentieth century as an opportunity to reassert traditional values—just as with AIDS today. And in the United States no value is more traditional than being uptight about sex. As one moralist put it in regard to syphilis, "perfect inhibition is the only guarantor of perfect health and perfect morality." Just so today. The emphasis is being put on returning to monogamy, not succoring people attacked with a virus; on altering behavior and further stigmatizing the already marginalized rather than ameliorating their suffering. . . .

Since the AIDS crisis began, many gay men have drawn back from their previous erotic pattern of multiple sexual partners, but the more radical among them insist that they've done so from necessity, not because they now view sexual variety as "immature" or as inimical to a satisfying life; in other words, they've put a hold on the sexual revolution, neither rejecting it nor their own past histories as having been morally (or even medically) misguided. Radical gay men (and in recent years, some lesbians) continue to affirm, even in the face of AIDS, the rightness of a sexual revolution that insists human nature is not monogamous, that a variety of sexual experiences are essential to self-exploration, and that these experiences do not compromise and may even reinforce the emotional fidelity of a primary relationship. . . .

In its February 13, 1989, issue, the *Nation* published [gay activist and writer] Darrell Yates Rist's article "The AIDS Obsession" and invited various people, myself included, to respond to it. In his piece Rist denounced the gay community's single-minded focus in recent years on fighting the AIDS scourge, characterizing it as "fashionable hysteria" and theorizing that our "keening" reflected a "compulsive . . . need to partake in the drama of catastrophe."

But the catastrophe, I wrote in response, was real "and the legions of the young in ACT-UP who have stationed themselves on the front lines deserve something better than being characterized [as Rist had] as 'clones' and 'chic street protesters.' " If the straight world, I argued, had shown more than a modicum of concern and involvement, gay people would never have had to rely so entirely on their own resources—which they've marshaled with heroic determination.

Rist had further denounced the ACT-UP demonstrators as "immoral because they are panic-mongering." To me that was a shocking mischaracterization of young men fighting for their lives, especially since Rist never paused to denounce a federal government whose indifference made such a fight mandatory. That was blaming the victim—and excusing the oppressor—with a vengeance. "The paradox," I wrote, "is that as a result of the successful mobilization of our own people in the fight against AIDS, so many have for the first time discovered their anger at heterosexist oppression that we may emerge from this crisis with the needed legions—at last— militantly to insist on an end to our persecution."

*   *   *

By 1990, gay activism surrounding AIDS had galvanized the community, heightened visibility, and produced some measurable political progress that would have been unimaginable a decade earlier. As late as 1986, President Reagan had refused even to utter the word AIDS, let alone allotted any resources to combat it, and his attorney general, Edwin Meese, had sanctioned firing anyone who co-workers merely *perceived* as having AIDS and causing them to fear contamination. That same year, William F. Buckley published a piece advocating that gay men with AIDS be tattooed on the rear end (and drug users on the arm). Three months after that pitiless prescription, the Supreme Court, in its notorious decision *Bowers v. Hardwick*, ruled that the state could legally arrest gay adults having sex in the privacy of their own homes.

By early 1990, more than fifty thousand people had died of AIDS, with double that number known to be affected with the virus. No successful treatment had yet emerged, but what had changed was the earlier attitude of pardon-me-for-existing. It had given way to a fierce assertion, led by vanguard activists and then by ACT-UP, of the right to be alive, and stay alive. ACT-UP not only demanded that the federal government release significant sums for research but also that full access to experimental drugs and treatments be open to everyone; with a new disease, they militantly argued, the afflicted were entitled to take their chances rather than simply wait around while new drugs wended their slow way through the pipelines of traditional research.

Some of the activists were privileged white men who'd grown up in the more permissive post-Stonewall climate and felt entitled not only to their sexuality but to all else. Passivity and helplessness weren't part of their makeup or vocabulary. Instead of collapsing, they became angry and resistant when confronted by obstacles. They formed buyers clubs to import promising drugs from abroad, they marched at home against drug companies that kept their prices high, and they pressured the Food and Drug Administration to release AZT before completing the usual three-phase efficacy trials (until 1991, it remained the only FDA-approved treatment—and a poor one—for AIDS).

As early as 1988, thousands of ACT-UP demonstrators from across the country gathered at FDA headquarters in Rockville, Maryland, where their representatives met with agency officials and, remarkably, succeeded in getting the FDA's drug approval process foreshortened. ACT-UP had confronted the federal government's indifference head-on and, through persistent protest had made notable dents in its defensive armor. The ACT-UP confrontations also produced considerable media coverage, and the images many Americans saw on television or in their newspapers contradicted the long-standing stereotypes of frightened sissies and their roughneck sisters. By 1990, there were fifty openly gay elected officials around the country (compared with half a dozen in 1980), and the Human Rights Campaign Fund, a gay lobbying group, ranked twenty-fifth on the list of the country's most powerful fund-raisers. In 1987, only 33 percent of adults believed that homosexual relations between consenting adults should be legal. By 1989, a Gallup poll revealed that the figure had jumped to 47 percent.

There were several downsides to this seeming success story. Many gay people, especially minorities, lacked health insurance to pay for the emergent drug therapies, and lacked, too, a place at the table with government officials that ACT-UP's all-white, all-male Treatment and Data Committee had gradually won. The members of that committee, having increasingly mastered the arcana of current viral science, had become insiders, and were sharply accused by other members of the gay community with advocating primarily for people like themselves; antagonism and fractiousness became so intense by 1992 that the Data Committee broke away entirely from ACT-UP and set up as the Treatment Action Group (TAG). In the meantime, the death toll from AIDS continued its relentless rise, even as one briefly touted medication after another—AL-721, dextran sulfate, Compound Q, DDI, AZT—failed to live up to its initial promise.

On other fronts as well, matters had pretty much stalemated. Draconian sodomy laws still remained on the books in twenty-four states, and the legislatures of only two states—Wisconsin and Massachusetts—had passed laws barring discrimination against gay

people (and only seven U.S. cities had as yet put "domestic partnership," which granted gay people some of the same rights as married
couples, on the books). At the same time, violence against gays and
lesbians had become an increasingly popular after-hours sport: in
1990, gay people were seven times more likely to become victims
of violent assault than other Americans. It was only with the brutal
murder of Matthew Shepard in 1998 that the American Psychoanalytic Association would hold its very first forum on homophobia
(there had been countless ones through the years on the "causes"
and "cures" of homosexuality).

DIARY

JANUARY 9, 1990:

Put in my usual Tuesday from two to six answering the
phones at PWA (People with AIDS Coalition). Dennis was
back after a bout with meningitis, back with full-throated
campy hilarity, insisting he's just waiting for his welfare check
before retiring to Atlanta—"the only place you can get a good
haircut." What great spirit they all have. . . . It was the same
when I visited John in the hospital on Saturday. There he is
with lymphoma and an untreated "blood clot on the brain"—
smiling and planning away. Vito [Russo], too, is a bundle of
positive energy, talking about "feeling a little better every day."
Is this merely denial? I don't think so.

MARCH 30:

At the end of the "Whose History?" panel last night at the
New York Historical Society (NYHS), a young man with a
large ACT-UP button on his lapel came up to me and said he
wanted me to know how I ended up (belatedly) on the panel:
"When I got the NYHS mailing," he said, "and saw that gay/
lesbian history had been omitted, I wrote in protest to the director of public programs." She wrote back that NYHS simply
couldn't afford another fee (a big $250). To which he responded,
"That simply isn't good enough. *One way or the other we* will *be*

represented at that event." The director got the message—and out went the call to me.

[As I later learned, the "young man" was in fact forty-five and his name was Bob Rafsky. He'd been a public relations executive until 1989, when he quit to devote his time entirely to ACT-UP, becoming its media coordinator in New York. Three years after the NYHS event, Rafsky died of AIDS.]

JULY 24:

At PWA today we stuffed envelopes with a grim letter describing the organization's desperate financial situation. . . . Meantime, the gloom thickens on other counts, too: Vito is in the hospital getting chemo; John felt so bad he had to leave PWA today and go home to bed; and Ken [Dawson], who was here for dinner last night, looked drawn and ill, and spoke in a low, energy-less voice light-years from his vibrant self— though he bravely stayed the full evening.

NOVEMBER 7:

Vito died this morning. With no hope of recovery, and with assorted medical interventions of the last two weeks doing little more than heightening his suffering, I suppose it's a blessing. . . . Getting to know him better than ever before over these past four months [I was part of his "team"], I came to admire his resilient will, the resolutely positive way he faced every crisis. Yesterday, when I entered his hospital room, he was shivering under a pile of blankets, yet insisting to the doctor that he felt decidedly improved. . . .

DECEMBER 21:

Vito's memorial yesterday upset me more than I anticipated. Some of it was the poignancy of the large turnout, the hugging and kissing, the sense of a genuine community, the unexpected reunions. Some of it was Vito's own omnipresence on film clips and posters—the vitality of his image in such sad contrast to the purpose of the day. Some of it was the bravery of so many: Ken [Dawson], Damien Martin, etc.—themselves weakened and endangered, in attending what must have felt, devastatingly, like a rehearsal for their own services.

OCTOBER 10, 1991:

We celebrated Ken's 45th birthday last night in his hospital room. Jed [Mattes, the literary agent] brought a cake, Eli and I party favors, and seven to eight people lifted their seltzer water. As Ken was about to blow out the candles, Jed said, "We're all wishing just what you are." We threw Silly Putty on the walls and ceilings, laughed at the hospital food, admired the pink amaryllis, and had something that actually approximated a good time. Ken's spirits *are* good. He reports that all of his tests have improved and that he hopes to be home by next week. What does he allow himself to know—that is, consistently? Does he hold out real hope of recovery? If terrors *are* gnawing at his innards, his smiling face belies it. This is more than WASP training, more even than a saintly disposition. . . . He had a tough battle with depression, but now jokes about naming each of his remaining dozen T-cells "after a strong woman friend." And the homophobes dare tell us we have a "character disorder"! . . . Ken started to tell us about the visit of a Boston friend who's raising a child, and couldn't hold back the tears—strangulated words about being glad that life goes on. . . . He's lost control over his sphincter. Plus a lung has collapsed. Yet on he struggles. . . .

NOVEMBER 13:

Ken's suffering goes on unabated . . . [He's] back in the hospital, lung again collapsed. They were due to operate this morning at 7:00 A.M., but now (2:00 P.M.) he still hasn't gone up—no explanation offered. The routine brutality of our medical system is appalling; and Ken is a middle-class white man!

NOVEMBER 14:

Ken is in agony. They had to take out more of his lung than hoped; apparently the pneumonia has severely damaged it. He just lies there, lips parched, each cough a knife through his body. . . . A little tea and a partial massage was all I could offer; makes me feel inadequate, awkward; such a dear man, so little anyone can do. . . .

MARCH 17, 1992:

Ken is drifting further away. At the hospital yesterday we ran into his doctor and got a full report. PML [progressive multifocal leukoencephalopathy] has been definitely diagnosed in the brain, which accounts for the in-and-out-again lucidity. Even when lucid, he now responds tersely. . . . He's showing remarkable tenacity in staying alive. . . . [Ken died on April 10].

JUNE 5:

Ken's memorial service yesterday had a powerful effect on me. . . . Several speakers found just the right loving words and phrases "decent, dignified, cautious, gentle, lonely" that encapsulate the man. John D'Emilio was especially effective, though everyone did well. What Ken stood for in the movement, beyond anyone else, was the insistence that we stop trashing each other and look for the *good* within our fellow activists. That is what "decent" means, and Ken was supremely decent—despite what Torie [Osborn] smartly called "the curmudgeon within."

The effect of AIDS on public opinion had by then become a double-edged sword: heightened fear of dreaded gay "carriers" counterbalanced by increased sympathy for their suffering. President Clinton's new administration in 1992 exemplified the contradiction: when his initial impulse to lift the ban on gays and lesbians serving openly in the military met with a barrage of opposition, he scurried for cover, settling with relief on a "compromise" solution of "Don't Ask, Don't Tell" that all at once fully exploited the military service of gay people while pretending they didn't exist as human beings.

At the core of homophobia, it has always seemed to me, lies the central fear of "differentness." Why the full, splendid spectrum of humanity should inspire terror in some people rather than joyful wonder is a puzzler. What can be learned from a neighbor whose expressions, habits, and values are a duplicate of one's own? "Nothing!" exults the crowd, "and that's exactly the way we like it. It was hard enough learning the dominant social codes; having finally mastered them, and feeling accepted and comfortable, let us alone!"

Yet the softening of homophobia was real. In a culture with a profoundly contradictory heritage of conformity and permissiveness, the way forward would necessarily be gradual (though only if the demands were for full and instant change; you ask for the whole pie in order to get a portion of it) and would periodically be marked by retreats—yet the fact would remain that nowhere else in the world was there a comparably vibrant and effective gay rights movement. In the 1970s, when the first gay civil rights measures were submitted to public referendum, only 29 percent of the voters reacted favorably; by the early nineties, the percentage had risen to 39 percent—and would continue to climb.

In 1993, a *Newsweek* article wrote us up as "the new power brokers" (a weird exaggeration) and the cover of an issue of *New York* magazine read "The Bold, Brave New World of Gay Women." Yet the early nineties also saw a 30 percent increase in assaults and hate crimes against gay people. The dragon of homophobia had hardly been slain. The slow increase in respect and acceptance amounted to no more than a fragile inclusion, and the inclusion was pretty much confined to those gay people who looked and behaved like "normal" folks—meaning primarily middle-class white men who put their faith in polite lobbying, eschewed confrontational tactics, and shied away (as the seventies gay movement had not) from left-wing issues relating to racism, sexism, and economic inequality. The April 25,1993, March on Washington, which I took part in, exemplified the turn away from "extremist" ACT-UP zaps; to me it seemed a bland, juiceless event more parade than protest—especially when contrasted with the earlier marches in 1979 and 1987.

By 1996, there were more than a million AIDS cases worldwide, 70 percent of them in Africa, and with still no effective treatment in sight (at the end of 1995, the FDA released yet another new drug, 3TC, which proved as useless as the preceding ones). At the same time, "compassion fatigue" had set in: donations to AIDS organizations began to decline steadily, paralleled by the sinking sense that the disease would never be brought under control.

And then, seemingly out of nowhere, the FDA also released saquinavir, the first of a whole new category of drugs known as protease inhibitors. Two others rapidly followed: ritonavir and indinavir. It quickly became apparent that—as FDA Commissioner David Aaron Kessler put it, "we now have some big guns in AIDS treatment." The year 1996 would prove a milestone in the long struggle against AIDS. A milestone—not a miracle. Almost immediately, reports came in of how the new drugs were reducing the amount of HIV in infected individuals, sometimes to the "undetectable" level, even as CD4 cell counts—essential to a healthy immune system—were correspondingly rising.

But what also became quickly apparent was that the new drugs did not work at all for some people, and worked only briefly for others. Besides, the exorbitant cost of the drugs (up to $15,000 for a year's supply) put them out of reach for most people suffering from AIDS. In the United States, drug-assistance programs existed in about half the states—but didn't initially cover protease inhibitors. Additionally, most of the leadership in the hard-hit Latino and black communities had learned to distrust "innovative" white medicine (in part thanks to the notorious Tuskegee Experiment, which had used black sharecroppers as human guinea pigs).

Many black church leaders, moreover, had long stigmatized AIDS as "a gay thing" and therefore—talk about massive denial—not a black (or Latino) issue. AIDS was not to be discussed from the pulpit, nor information about its treatment made available in the lobby. But it soon became undeniably clear that HIV had increasingly become a disease of color; AIDS decimated the African continent and in this country cut a horrifying swath through black and Latino communities. By 2007, African Americans, just 13 percent of the U.S. population, accounted for more than 50 percent of new HIV diagnoses, and those in black leadership positions finally proved willing to engage with the issue.

In the interim, President Clinton, having (unlike his predecessors) directly addressed the AIDS crisis and increased funding for research and services early on in his administration, then showed little sustained interest or resolve. Despite the findings of the National Institutes of Health, for example, that needle-exchange programs unquestionably lowered the incidence of AIDS, and despite the support of his own senior health officials (including Secretary Donna E. Shalala) for such programs, Clinton refused federal funding for them. Instead, he signed the 1996 Defense of Marriage Act, which denied same-sex couples the right to have their unions legalized—thereby serving notice that recent progress in the acceptance of gay people (itself pretty much confined to the most assimilable segment of the gay population) shouldn't be equated with any inevitable march toward first-class citizenship—or even second-class for the truly, proudly different (which is to say, in mainstream lingo, the freaks).

Most gay teenagers didn't need to be reminded that they weren't considered quality goods, but by the midnineties many in the gay world, and particularly in the more tolerant urban areas, did choose to believe that equality was around the corner, bound to happen, that a little more tidying up around the edges—perhaps best done by pushing the freaks as far offstage as possible—and the struggle would be over.

Paralleling the rise of optimism about the goal of converting AIDS to a "manageable disease" was a surge of conviction that as a people we were now unstoppable. Some prominent gay leaders and organizations, and in particular Elizabeth Birch and the influential (largest and wealthiest) Human Rights Campaign, were entirely in accord with the goal of assimilation and with fostering an image of gay people that would accelerate that process. That meant replicating themselves, featuring one segment only of a diverse gay community: mostly white, educated, well-spoken folks who dressed for success and held mainstream values.

Those gay people with left-wing politics saw assimilationism as defeat and deceit—a misrepresentation of the many different communities that constituted the gay world and a denial of the subversive potential of our distinctive values and perspectives. The lefties didn't want to serve openly in the military; they wanted to destroy the war machine. They didn't want to settle down into traditional marital relationships, nor give them privileged status; they wanted to challenge sexual monogamy, gender stereotyping, and traditional patterns of child rearing.

But left-wing gays had shrunk by the midnineties, in contrast to the early seventies, to a small, nearly silent voice in the community as a whole. The majority of gay people chose to see themselves as "just folks"; their highest aspiration was to join the mainstream, not to challenge its orthodoxies.

Many ACT-UP chapters had ceased to operate by the late 1990s and others had refocused their efforts on the global issue of getting affordable versions of the new drugs to poor countries. By this point the gay movement as a whole had drifted decidedly to the right, with the issues of gay marriage and gays in the military leapfrogging to the top of the agendas of the most powerful movement organizations (and especially the Human Rights Campaign). As early as 1994, during the celebrations of Stonewall's twenty-fifth anniversary, one of the top fund-raising events—to the disgust of everyone one inch left of center—was held on the deck of the aircraft carrier *Intrepid*; for weeks before, ads for credit cards with rainbow flags appeared in the gay male press. That press, incidentally, was itself becoming unrecognizably different from the politically aware publications (*New York Native*, *QW*, etc.) that had once held sway. By the late nineties, the popular favorites were *Genre* (specializing in poolside swimwear) and *OUT*, which as late as 2008 boasted a five-man fashion department, but not a single literary, theater, or politics editor.

—from *Midlife Queer* (1996) and *Waiting to Land* (2009)

POLITICS AND
ACTIVISM

Racism in the Gay Male World*

In the dozen years since Stonewall, most of the radical goals set by the early gay liberation movement have been diluted or discarded. As our movement has grown in numbers, its initial values have atrophied. Originally, the gay movement strove to speak and act boldly against entrenched privilege based on gender, racial, ethnic, and class discrimination. That commitment has been largely displaced by "liberal" goals and strategies that emphasize the need to work within the established system to secure social tolerance and legal redress.

Worthy goals, to be sure. And ones which we have made some notable progress in advancing in recent years. We've gained greater visibility and protection. We're more "tolerable" to the general public. But at no small cost: the cost of making ourselves over in order better to conform to an acceptable public image, the cost of bending

---

*In its original form, this was a presentation speech awarding a "certificate of merit" to the gay organization Black and White Men Together (since changed to Men of All Colors Together) at the seventh annual Lambda Legal Defense Fund dinner in October 1982. As if in confirmation of my remarks, a number of gay white men angrily walked out in the middle of the speech and others later expressed strong disapproval of what they called my "inappropriate and offensive" comments.

our energies toward adjusting to mainstream mores, to becoming Good Americans. The inevitable concomitant has been to downplay differences we once proudly affirmed, to discard radical social analysis, soft-pedal our distinctiveness, discourage and deny the very diversity of behavior and lifestyle our conformist society stands most in need of.

This quest for respectability first publicly showed itself in 1982 when we filled the Grand Ballroom of the Waldorf-Astoria—1,000 strong and paying $150 a plate—to celebrate the first annual Human Rights Campaign dinner. Resplendent in our finery, we gave Walter Mondale, chief speaker of the evening, a standing ovation— roared our enthusiasm for what in fact was a standard (and tedious) anti-Reagan stump speech that never once directly addressed the reason for the occasion: the cause of gay rights. Nor was any resentment apparent when Mondale, the instant he finished his speech, quickly left the platform—missing the subsequent presentations and resolutely refusing any comment to the crowd of reporters that awaited him at the Waldorf's exit.

It's no coincidence that the dinner crowd, which so lustily cheered Mondale's shameful performance, was composed almost entirely of dinner-jacketed white males (along with a handful of women, and almost no blacks or Hispanics). Surely the nature of Mondale's audience goes far toward accounting for their grateful, even enthusiastic, response to him. A leading member of the ruling patriarchy had—at last!—graced a gay white male event with his actual presence, given it at least token legitimacy. What matter how minimal the gesture; the symbol was what counted. With Mondale appearing at an openly gay affair, surely the time was not distant when the ruling elite would grant full admission to the inner sanctum of white male privilege.

We can take some hope in the fact that at least some gay men have banded together to form an organization, Black and White Men Together, devoted to confronting rather than evading the endemic racism in our community. The ultimate impact the organization will have is unforeseeable. But what can and should be said is that it has already punctured the reigning complacency, insisting we face up to serious problems dividing and disfiguring our community, encouraging us to reclaim our radical roots, to rechart our course.

The gay movement's evolution from radicalism to reform is typical, alas, of how protest movements in this country have always (and, usually, quickly) shifted their priorities. Originating in fierce anger and initially marked by broad-gauged demands for social change, they rapidly evolve into well-behaved, self-protective associations, and in the process abandon demands for challenging the vast inequities in our social and economic systems, substituting (at best) token liberalism.

No movement born to protest inequality can hope to accomplish contradictory purposes. In its current guise, the gay movement may well succeed in gaining broader access to the preexisting clubhouses of power, but it can't pretend that it's centrally devoted to a struggle for improving the lot of the many. The gay movement can't opt for putting its primary energy toward winning mainstream America's approval and simultaneously pretend not to have jettisoned its earlier determination to address the plight of *all* gay people: the invisibility of lesbians, the discrimination against nonwhites and gender nonconformists, the scornful disregard of the rural poor.

Of the national gay organizations, none focuses its current efforts on behalf of those nonaffluent, nonprivileged gays who constitute our actual majority, who everywhere dot the land, doing its dirty work, unacknowledged and unorganized, self-esteem disfigured, future hopes dim. Who among the leaders of our burgeoning gay officialdom speaks to those needs, acknowledges their existence? When has *one* of the proliferating weeklong strategy conferences that our national organizations proudly sponsor included such concerns prominently in its agenda or issued in its imposing statements of purpose any awareness of the terrible daily burdens that weigh down the lives of so many of our people? Having at one period attended many such gatherings, I bear my share of responsibility for this callousness, now endemic.

As the black-tie dinner at the Waldorf demonstrated, the gay movement has finally managed to secure the allegiance of—by surrendering control over its priorities to—prosperous white male recruits who'd previously disdained association with a movement they regarded as controlled by "impractical, noisome visionaries." The more those who earlier eschewed the gay movement have now joined it, the more their bland deportment and narrow social perspectives have come to dominate: they have "upgraded" our image while diluting demands for substantive social change, shifting organizational policies into comfortable conformity with their own reformist goals.

The gay movement, radical at its inception, has lost courage. Its national organizations are currently dominated by skilled lobbyists pressing for narrow assimilationist goals through traditional political channels. Its chief priority is to win acceptance for the most conformist, most conservative, mostly privileged, mostly male few.

It is a perilous path. The drive to establish our credentials as mainstream Americans is inextricably yoked to deemphasizing our "differentness"—and that, in turn, is tantamount to falsifying our unique historical experience and the subculture it has generated. The result is not only to rob gay people of their heritage but also to negate the potential contribution our "off-center" lifestyle(s) held out for challenging reigning assumptions—for contributing our special perspectives on the nature of partnership, family, gender, and friendship.

The "official"—organized, national—gay movement's current emphasis on winning short-term gains for the few *has* produced its notable successes and *has* increased "tolerance." But it may have done so at the expense of producing any substantive long-range impact on the nation's institutionalized inequalities. The more we press for limited gains, the more we twist our identity to conform with mainstream values, the more we jeopardize our chance to offer new perspectives to a nation desperately in need of them.

—from the *New York Native*, June 20 and July 3, 1983

Postscript

The birth of ACT-UP in the mid eighties went a long way toward restoring *some* hope that the gay movement might return to its roots. Indeed, when I dedicated a plaque at an outdoor ceremony in June 1989, renaming a portion of Christopher Street as "Stonewall Place," I devoted most of my speech to hailing ACT-UP as "a potential reincarnation of the radical, broad-gauged Gay Liberation Front of the early seventies: what we are seeing are gay men and lesbians acting in concert, welcoming and appreciating each other's differences, and also welcoming other minority people."

Since the midnineties, however, that radical spirit has mostly dissipated and liberal goals (gays in the military, gay marriage, etc.) have once again come to dominate the movement. I'm far from alone in regretting this. In 2007 some twenty queer activists hammered out in a two-day conference a document ("Beyond Same-Sex Marriage") that was subsequently signed by hundreds and hundreds of movement people, myself included. The statement offered a clear, eloquent, densely argued challenge to current strategies for "marriage equality" being pursued by the major LGBT organizations. It aimed at honoring the diverse ways people actually "practice love, form relationships, create . . . networks of caring and support, establish households, bring families into being, and build innovative structures to support and sustain community."

"Beyond Same-Sex Marriage" reminded us that the majority of people in the United States do not live in traditional nuclear families. Rather, diverse households are already the norm and range from kinship networks and extended families to senior citizens living together to single-parent households. Marriage and the nuclear family, the statement argued, "are not the only worthy forms of family or relationship and should not be legally and economically privileged above all others." The call is for a new vision of human relatedness and a civic commitment to recognizing and securing the wide diversity of household arrangements that actually characterize the country's domestic topology. Lifetime monogamous pair-bonding (whether "legally" sanctioned or not) isn't the only path to human happiness and may not even be among the best: 50 percent of marriages now end in divorce and the figure would probably go higher if more women with limited education and job histories could figure out how to independently support themselves and their children.

On the specific topic of racism in the gay male world, a seven-minute video entitled "The (White) Gay Rights Movement" began making the rounds on blogs and social networking sites in 2012. In response, one black gay man wrote that in his ten years of experience in the movement, he found "that the LGBT community and movement . . . is almost as unwilling as the GOP to deal openly and honestly with race . . . and the inclusion of people of color."

Cuba

To write this piece, I began by taking Samuel Flagg Bemis's *A Diplomatic History of the United States* down from my bookshelves. It was the text we'd used when I was an undergraduate at Yale in the early 1950s for a course on American foreign policy taught by Bemis himself—then widely regarded as the "dean" of American diplomatic historians. I turned to the sections in the book on Cuba and was startled at their jingoistic content and embarrassed to see that I hadn't scribbled a single note of protest in the margins. At the time, obviously, Bemis's views in no way offended my understanding of the world and of our country's role within it. Yet among his statements are the claims that our "trusteeship of Cuban independence . . . has stood as a notable example to the powers"; that we intervened in Cuban affairs and set up provisional governments "with great reluctance"; that the Cuban people, "who had not submitted to two hundred thousand Spanish troops in 1898, made no resistance to a handful of soldiers in the second American intervention because they had confidence in its righteousness"; and that our special relationship with Cuba had allowed its people to enjoy "a rousing economic prosperity."

Bemis's views seem shocking today but at the time were representative of his generation of diplomatic historians—which should give us all pause about the "objectivity" of scholarship. Starting in the 1960s, the revisionist work of historians like Gabriel and Joyce Kolko, Lloyd Gardner, Ronald Steel, William Appleman Williams, and Walter Lafeber shook that consensus view of the fifties to its roots. Students have also grown more skeptical about their professors' opinions, and citizens of their government's professed benevolence.

Yet perhaps not skeptical enough. The dimensions of our historic imperialism are still not widely enough known or, if known, not widely credited. As regards our relations with Latin America in general, the long-standing ignorance of the public as a whole— a compound of disinterest and disbelief—still holds. As regards Cuba in particular, our lazy susceptibility to the limited materials fed us through government channels, the media, and those few historical works that reach a wide readership—for example, Arthur Schlesinger Jr.'s *A Thousand Days*—are suffused with unacknowledged value judgments that sustain the image of the United States as a kindly parent and of Cuba as a mere Soviet satellite.

Yet as revisionist scholarship has made clear, the 1961 invasion at Playa Giron has a long, dishonorable ancestry; it was but the latest in many direct interventions on our part in the internal affairs of other countries, itself illustrative of our continuing sense that we have a divine right to determine other peoples' futures. As regards Cuba itself, if we dig into the history of our relations with that country at almost any point, we unearth an appalling stench. The malodorous high point in the pre–Civil War period was probably the famed Ostend Manifesto of 1854.

In their eagerness to secure Cuba from Spain, President Franklin Pierce and his advisers arranged a conference of the American ministers to London, Paris, and Madrid. The three worthies duly conferred, and issued to the world a "memorandum" bluntly declaring that if Spain refused to sell the island of Cuba to the United States, "then by every law human and divine, we shall be justified in wresting it from Spain, if we possess the power." Most of the world read those laws differently. Indignation was so widespread (an indignation shared, it should be said, by many Americans— "Manifesto of the Brigands" was the *New York Tribune*'s title for the memorandum) that President Pierce backed down and American rapacity was thwarted for some forty years.

But at the end of the nineteenth century, as Cuba's great poet and revolutionary José Martí feared, independence from Spain was no sooner achieved than it rapidly gave way to almost total dependence on the United States. In 1901 our government forced the Platt Amendment into the Cuban constitution, affirming Cuba's obligation to sell or lease lands to us for coaling or naval stations and our right to intervene "for the protection of life, property, and individual liberty." That right has since been exercised many times and under many guises, from landing the marines in 1906, 1912, and 1917, to FDR's more "liberal" approach of simply sending warships into Cuban waters to register our displeasure with (and thereby bring down) a government of which we disapproved.

Business, as usual, followed the flag. American corporations moved into Cuba soon after the 1898 war with Spain, and the investment from such giant firms as the United Fruit Company and the First National City Bank of New York rose from $50 million in 1895 to $1 billion in 1959, the year Fidel Castro came to power. By then, it's no exaggeration to say, American interests had long since come to dominate all strategic sectors of the Cuban economy, turning the island into a giant plantation and the vast majority of its citizens into servants of American corporate enterprise. That Castro would change all this was immediately apparent to the American power structure. In a confidential memorandum written in April 1959 for distribution to the CIA, the State Department, and the White House, Richard Nixon suggested that a force of Cuban exiles be armed to overthrow the Castro regime. President Eisenhower adopted this suggestion in 1960, and President Kennedy implemented it in 1961 at Playa Giron. Of Kennedy's advisers, only Senator William Fulbright openly opposed the invasion.

The landing at the Bay of Pigs, in short, was not an aberration, an inexplicable deviation from our traditionally benign stance toward Cuba. Instead it was of a familiar piece with our long-settled view that we have the right to intervene—and by force—in the internal affairs of other countries whenever our "interests" appear to be threatened. And *we* define the nature of those interests and the reality of the threat. Sadly, it's questionable whether the fiasco at the Bay of Pigs has taught us anything—other than the need to be more circumspect in our tactics and more determined upon our goals.

The literature currently (1974)* available in English on the Cuban Revolution contains huge discordancies: vilified in some books, Castro is elevated to sainthood in others. What has most surprised me, though, has been the range of views expressed among my *own* friends, good leftists all. They deplore the historic role the United States has played in Cuban affairs and regard the Bay of Pigs invasion as wholly disgraceful. But some disagree with the common tendency to place exclusive stress on economics as a sufficient explanation for our country's role; and others question the totalitarian aspects of Castro's revolution as it's developed over time.

My own views have wobbled considerably and I can't pretend to have fully unraveled them, even to my own satisfaction. What I am certain of is that in the first decade or so of the revolution it was a gross oversimplification for our leaders to assume that "anticommunism" sufficiently justified their decisions to cut off diplomatic contact and impose an embargo. The Johnsons and the Nixons have unquestionably been sympathetic to the view that what's good for American business is good for the world—and their policies have reflected that sympathy. But saying that does not *summarize* their ideology, nor unravel its complex strands.

Our leaders, like most of us, are capable of sustaining varied loyalties: in their case, to "free enterprise," American profits, God, "individualism," and parliamentary democracy. That these loyalties have almost always been mutually reinforcing does not justify the assumption that they are interchangeable. To recognize, moreover,

---

*For an updated bibliography and a fine reassessment, see Samuel Farber, *Cuba Since the Revolution of 1959* (Haymarket Books, 2011).

that Johnson, Kennedy, Nixon, et al., have certain *non*material commitments is not to soften the indictment against them but to clarify it. Marxists tend to see ideas (except those of Marx) as having no authentic or independent life apart from the "material relationships" that brought them into being and for whose protection they are publicly employed. Not only does this undervalue the powerful role that a "mere" idea (such as "manifest destiny"—or Freud's concept of the unconscious) can play in human affairs, but it minimizes as well the ability of individuals to act other than along predictable socioeconomic lines. That Castro and most of the other guerrilla leaders in the Sierra Maestra came from the middle class should alone give pause to the dialecticians among us.

It's still difficult to grasp whether the island's brand of socialism is peculiarly Cuban (its Marxism derivative, superficial, original, confused, or cynical) and whether the pivotal role of the Castro brothers in making policy is a substitute for or a necessary transition to popular control. Some of the revolution's central contradictions seem to have intensified with time, as has the definition of acceptable individual deviation: the publication of the avant-garde *Lunes* has been suspended; the poet Heberto Padilla made to confess publicly his literary/political sins; homosexuals rounded up and put in isolated prison camps (a repression that has now given way to subtler but still real forms of ostracism). As Miguel Angel Quevado, the editor of *Bohemia*, wrote as far back as 1960, "To carry out a profound social revolution, it was not necessary to install a system which degrades man to the condition of the state." Angel suspended his journal, sought asylum—and died by his own hand in Caracas in 1969.

A revolution made in the name of the masses, one that has taken large steps in eliminating the vast inequalities that earlier existed between rich and poor, white and black, urban and rural Cubans, has yet to find institutional means for ensuring that the people can have a direct and continuous voice in deciding national policy. I've long been persuaded by Fidel's argument that *before* the revolution, elections and political parties had served only to legitimize and preserve the interests of the privileged. But I'm not persuaded that the exploitative purposes for which these institutions were used under an oligarchy need automatically discredit their potential value under socialism. The fact that some of Castro's policies have never had to stand the test of popular ratification doesn't encourage the belief that present-day Cuba has yet found substitute channels for the expression of dissent.

We know that political parties and elections bring with them the dangers of counterrevolution. We know, too, that a "free press" is often the handmaiden and alter ego of the privileged elite in power. But as Salvador Allende showed in Chile, we also know that parties can serve as authentic alternatives to, rather than mere echoes of, privilege. And as the *New York Times* demonstrated with the Pentagon Papers and the *Washington Post* during the Watergate scandal, we also know that far from being a mockery of justice, a free press can sometimes be its agent.

A devoted friend of the Cuban Revolution has asked me to remember that it must be judged not from where we are, but from where Cuba *was*. It's an injunction bewildering on several counts. No one (on the Left, that is) would want to deny that Cuba initially made impressive headway against the vast disparities that once existed in income, job opportunity, health services, diet, and education. No one would want to claim that the United States, proportionate to its resources, has made comparable strides. It therefore hardly makes sense to patronize a country whose performance thus far has been superior to our own.

Unless, that is, other kinds of costs seem to overbalance the material gains. And unless the material gains themselves seem in danger of becoming the resting place—rather than the starting point—of the revolution. Hugh Thomas has written, "Health and education are only aids to the good life. . . . The multitudes in uniform are surely supposed to be marching to a spot where they can disband."

A growing number of people no longer locate that spot, or even the march to it, along the older utopian continuum of "man free from material want." They search for a new utopia in the area of psychosexual transformation, envisioning a gender revolution in which "male" and "female" have become outmoded differentiations, individual human beings instead combining in their persons the qualities previously thought the preserve of one gender or the other. It's possible to argue that this new vision, when most of the world still goes to bed hungry at night, is a luxury and an illusion, the decadent yearning of a society already sated with possessions—but not with the satisfactions they were supposed to have brought in train.

The point here is that those who see the redefinition of gender and sexuality as the cutting edge of the newest revolution tend also to regard the contours of Castro's "new man" as distressingly old. "Honor" and machismo on the one hand, and statism and authority on the other, combine to suggest an image that may not do justice to the Castro brothers' *ultimate* intentions but does seem descriptive of their current emphases. Perhaps they have no choice. Doubly beset as Cuba is by the ingrained aggressiveness of our country and the ingrained gender stereotyping of its own, the government may think it neither wise nor possible to push the revolution into still further areas of innovation. The danger is that it may not want to. Or that it may be a willing prisoner of the Marxist paradigm that sees changes in material relationships necessarily preceding changes in culture. Or it may be that even if the ultimate goal *is* a sexually liberated, stateless communism, the Castros may find, as have so many visionaries before them, that ultimate goals forever recede as they forever approach.

We do not know. For the vast majority of people in the world, the "older" vision of freedom from material want is still so distantly utopian that perhaps only a citizen of the United States could be provincial enough to doubt its continuing centrality. Or arrogant enough to suggest that a more encompassing vision, the redefinition of gender and sexuality, awaits us, that the redefinition cannot proceed without absolute freedom of inquiry and expression, and that it is in the presumed heartland of counterrevolution, the United States of America, that we are beginning to glimpse its emerging contours.

—from the Introduction to *The Havana Inquiry* (1974)

On the Death of Ronald Reagan

On his death, the mainstream media is sanctifying Ronald Reagan as a man of compassion, grace, and kindness.

Go tell it to the many thousands dead from AIDS because Reagan wouldn't lift a finger to foster research or to combat the mounting epidemic in any way. Mr. Compassion couldn't even say the AIDS word. And he's on public record, when governor of California, as declaring that homosexuality was an affliction and a disorder.

Go tell it to the thousands tortured, mutilated, and dead as a result of his support for the contras in Nicaragua.

Go tell it to the minorities in our own country, and in particular to African Americans, whose civil liberties he did so little to protect, and whose opportunities so little to expand.

You needn't tell it to the world's corporate heads, generals, and dictators. They felt in full Ronald Reagan's beneficence.

Historical truth matters. As a nation we care little for it, much preferring simplistic distortions that sustain our national myths about "freedom," "opportunity," and "democracy." You can't grow into adulthood when you're fed pablum all your life. And that's why we remain a nation of adolescents, with a culture concerned far more with celebrityhood than with suffering.

—from *Waiting to Land* (2009)

Pleasuring the Body:
Reflections on Gay Male Culture

In an essay in the spring of 2002, I elaborated on many of the views on gay life that I'd been developing over the previous decades. I started with a quotation from Herbert Marcuse (in *Eros and Civilization*) nearly fifty years ago, that had long been a kind of mantra for me: because of their "rebellion against the subjugation of sexuality under the order of procreation," homosexuals might one day provide a cutting-edge social critique of vast importance.

Marcuse's prophecy may be coming to pass. Or so some are claiming. There is mounting evidence that a distinctive set of perspectives has emerged among gay people (despite enormous variations in their lifestyle) in regard to how they view gender, sexuality, primary relationships, friendships, and family. One even increasingly hears the claim that gay "differentness" isn't just a defensible variation but a decided advance over mainstream norms, that gay subcultural values could richly inform conventional life, could open up an unexplored range of human possibilities for *everyone*. That is, if the mainstream was listening, which it isn't.

The mainstream's antennae remain tuned to a limited number of frequencies: that heterosexuality is the Natural Way; that (as we move right of center) lifetime monogamous pair-bonding is the likeliest guarantee of human happiness; that the gender binary (everyone is either male or female, and each gender has distinctive characteristics) is rooted in biology. Those queers who look and sound like Normal People (or are at least able to fake it) are being welcomed into the mainstream in mounting numbers. But the armed guards at the gates continue to bar admission to the more transparently queer. The mainstream somehow senses that the more different the outsider, the greater the threat posed to its own lofty sense of superiority. Fraternizing with true exotics can prove dangerously seductive, opening up Normal People to possibilities within themselves that they prefer to keep under lock and key. . . .

In allowing increasing numbers of the clean-cut variety of gay white men into the clubhouse, there's a widespread assumption that at least *these* people are "normal" in their traditionally defined masculine values and behavior. But evidence to the contrary is building. According to one large-scale study, gay men volunteer 61 percent more time to nonprofit organizations than their heterosexual counterparts. Moreover, they consistently score higher than straight men on studies that attempt to measure empathy and altruism. We perceive discrimination against others more readily than other men do, and we're more likely to have friends across lines of color, gender, religion, and politics.

Many gay men, moreover, put a premium on emotional expressiveness and sexual innovation; we've reworked the rules governing erotic exploration, friendship, and coupledom. In the latter regard, for example, the community ideal (even if only approximated in practice) is one of mutuality and egalitarianism—which again sets it apart from stereotypical straight men, some of whom spout egalitarian rhetoric but few of whom carry their fair share of domestic responsibilities.

Whether the relationship, moreover, is between two men or two women, a growing body of scholarly evidence (a convenient summary is in the *New York Times*, June 10, 2008) suggests that same-sex couples significantly diverge in behavior from their heterosexual counterparts—and in ways that "have a great deal to teach everyone else." Same-sex couples are (in the words of the *Times*) "far more egalitarian than heterosexual ones" in sharing responsibility for both housework and finances—unlike heterosexual relationships, where women still do much more of the domestic chores (and live with a lot of anger as a result) and men are more likely to pay the bills. Perhaps in part as a result, gay and lesbian couples "have more relationship satisfaction"—though no less conflict between the partners. Yet when conflict arises, "belligerence and domineering" are less frequent when gay couples fight, the partners make fewer verbal attacks on each other, are better at using humor and affection to defuse confrontation, and show much greater ability at "seeing the other person's point of view."

The larger point is that there really is a gay subculture, a way of looking at life and coping with its joys and sorrows that has much to offer the straight world—if it would bother to listen—and also to offer the multitude of gay people who prefer to claim that we're just like everybody else. We're not, and to insist that we are contributes to the destruction of a special set of values and perspectives that could do much to provide needed shifts in mainstream patterns. Gay people are entitled to all the *rights* straight people enjoy, but aren't carbon copies of straight people.

All of this, to be sure, can be overdrawn. Experimental patterns in sexual behavior and partnership relations date at least from the countercultural 1960s—not to mention the nineteenth-century Oneida community, the Bloomsbury crowd, or the bohemian Greenwich Village of the 1920s. It's also vital to acknowledge notable shifts in attitude among many of today's younger generation of heterosexuals (especially in urban areas): a "what's the big deal" view of same-gender sexuality, and a willingness to ask "what's a 'man,' what's a 'woman,' what constitutes a 'family' or a 'good' relationship?"

Besides, a segment of the gay male community aims at a "harder," not a softer, self-definition of masculinity, wants to outmacho the macho straight male. Though I try my best to follow a "let-a-thousand-flowers-bloom" philosophy, I confess to the view that the gay man striving to outlift his straight counterpart—and to match him in emotional constriction as well—seems to me misguided. The toned and healthy body, yes. But the plaster-cast Hercules, devoid of mere mortal feeling, no. To me that's literally a disfigurement. It's also a denial of the dominant cultural differences, past as well as present, between gay and straight men.

In regard to the past, I follow the views and findings of that currently towering figure in Talmudic studies, Daniel Boyarin of the University of California at Berkeley. His 1997 book, *Unheroic Conduct*, is a work of immense importance, all at once erudite, witty, playful, and boldly speculative. Boyarin's basic thesis—though this summary won't do justice to its supple byways—is that traditional Ashkenazic Jewish culture produced, in opposition to the Roman model of the powerful, aggressive, violent warrior, a cultural ideal of masculinity that valorized gentleness, nurturance, emotional warmth, nonviolence, inwardness, and studiousness. These characteristics were associated with sexual desirability, not sexlessness—in contrast to the somewhat comparably pacific early Christian model of maleness associated with the *de*sexualized St. Francis. This doesn't mean, Boyarin emphasizes, that orthodox Ashkenazic culture was sympathetic to women (who were excluded from power) or to homoeroticism (male sexual attraction seems to have been considered abnormal).

Boyarin's Ashkenazic Jews—men whose avoidance of what we call "rough and tumble" play would, by contemporary standards, be branded as "sissies"—were in their own culture esteemed as ideal representations of maleness. But by the nineteenth century, the now stereotypic figure of the "feminized" Jewish man had become, in the minds of many Jews, a roadblock to assimilation, and a successful effort (joined by Freud and Theodor Herzl, among others) was made to discredit the once privileged model of a gentler, more nurturant masculinity as either the pathological product of the Diaspora or a figment of the anti-Semitic imagination.

Boyarin wants to reclaim that earlier tradition. He believes, and I agree, that restoring the once-revered model of gentle, nurturing masculinity would greatly help to destabilize binary notions of gender, would emancipate men *and* women from roles that currently constrict their human possibilities. "The critical recovery of the past" would, in Boyarin's words, "make for the redemption of the future." The implications of Boyarin's work are breathtaking. By reclaiming a radically different—and socially constructed—model of masculinity, he all at once wreaks havoc with simplistic biological determinism and offers us a previously unsighted path toward social change.

As a champion of the gentle, inward male, Boyarin has to confront the macho muscularity of the gym culture, and does so in a typically nuanced way. Himself an openly gay man, Boyarin has no trouble appreciating, on one level, the beauty of the well-built male body. But Boyarin warns that the emphasis on powerful muscularity reinforces "the dimorphism of the gendered body and to that extent participates in the general cultural standard of masculinity rather than resisting it." In contributing to the notion that only one kind of male body is desirable, the gym stud-bunny is helping to reinforce the valorization of "topness" over receptivity that already dominates our culture, sexual and otherwise.

The macho-looking gay male is also serving another negative function. The gym-built body, imitative of stereotypical maleness, all but announces that "No Sissies Live Here," thereby encouraging gay men (including the stud-bunnies themselves) to bury and deny the gender-discordant traits that made so many of us feel painfully different in childhood, to repudiate, in other words, "woman-identified" aspects of the self.

In a 1999 paper in the journal *Psychiatry*, Richard Isay insists that all of the several hundred gay men he's treated over the past thirty years exhibited gender-discordant traits in childhood. Such traits, it should he pointed out, are not confined to children who later develop a same-gender erotic preference: some thirty-five years ago, Richard Green, in a much-contested book, *The "Sissy Boy Syndrome" and the Development of Homosexuality*, found that roughly a third of the gender-discordant male children he studied became, as adults, heterosexual in orientation.

Leaving aside that segment of the gay male population that wants nothing more than to be seen as hyperstraight, the differences between gay culture on the whole and that of the mainstream are real and consequential. But it doesn't follow that those differences are hardwired—even if most of the LGBT world would itself concur—that biology, not culture, is the root source of the differences. Even the summary notion that lesbians are "tougher" and gay men "gentler" than their straight counterparts needs complicating. Gay men, having been subjected for generations to street bashing and police brutality, have learned, out of prudence and fear (not genes), to restrain their anger publicly. Tellingly, it does show in private: the rate of domestic violence among both gay men and lesbians approximates that of heterosexual violence. (The latest of many studies to confirm that is *No More Secrets* by Janice Ristock.) We're not devoid of rage; as a survival tactic—especially before Stonewall—we became adaptively passive-aggressive (a central ingredient in classic camp as well), taking out the aggressive side in the comparative safety of our homes—or on ourselves, through the abuse of drugs and alcohol.

At any rate, the widely and stubbornly held view that sexual orientation is hardwired flies in the face of most of the known evidence. A number of "scientific" studies (like Simon LeVay's on the hypothalamus, or the various hormonal and twin studies) have proclaimed themselves "proof" of the genetic theory, but on further inspection have turned out to be unduplicative or based on shoddy methodology. As the biologist Joan Roughgarden has put it, "Nature abhors a category."

Just as there's no single, proven, causative path to homosexual behavior, so too there's no fixed gay—or for that matter, straight— identity through time and across cultures. There have been huge variations in what constitutes proper (or improper) female and male activities, attitudes, movements, attire, even eating habits. Cultural taboos or mandates have differed radically in human history in regard both to gender and to same-sex relationships.

Yet in the face of overwhelming evidence to the contrary from science, history, and anthropology, gays and straights alike remain addicted to the shaky notion of a predetermined sexual orientation and a fixed identity. Which is one reason the younger generation prefers "queer" to "gay": it's a more inclusive term that potentially embraces a wide variety of "differentness" and is more suggestive of the complex, fluid, contradictory nature of our actual impulses and fantasies (anyone who pays attention to their dreams can readily see that we all have a pronounced, undomesticated, anarchic side).

Why then the general preference for fixed, genetic explanations for human behavior? It simplifies a number of matters, and offers a variety of comforts. If there are predetermined states of being—categorical, airtight, distinctive (and therefore not susceptible to change)—it becomes far easier to accept oneself. "I was born this way, it's my essence, my destiny." Under the banner of a fixed identity, it's also easier to justify creating a political movement aimed at achieving the rights of those who share that identity.

The genetic explanation for sexual orientation also serves heterosexuals well—thus the huge coverage (front page of the *New York Times*) of LeVay's claim that gay brains were "different" from straight brains and the media's absolute failure to report the inability of other scientists to duplicate LeVay's findings. Most heterosexuals are delighted with the suggestion that homosexuality is inborn. It then becomes a trait confined to a small number of people who are distinctly Other, wholly unrelated to oneself (last night's half-buried dream about sucking the garage mechanic's cock was due to food poisoning).

This may be convenient self-deception, but isn't objectively sustainable in the face of the known evidence. Way back in 1979, in *Homosexuality in Perspective*, Masters and Johnson published their preliminary findings from twenty years of studying sexual fantasies. They concluded that among gay men and lesbians, overt *heterosexual* interaction was their third-highest fantasy; to an only slightly lesser degree, straight men and women fantasized about overt *homosexual* interaction. What made the latter finding especially remarkable was that the heterosexual cohort all ranked zero ("exclusively straight") on the famed Kinsey scale and during personal interviews had described same-gender sex as "revolting" and "unthinkable."

Though Masters and Johnson recoiled from their own findings, it's plausible to argue that the widespread (if deeply repressed) existence among confirmed heterosexuals of same-gender sexual fantasies suggests (as had Freud) that almost everyone is potentially receptive to bisexual contact, that even when we've grown up in a homophobic culture that emphasizes the genetic separation of "straight" and "gay," the wish to be both retains a strong subterranean hold.

If we can say nothing definitive about the origins of sexual orientation (not to mention those who develop fetishistic attachments to "water sports," leather, big breasts, small breasts, whipping, or ladies' high-heeled shoes), the same is true about gender nonconformity and its possible link to homosexuality. Recent research findings are complex and controversial—though it's become increasingly clear that we need to emancipate ourselves from a binary view of gender that restricts possibilities in both women and men. Commonplace assumptions ("women are more emotional, men are more aggressive") are, as with stereotypes about sexual orientation, grounded in a presumed hardwiring that is in fact much contested. Simplistic biological determinism has been undermined recently by the work of many other scholars, especially in anthropology, primatology, and history.

I suspect that if we really do care about breaking down the gender binary, the place to look for inspiration is not Gold's Gym but the increasingly visible transgender movement, offering as it does a radical remodeling of traditional "masculinity" and "femininity." Gender-discordant behavior hasn't been a front-burner topic since the early 1970s, when radical gay liberationists championed an androgynous ideal. ("Gender-discordant" is a necessary but troublesome term, implying as it does that we know what a gender-concordant model looks like, that it exists cross-culturally and should be viewed in a superior light.)

I myself ascribe to the queer theory argument that "male" and "female" social roles are not to any significant degree intrinsic—that is, biologically determined—but are primarily, and perhaps even exclusively, the products of learning and repetitive performance. In this context, "gender discordance" becomes something of a *non sequitur*: where all boys are capable of (perhaps even, in the earliest years, inclined toward) a female-identified—which may be comparable to saying transgendered—self-image and presentation, then no particular gender configuration can legitimately be seen as "deviant."

The currently fashionable incantation—itself harking back to Jungian twaddle about "anima" and "animus"—that men "need to get in touch with their feminine side" doesn't go nearly far enough in meeting the need to reinvent for everyone, male and female, more fluid, expansive self-definitions; it's about moving beyond gender conformity, beyond gender itself, to molding individually satisfying selfhoods.

Currently, gender-discordant boys and girls, taunted at school and berated at home, internalize the view that something is "wrong with them," that they're "not okay." And most of them, from an early age, struggle to divest themselves of the disapproved behavior. The psychic cost is high. In repudiating aspects of the self that could he read as "discordant" for traditional gender behavior, these children do deep injury to their affective lives; many, as adults, avoid relationships that might evoke any resurgence of the "wrong" gender traits.

As regards the ongoing debate about whether gay male "promiscuity" is meretricious or praiseworthy, we need to begin by remembering that there is enormous variation in how gay men lead their sexual lives. Even before AIDS, only about 20 percent of the gay male population pursued "sexual adventuring" in any sustained way—about the same percentage as those who chose celibacy. Roughly three-quarters of gay male couples do define "fidelity" in terms of emotional commitment rather than sexual faithfulness—a much higher percentage than is found among either lesbian or heterosexual couples.

Although I've become a less zealous defender of the uncomplicated joys of sexual adventuring than I once was—that doesn't put me in the camp of those who celebrate the transcendent wonders of monogamy, or make claims for its "naturalness" by citing the universality of the practice among other species. The latter simply isn't true, as the latest researchers (see especially Bruce Bagemihl, *Biological Exuberance*) have made abundantly clear. Monogamy exists in the animal kingdom, but is rare—unlike homosexuality, which, as we've also learned recently, is rampant. Far from being universal, monogamy doesn't even exist among birds, those previous exemplars of domesticity and mating. Which is not to say, either, that so-called "open" relationships provide, among humans, any greater measure of happiness (as I also once argued). Apparently the safest guideline here is "different strokes for different folks," so long as partners to any relationship are honestly committed to its boundaries.

It's difficult, given our puritanical traditions, not to argue against pleasuring the body. That isn't my point. My main concern is that too great a focus on glutes and orgasms often seems yoked to an undernourished political sense and seems, ultimately, a kind of provincialism, an indifference to the survival issues that dominate and defeat most of the planet's inhabitants—including most of its gay people.

Celebrating rather than apologizing for gay male sexuality is a needed antidote to generations of negative stereotyping. But celebration alone can become incantatory, a repetitive chant that ultimately forgets precisely what we're glorifying and why. One gay male writer has defended promiscuity as "diffuse intimacy." "Diffuse" it certainly is, but does that enhance intimacy or spare us its embrace? We need to be on guard against the temptation to replace the apologetics of the past with an era of too easily bestowed, and perhaps unwarranted, self-congratulation.

—from *Waiting to Land* (2009)

The Center for Lesbian
and Gay Studies

The 1980s were probably the first moment in time when an attempt could be made in this country to formalize LGBT studies within a university structure. (That had already happened in the Netherlands as early as 1981, but in no other country.) Thanks to fifteen years of political activism; an AIDS crisis that in the public eye had humanized (as well as demonized) gay people and created more sympathy for them; and the accumulation of a substantial body of work (by, among others, John Boswell, Alan Bray, Blanche Wiesen Cook, John D'Emilio, Lillian Faderman, Jonathan Ned Katz, Joan Nestle, and Leila Rupp), the time was at least potentially ripe.

The ground had become fallow for lesbian and gay studies for reasons that go back even further. Major credit belongs to the advent, following the Stonewall riots, of an organized gay political movement—as always, activism precedes academics. Behind that, in turn, was a whole series of developments in the 1960s: a counterculture that challenged traditional pieties and authorities; a black struggle that contained at its core ("black is beautiful") the assumption that it was fine—maybe better than fine—to be different; and a feminist movement that boldly confronted the inevitability and "naturalness" of binary gender roles. Had there not been this across-the-board assault on long-standing norms, the gay movement (and the emergence of gay studies that followed in train) would never have been possible.

After the first dozen years of research into historical material, it became obvious that information regarding whole centuries and several national histories were virtually nonexistent. And what preliminary findings we did have related mostly to the behavior of white men, and a few white women. Efforts to reclaim the gay past, moreover, had thus far primarily focused on two areas of research: biography and the history of repression.

By the end of the 1980s, scholars of the gay past had expanded their search to include how gay people have viewed themselves through time. Here a polarizing debate opened up that in evolving form continues to the present day, and engages many more disciplines than history in the social sciences and humanities. Essentially the debate recapitulates the ancient "nature versus nurture" argument. Gay people themselves overwhelmingly opt—gay men perhaps more than lesbians—for the "nature" explanation ("I was born this way") and are devoted to the notion that a consistent homosexual presence, personality, and set of behavioral patterns can be perceived through time and across cultures.

But the scholarly world has just as solidly come down on the opposite side of the debate, insistent on the contingent nature of erotic desire and sexual identity. Most gay and lesbian scholars deny that the categories "homosexual" and "heterosexual" are real and persistent aspects of the human psyche that can be identified very far back in time. They argue that such either/or distinctions, rather than being an innate, universal grammar, are not found through time and across cultures, nor are the taboos, judgments, and penalties attached to particular sexual acts.

Historically, same-gender erotic desire has been organized in many different ways—sometimes shaping itself around substantial differences in age or social class between the two partners, sometimes creating "third gender" figures, sometimes insisting that homosexual behavior be understood according to traditional gender roles (he who penetrates is "male"; he who gets penetrated is "female"). Our sexual behavior, as well as our sexual identity, is, like everything else about our humanness, a product of the particular society in which we live, a reflection of its time-specific norms and values. Queer theorists, moreover, have additionally complicated the picture by modifying the triumphalist emphasis, since Stonewall, on "proud to be gay" to include the melancholic effects that homophobia has had on gay lives: the shame produced by stigmatization has made a significant contribution to certain formative aspects of gay culture.

To become even superficially aware of the range in the past of what were considered ideal, permissible, mandated, or tabooed patterns of same-gender erotic relationships is to become aware of the astonishing diversity of human behavior and of the variety of cultural norms. In Periclean Athens the adult male citizen who did *not* find teenaged young men sexually desirable would himself have been considered aberrant. Among certain tribal cultures in New Guinea, the oral ingestion of semen is considered essential to the youngster's growth into full manhood; on a regular basis, boys fellated men—and "as a result" themselves grew into heterosexual manhood in an apparently unproblematic way.

Adult women in late nineteenth-century, early twentieth-century America set up housekeeping together so frequently as to become known as "Boston marriages." Yet those who lived on into the post–World War I period, when the term "lesbian" became commonly used, vigorously denied that their relationships had had a sexual component. The historical rarity seems to have been what today is regarded as the most commonplace and acceptable arrangement of two adults of the same gender settling down together in a relationship whose intent was monogamous and lifelong.

About all of this we still knew little in the mid-1980s. The book of same-gender relations was so filled with entirely blank pages that in truth we knew very nearly nothing at all. The time seemed obviously right to encourage reliable additional scholarship and to disseminate that scholarship to a wide audience. And thus it was that, late in 1985, I came up with the idea of a university center devoted to LGBT studies. A longtime friend of mine, the documentary filmmaker Helen Whitney, was then married to Benno Schmidt, who'd recently been named the new president of Yale University (my own alma mater) to replace the outgoing Bart Giamatti. Benno hadn't yet formally assumed his duties, but the time seemed ripe to approach him with my new idea.

The diary I kept at the time picks up the story from there:

JANUARY 19, 1986:

A very friendly, helpful call from Benno. He takes well to my letter and has already sounded out Bart on preliminaries. Bart, predictably (given his antigay reputation), immediately objected to establishing a center devoted to "gay" anything: "gay," according to Bart, is an "advocacy" word. Benno says he hasn't yet made up his own mind on that issue. I drew the parallel with black studies. Would Yale insist on a center devoted to research about *colored* Americans, because some might regard "black" as an advocacy word? Don't people have a right to name themselves? Benno said that Bart suggested I shift from "gay" to "human sexuality." No, I said; along with the Kinsey Institute, there's plenty of grant money and research already devoted to that subject. There's none for gay studies. How about using the word "homosexuality?" Benno suggested. No, I said, that's a clinical designation, loaded with moralistic implications. We dropped the subject of terminology for now. . . .

Pending any decision from Yale, I invited some half-dozen gay and lesbian academics, a group that gradually expanded in size, to meet monthly in my apartment to begin discussing what our ideal qualifications were for such a center.

APRIL 8:

Pretty much everyone asked to the April meeting about the possible new gay studies center has accepted enthusiastically . . . though many of the women are rightly leery of the male bastion

Yale. It's a toss-up between attraction to Yale as a prestigious legitimizing agency and repugnance to it as a traditional dispenser of elite male privilege. . . . The primary goal is to gather a group of people and create the kind of structure that will serve *gay* people; to use the opportunity Benno's administration represents for *our* purposes. . . . If Yale should try to impose conditions—for example, requiring a high percentage of PhDs or full professors on any governing board—which would run counter to our vision of what is appropriate (in this instance, those *without* "proper" academic credentials who have nonetheless made significant contributions to gay studies), then we would have to try to establish the center elsewhere.

APRIL 19:

Thirteen of us gathered in my apartment—the "Organizing Committee" for the gay center, as we have now designated ourselves. . . . On the whole it went well . . . though John Boswell [the Yale historian, and author of the pioneering *Christianity, Social Tolerance, and Homosexuality*] started huffy, "warning" us that Yale would insist, rightly in his view, on laying down essential guidelines for any center sporting its name. Carole Vance [co-author of *Pleasure and Danger: Exploring Female Sexuality*] issued an eloquent counterwarning that in the search for the legitimizing of gay studies, we have to remain vigilant that a rapprochement with traditional academia does not end in an accommodation to *its* norms. I sided with Carole, though I think Boswell's traditionalist values (shared by Ralph Hexter and Al Novick [professor of biology at Yale], but not by Tony Appiah [then a professor of philosophy at Yale and the author of a number of important books, including *In My Father's House*], will aggressively reassert themselves in what is bound to prove an ongoing struggle to maintain the integrity of gay differentness as we push for mainstream institutional affiliation. It's the old American story of balancing a radical vision against the urge to operate in a broader arena (the vision invariably diluting as dissemination spreads). . . .

JULY 9:

Benno invited me up tonight to talk over prospects for the gay center. We spent less than two hours, and no more than half that time was on the center, but a lot got said. Benno reiterated his enthusiasm for a *research* center—[as distinguished from] an undergraduate major in gay studies or a policy-oriented public affairs institute. That's precisely our committee's chief interest, so I had no trouble reassuring him that we were proceeding on parallel paths. (Benno is not naive: he fully recognizes—and welcomes—the intrinsically *political* mission of any center devoted to disseminating information, increasing understanding, changing minds, about gay people). He expressed awareness that the alumni, or segments of it, will likely chew his ass out for sanctioning even a purer-than-Caesar's-wife scholarly think tank devoted to gay subject matter, but seems prepared to face down that storm. I think he can be taken at his word; he seems genuinely committed to the proposal. He offered to appear at select fund-raising events as a further indication of his commitment.

SEPTEMBER 29:

Boswell, it turns out, is prepared not only to resign from the center, but to destroy it. Today's letter from him—a copy of which he sent to Benno—effectively seals the prospects of negotiation. Benno feels he can't proceed without the support of Yale's "gay star." Since Boswell has characterized the committee's deliberations as "unremittingly hostile" to Yale, Benno can be pardoned for forgoing an affiliation that promised in any case to bring him maximum trouble with the alumni. I'm shocked and angry at John Boswell's behavior; isolated at the last meeting, failing to secure control of the center for himself, he sets out to sabotage it—at Yale, anyway. . . . A now-consolidated organizing committee can at least try to set up shop elsewhere. . . .

MAY 8, 1987:

A wonderful outcome to our meeting today about the center with Harold Proshansky [president of the CUNY Graduate School, where I taught—as well as at CUNY's Lehman campus]. He's for it, straightforwardly for it! He thinks the time is if anything overdue, thanked us for bringing it to CUNY (what a happy contrast to Benno's hesitations and retreats), and will work actively with us to prepare strategies for getting the Board of Trustees' approval. . . . it was nice not to have to justify our lives for once, to have the legitimacy of who we are and what we're trying to do taken respectfully for granted. . . . Proshansky emphasized that a great deal of hard work lies ahead. He plans to approach Chancellor [Joseph] Murphy first (he's widely viewed as a great champion of minorities) and then to ask a select group of the campus presidents each to kick in $5,000 from their slush funds. That way, should our own fund-raising falter, we'll still have a minimal budget to get started with. . . .

MAY 11:

Murphy has turned Proshansky down for money and forbidden him from approaching any of the campus presidents. Here we go again: a "radical" being radical on every issue but ours. . . . Well, the project hasn't been smooth up to now, so why should it suddenly become so? (Except that it seemed for a moment that it might). . . .

Our committee—its personnel shifting somewhat through time—continued to work hard to make the center a reality. But by the spring of 1988, the center had been turned down by all the foundations we'd applied to for grants, and was still nowhere near raising the $50,000 Proshansky had set as the start-up budget needed to establish our viability. As a result of passing the hat at two public events we'd held—both of which drew standing-room-only crowds, thereby demonstrating the strong need that existed in the community for such a center—as well as small donations from individual contributors, we did have nearly $10,000 in the bank. But that had taken us two-and-a-half years to raise. At that rate, we'd still be at it in the twenty-first century.

We tried not to think about that, taking heart from the fact that here and there a course or a conference relating to lesbian and gay studies had started to surface. Nowhere in the country did a department or a scholarly research center exist, and only rarely could a brave student find even minimal fellowship money to pursue a topic in LGBT studies. On the few campuses where a course had been offered, it stood alone, wasn't always repeated, or had trouble finding students brave enough to enroll.

The organizing committee of what would ultimately become the Center for Lesbian and Gay Studies (CLAGS) continued to plug along. In 1989, out of the blue, David Clarke, a gay man who died of AIDS in San Francisco and who none of us knew, left the center a $20,000 bequest. That same year we finally hit pay dirt with a foundation; the executive director of the Rapoport Foundation (the legacy of another gay man dead of AIDS), gave us a $10,000 grant (and continued to support us for years to come). Then, in November 1989, our first benefit netted us an additional $11,000—and suddenly, after five years of trying, we'd reached the stipulated goal of $50,000.

I started in on the rounds of calls and meetings requisite to getting CLAGS put before the CUNY Board of Trustees. They eventuated, in April 1991, with CLAGS being formally designated an official research center of the CUNY Graduate School. Having climbed that hill, we were, predictably, immediately confronted with another: persuading the authorities to give us an actual office. Ten months after becoming formally established, my own graduate school office was still doubling as the CLAGS office; space, I was told, was "tight." When one was finally found for us, it proved literally unusable. Containing one desk and one chair, it had no lighting in the ceiling, paint peeling off the walls, a single window so covered with filth that one could just about make out the brick wall it faced, ancient (and limited) file cabinets, loose wires scattered all over the floor, no typewriter or computer, no working phones—not even a key to the bathroom.

When my complaints went unheeded, I finally did a one-man sit-in outside the office of the vice president of the graduate school. After an hour's wait in the corridor, he finally agreed to see me in his elegantly appointed office, swiveling luxuriously in his Eames chair, puffing cigar smoke in my direction. I should have laughed, I suppose, but my anger won out: "We don't, of course, expect fancy chairs, like yours, but it'd be nice to have two beat-up old ones, and—perhaps you'll think this excessive—one 40–watt bulb so that when a visiting scholar comes to call, one of us wouldn't have to stand throughout and we could at least make out the contours of each other's faces." The vice president showed no sign of chagrin, though in the following weeks, the needed ingredients to make the CLAGS's office habitable did slowly appear.

As a result of articles in the *Chronicle of Higher Education* and the *Advocate*, word had earlier spread that we were about to open our doors, and for some time I'd been getting a steady stream of letters from would-be graduate students eager to enroll in what they presumed was a doctorate program in lesbian and gay studies. Alas—as I tried to explain to the many people who wrote to me—we'd barely gotten a leg over the barricades, and the only way CLAGS could have gotten formal accreditation at all was as a research center, not as a department that could hire faculty and offer courses or degrees. One undergraduate major in lesbian and gay studies did exist at the City College of San Francisco; and San Francisco State, in 1990, soon hoped to offer a minor in the field. That was it. Gradually CLAGS would be able to offer research grants and to employ a tiny, part-time staff, but even today, more than twenty years later, no PhD in LGBT studies exists anywhere in the country.

More and more activists and academics in a growing number of localities began to explore available source materials. As a result, long-buried and uncataloged archival sources began to surface in manuscript libraries, providing needed research materials for an emerging generation of LGBT scholars. The 1990s would see a proliferation of books and articles, as well as new academic journals (*Genders*; *The Journal of the History of Sexuality*; *OutLook*; *GLQ*).

There had, of course, been a few precedents: as long ago as 1897, Magnus Hirschfeld and associates had established the Scientific Humanitarian Committee in Berlin; and in this country, the late 1950s had seen the creation in California of ONE, Inc., which had developed a research facility. Still more recently, the Canadian Gay Archives had opened its doors. And as the view of homosexuality as pathology began to subside, increasing numbers of graduate students and faculty came out, and gay-themed course offerings in a wide variety of fields began to be offered at the university level. Stimulated by the existence of CLAGS, the CUNY Graduate School became a focal point for LGBT studies, and a critical mass of openly lesbian and gay students was soon enrolled. A considerable number of them, on reaching the dissertation level, would opt for writing their doctoral theses on gay-themed subjects—even while being fully aware that they were limiting their employability. To this day, some of those who do manage to find full or part-time academic jobs do so under general rubrics like "cultural studies" or "gender studies."

The presence on many campuses of a significant number of liberals ("Of course gay people are entitled to the full rights of citizenship") proved critical in allowing lesbian and gay studies to gain a toehold. But as I kept discovering, unpleasantly, a willingness to grant us basic rights wasn't remotely the equivalent of actually wanting to know about our lives—let alone of believing that our distinctive insights might have anything of importance to say to *them*. Even as these liberals announced their own tolerance of our existence, they seemed clueless about the limitations of their openness to our knowledge and perspectives.

This was far truer of straight white male scholars than female or minority ones. The latter, after all, knew a great deal about being kept outside the centers of power—and how being on the margins often provided insight into the psyches and behavior of the Big Boys. But if we knew something about their lives, they wanted to know as little as possible about ours. The liberal mantra "What gay people do in the privacy of their own homes is no concern of ours" masked inherent disdain for the notion that the patterns of our sexuality, relationships, friendships, and families might contain information relevant to their own lives. The liberal adoption of "the privacy principle" is an effective shield against letting too much subversive information get through, the equivalent of building a wall between gay and straight that not only perpetuates the fallacious hetero/homo binary but conveniently protects the straight world from questioning some of its own assumptions about human behavior. Even male scholars further to the left of "liberalism" (Eric Hobsbawm, say, or Bogdan Denitch) seal themselves off from the realities of gay experience—or as Todd Gitlin scornfully put it, "what they imagine to be their identities."

Many left-wingers, on campus and off, position themselves as radicals on race and class issues but are utterly traditional in regard to feminist and gay concerns. Zealous in challenging the economic status quo, they're no less zealous in defending the status quo when it comes to cultural issues. Michael Tomasky, to give one example, has cavalierly dismissed "supposedly oppositional" gay culture with its "superficially transgressive ideas." Supposedly? Superficially? None of these left-wing traditionalists could conceivably express such views if they'd read a word of Eve Sedgwick or Judith Butler. If they had, they'd have to take seriously some of the basic insights of queer history and theory: the performative aspects of gender, the viable parameters of friendship, the shifting shape across time and culture of such purported universals as the nuclear family, monogamy, lifelong pair-bonding, and the uncertain linkage between love and sex—as well as the omnipresence in all of us of a wildly anarchic, unorthodox range of erotic fantasy and desire.

* * *

When I accepted an offer to join the CUNY system back in 1972, I'd been asked to teach at the Graduate Center as well as on one of the undergraduate campuses. For the time being I'd declined, preferring for a while just to teach undergraduates. I'd grown tired in recent years of the dutiful way graduate students wrote down everything I said as if it was Truth. But I did offer to sit on PhD exams and read PhD theses until the urge to produce scholarly offspring returned.

By the midseventies, I'd become increasingly involved in the brand-new field of the history of sexuality and at that point I went back to the Graduate Center and said that I'd be willing, after all, to offer a course on that subject—that I needed older students with more information and experience to bounce ideas off. The reaction was immediate: no. Gertrude Himmelfarb, chair of the Graduate Center History Department at the time, acerbically told me that the department felt that sexual history wasn't "real" history at all; it had been spawned by political polemics, not scholarly necessity. My standing as a legitimate scholar, she told me, might well be at stake. As if activism hasn't always ignited scholarship—the feminist movement and feminist studies, the black movement and black studies. As if a scholar's political and social views don't always, consciously or not, color their narratives (Himmelfarb herself, a right-wing conservative, being among the more notorious current examples).

I wasn't entirely surprised. Back in 1974, Dennis Rubini, an openly gay historian at Temple University, and I had submitted a proposal for a panel on "the history of sexuality" (not the more inflammatory "lesbian and gay history") for the American Historical Association's annual convention; not getting any response, we'd inquired and had been told that the proposal "seems to have gotten unaccountably lost." We'd resubmitted the following year, and that time were formally rejected.

I was prepared for Himmelfarb's reaction, but it nonetheless angered me and I reached for the only card in my deck. If my scholarship was now regarded as tainted, I told the history faculty, then surely it wouldn't want me contaminating its innocent students:

surely it would be best if I no longer sat on PhD exams or read PhD theses. Should the faculty decide at some future point that the history of sexual behavior was a legitimate subject, I'd be glad, once more, to serve as a PhD examiner and mentor.

And there the stalemate held for some fifteen years, as the national, and Graduate Center, climate slowly changed. Finally, in 1991, coinciding with the establishment of CLAGS, my graduate seminar on gay and lesbian history was formally approved. I pick up the story in my diary for that year:

FEBRUARY 7, 1991:

Thirty-seven students showed up last night for the seminar ("Reclaiming Gay/Lesbian History, Politics, and Culture") at the Graduate Center—including two faculty members, students from NYU, Rutgers, and the University of Rochester, and representing nearly every conceivable field (yes, even Japanese literature) *except* history (Joe W. says the history students are afraid to sign up because the dept. is notoriously conservative). The official registration list had only sixteen names and the actual turnout stunned—and thrilled—me. It confirms the wish/need for gay/lesbian studies and sends a clear message to the university's powers-that-be.

Since my whole point in giving the course is to excite interest in the field, I'm not going to turn anyone away, though I'd originally cut off enrollment at twenty, wanting to preserve an intimate, informal atmosphere. But I told the students last night that they were all welcome and to keep the size manageable I'd break the group into two parts and give a second seminar on another evening. We'll put that decision off until next week, to see if the same number turns up. Anyway, I'm hugely excited, and gratified. . . .

FEBRUARY 14:

Not only did the seminar number hold last night, but it went *up* to forty! I've divided them into two separate groups, Monday and Wednesday nights. It's going to complicate my life. I was feeling overextended without the additional seminar— but I couldn't in conscience do otherwise. The actual session was an eye-opener. This *is* a different gay generation! At times during the discussion, I felt as if I was scrambling to keep up; the new deconstruction terminology, of which Amanda and Liz seem especially adept, indeed dazzling, had me recharging every remaining synapse. I was so excited when I got home that I didn't fall asleep until 3:00. . . .

FEBRUARY 21:

My first talk of two [on "Gay and Lesbian Studies"] at the Museum of Natural History went well—about four hundred people showed up. It had the excited feel of an historic occasion—the first time one of NYC's major cultural institutions opened its doors *fully* to gay/lesbian subject matter. It became clear why in the dressing room prior to my going on. Malcolm Arth, head of programming at the museum, came by to get some info for the introduction and came out to me directly (though he says he's in the closet still at the museum). From what I could gather, he dislikes the new administration, has chosen to retire at the end of this year, and saw this two-part series as a kind of nose-thumbing at the powers-that-be. He also said that the museum is honeycombed with gay curators, none of whom are out, all of whom would be in avid attendance at the lecture.

OCTOBER 6:

It's two days since CLAGS's inaugural event. On one level it was a flat-out triumph. Four hundred fifty to five hundred people attended, $26,000 grossed, the speeches brief and effective, the food superb, Alice Walker [who co-chaired the event with Adrienne Rich] gracious and focused, the mood throughout buoyant. And I was able to announce Dave's $110,000 gift with Dave present [David Kessler, an old friend of mine, had endowed an annual lecture/celebration of a noted lesbian or

gay scholar; over time, "the Kessler" became a significant community event and the first ten years of lectures were published
as a book]. As several people said, "I can't believe a fledgling
organization put this together."

With CLAGS now formally established, we steadily expanded
our public offerings, even as we continued to search for the funds
to support them—the Graduate Center still not providing a dime in
direct financial support. Ironically, the more frequent and elaborate
our offerings became, the more the impression grew that we were
rolling in money—what else could explain our productivity? Similarly, when we won the $250,000 Rockefeller Humanities Fellow-
ship it was widely assumed that the award was meant for the Center
for Urban Community Services. We were as astonished as everyone
else at receiving the prestigious grant—even if, in fact, we got to use
a mere $15,000 for operating expenses.

By 1992, CLAGS was increasingly producing a number of major
(one- to three-day) conferences, and maintained a monthly colloquia series as well, an informal gathering at which scholars presented works-in-progress. A scholarly directory—the first of its
kind—of university faculty offering courses or doing research on
lesbian and gay subjects was, after two years of gathering and check-
ing listings, about to go to press. Also, through specially earmarked
gifts, we were now able to offer an increasing number of grants and
awards that ranged from $500 grants-in-aid for CUNY graduate
students to two $5,000 research grants in lesbian and gay history,
to the broad-gauged two yearly Rockefeller Fellowships of $35,000.

Yet perhaps predictably, criticism of CLAGS continued from
various quarters, and included a range of grievances. One prominent lesbian psychologist, for example, wrote to me early in 1992
to complain that our public programming inadequately reflected
lesbian perspectives. This, I thought, was patently unfair, though
I adopted a gentle tone in response. Our governing board, I pointed
out, had absolute gender parity, and both its co-chairs were women;
the first Kessler awardee had also been a woman (Joan Nestle). In

regard to our public programs, our most recent conference, "The Brain and Homosexuality," had four female and four male panelists. Our upcoming two-day conference on "AIDS and Public Policy" would devote one full day to "Women and AIDS." Seven of the nine speakers at our panel "Feminism and Lesbianism," organized by Judith Butler, were women. "In this male-haunted world," I wrote the psychologist, "I think we're doing pretty well. I hope you'll eventually come to agree." She didn't respond.

SEPTEMBER 1, 1992:

CLAGS has been keeping me going at a furious clip. Multiple meetings are the least of it. The calls and letters are reaching flood tide, and I have to be corresponding secretary along with stamp licker and room renter. This is the kind of success I hoped for, but the ten-hour-day reality leaves little room for much else. ("And isn't that," whispers the wise little voice, "what you *really* hoped for?") . . .

MAY 4, 1996:

The organization is probably in the best shape ever—$115,000 in the bank, fellowships endowed, a series of books in the works, a pioneering directory published, and a solid network of contacts established with foundations, members, and donors. The rock of Gibraltar we're not, but given the original odds and the repetitive ambushes along the way, we're far more solidly established than I would have thought possible even a few years ago.

AUGUST 10, 1996:

I stepped down as the executive director of CLAGS, nearly ten years to the day in 1986 when I gathered a small group of friends in my living room to discuss the possibility of setting up a lesbian and gay research center. Out of that initial gathering, CLAGS had been born, though it took five years of struggling to raise money, support, and visibility before we became formally established as a center at the CUNY graduate school.

I feel strongly that the right time had arrived for me to step away, to let a new generation reconfigure CLAGS in its own image. And I really will step away. I understand that the new director has to have a clear field. I'll make myself available for information or advice, but only if asked. The break is clean and without regret.

There's much, in retrospect, to feel good about. Today, CLAGS, though always in need of money, has a large mailing list and has become well-known as a centerpiece and clearinghouse for the burgeoning new field of lesbian and gay studies. And the center had kept to its original mission and principles. Through a series of fellowships, publications, and a remarkable (especially for a new organization) number of colloquia and conferences on major issues relating to gender and sexuality, we've increased the amount of reliable scholarship on the LGBT experience, and disseminated it to a general public. And—despite some brief periods of imbalance— we've basically stuck to our principles of gender parity, multicultural perspectives, and the inclusion, in terms of both fellowship awards and board membership, of scholars who aren't academically affiliated.

—from *Waiting to Land* (2009)

Queers for Economic Justice

Diary

APRIL 26, 1996:

Sat through most of the "Future of the Welfare State" conference today at the Graduate Center. The conference was both stirring and depressing. The panelists were mostly heterosexual white men over fifty, all (rightly) wringing their hands over the growing global disparities between rich and poor, but all spouting mostly tired analyses and almost all (the Swedish diplomat Pierre Schori the major exception, in regard to women) showing little interest in or comprehension of recent work in feminist or gay studies. Not that such work should supplant prior emphases on class, but it might at least, if acknowledged, provide supplemental insights. The omission of any reference to gays and lesbians as either objects of concern or subjects of active agency was especially glaring. The entire first panel was (devoutly) concerned with "strengthening dialogue with mainstream religion," with E.J. Dionne worrying about the Left embracing assisted suicide.

Norman Birnbaum deplored the Left's "ideological stubbornness" in preventing new ideas from emerging—yet never mentioned the current ferment over traditional gender/sexual models as one possible source for new ideas. Joe Murphy (he who, when chancellor in 1987, made it clear to Proshansky that he would not openly oppose but would not lift a finger in favor of establishing CLAGS) seemed smugly self-congratulatory about a new Ethiopian constitution he's involved in formulating that *rhetorically* declares for the needed liberation of women—even as he freely predicts it will take "a long time" before that liberation begins to be implemented. Bogdan Denitch warned against "feel-good" politics and focusing on "cultural" issues; I'm delighted, he said snidely, that Clinton favors gays in the military, "but that is (broad smile) obviously not the most urgent issue facing us." I happen to agree with him, but wouldn't have smiled.

All of which confirms the need for raising awareness—and attempting linkages. The straight Left needs to be kicked in the butt for its alternating ignorance, silence, or even opposition over gender/sexual issues. And the gay/lesbian world has to awaken to the horrendous plight of the unemployed, the homeless, and the working poor. The global horror of poverty, racism, and ethnic cleansing reinforce my conviction that the gay movement must be reconfigured (à la GLF [Gay Liberation Front] in 1970) to become a site for contesting, in coalition with others, established concentrations of power.

JANUARY 12, 2002:

The climate within the national gay movement hasn't proved congenial to a left-wing turn. In 1999, when a range of progressive organizations came together to protest the policies of the World Trade Organization, of which the "Battle of Seattle" in November 1999 was the high-water mark, none of the major LGBT national organizations joined in and left-wing gay people participated as individuals only.

Similarly, the Human Rights Campaign (HRC) and the United Fellowship of Metropolitan Community Churches— neither known for their vanguard agendas—have apparently decided, without consultation with other LGBT groups, to co-sponsor for the next year a so-called "Millennium March" on Washington. With its corporate sponsorship and its emphasis on gays being "just folks," the apolitical nature of the march is to some of us in shocking contrast to the three previous marches (1979, 1987, 1993). Certain that this one provides no hint of a challenge to "regimes of the normal," most gay left-wingers are staying home.

"At this point in the LGBT movement's evolution," as Liz Highleyman has put it, "it's worth asking whether gay, lesbian, bisexual, and transgender people are in fact a progressive constituency. . . . As LGBT people gain mainstream acceptance, many feel a decreased need or desire to align themselves with marginalized groups or radical causes. . . . Does it make more sense to join forces with the progressive multi-issue movement [the Battle for Seattle, for example] rather than trying to influence the LGBT movement? . . . Who are our best allies? Mainstream and conservative LGBT people, or progressive and radical heterosexuals?" Those questions need asking, but since the receptivity of most progressive straights is decidedly in doubt, for me it boils down not to "either/or" but, alas, "neither/nor."

I was unexpectedly given direction, in a chance conversation with Terry Boggis. She told me about a group of progressive queers involved in the Economic Justice Network, and invited me to the network's next meeting. I went, and met Joseph DeFilippis, a dynamo in his early thirties. We talked about the importance of setting up a nonprofit centered on the needs of the gay poor—people in shelters, prisons, unemployed, on welfare, without health care.

These aren't people available for taking on liaison work with progressive groups—their survival needs are simply too great. But they are people whose desperate situations are being largely ignored by the national LGBT movement. Joseph and I found that we were very much on the same wavelength politically, and we both wanted to move full steam ahead in setting up the new nonprofit. Joseph, forty years younger than me, had the much fuller head of steam; my impulse is intact, but my follow-up drive less so. Anyway, Joseph and I have both learned from painful past experience that not everyone appreciates the locomotive pace, nor the expectation that every task would be completed on the promised date.

Still, by May 2002, thanks mostly to Joseph's untiring efforts, we were actually holding our first planning meeting. Spirits were high but attendance disappointingly low. Only a dozen or so people had shown up out of the thirty-two who'd expressed "strong interest." Of most concern was that many of the no-shows were people of color; Joseph, who'd done almost all of the groundwork for the meeting, was deeply puzzled: he thought he'd had firm commitments. The people at the meeting I didn't already know profoundly impressed me; most were in their twenties, urgent, radical, and already devoting their lives to full-time work for a variety of social justice organizations (such as Coalition for the Homeless).

But we all agreed that we couldn't proceed to a second meeting until (as I wrote in my diary) "a good representation of people of color is invited to tell us whether this new enterprise really does feel congenial to them, and if not, how we can make it so." A number of people, with Joseph again taking the lead, volunteered to sound out those who hadn't shown up. The soundings proved fruitful, and in July we held our second meeting—with eight of the fourteen attendees people of color. Two months after that, we had a full-day retreat; this time, only five of the fourteen people were white, though the gender breakdown was less good (nine to five male).

It was an exhilarating day. We started to form committees, put some structural building blocks in place (Joseph, by acclaim, became coordinator), and chose a name for ourselves: Queers for Economic Justice (QEJ). Consensus was rapidly achieved on nearly every issue, and good will was endemic (inevitably, the honeymoon will give way to occasional squabbles, but hopefully fewer than I've experienced in other organizations).

During the course of the meeting, concurrence quickly developed over the scandalous avoidance in society at large and within the gay community itself of issues relating to welfare reform and prison conditions, LGBT homelessness, lack of access to health care, and antigay violence at low-paying worksites. The uniform view was that poverty is most acute among the LGBT young, the transgendered, and the elderly. I left the retreat, as I wrote in my diary, "full of enthusiasm for the work ahead."

By 2004, the total income for QEJ was a little under $90,000. That allowed us to employ Joseph DeFilippis as coordinator, Jay Toole as a part-time organizer to work with LGBT people living in shelters, plus a part-time consultant to help us generate additional funds. Our ambitions were larger than our budget: high among our priorities were developing "Know Your Rights" programs for LGBT people who are homeless or in need of public benefits; holding community forums on neglected issues like providing shelter for transgendered people and LGBT youth; doing outreach to other small LGBT groups (FIERCE!; Al-Fatiha; the Neutral Zone; Latino Gay Men of New York; SONG; the Queer Immigration Rights Project, etc.) attempting to do comparable work; and teaching people to advocate for themselves.

In September 2004, [my partner] Eli and I gave a fund-raiser in our apartment for QEJ. The main point was "cultivation"—letting wealthy individual donors know that we exist—and we did collect nearly $7,000. But no thanks to the prosperous; exactly one prominent gay philanthropist attended. And no straight lefties, wealthy or otherwise. None of them even bothered to RSVP, let alone send a check. I guess I should stop being surprised at how little the heterosexual Left incorporates us into their vision of a better future; we get the lip service of tolerance, not the embrace of camaraderie. Anyway, the following year, QEJ became officially incorporated and—thanks to the support of a few small gay or left-leaning foundations (North Star, Open Meadows, Paul Rapoport, RESIST, Open Society, etc.) has continued to survive, with a slow rise in its annual budgets and its offerings. For QEJ actually to thrive would require a considerable transformation in national values, and I include gay ones.

In the upshot, I stayed on the QEJ board for three years, until I finally had to turn full-time to completing *The Worlds of Lincoln Kirstein*. QEJ remains alive, though not robust. Its budget and projects rise and fall year by year. Compared with the giant gay organizations (the HRC has eight hundred thousand members and an annual budget of $40 million), QEJ is still barely known, and woefully underfunded and understaffed. Yet in serving a poor, silent, and otherwise ignored segment of the LGBT community, it holds, in my view, the commanding moral ground.

The 2005 National Gay and Lesbian Task Force "Creating Change" conference [a gathering each year of LGBT activists and organizers to exchange views and strategies] gave off more than a few glints of hope that the cycle may again be turning, that the number of progressive voices within the LGBT community could shortly become a ringing choir (well, maybe an *a cappella* minichorus). The hope resides almost entirely with the younger generation, and with activists working outside the national LGBT organizations—like those from QEJ. Discontent with the narrow scope of the gay agenda—with its preeminent issue of gay marriage—is notably on the rise. The HRC Campaign may currently dominate the LGBT political scene but its grip on the future no longer seems assured.

HRC's legions represent the older, more prosperous segment of the LGBT community, those who grew up under terrifying threats of punishment, disclosure, and criminalization. They're understandably thrilled at the recent change in climate—at being normalized by clinicians and *courted* by straight politicians. They want more of the same and don't want their new status threatened by association with advocacy for the homeless and the poor. It's like the history of immigration: the newly assimilated want nothing to do with the newly arrived.

The surge in progressive values is taking place among the

seventeen-to-twenty-nine age group regardless of sexual orientation, providing hope that not only the gay movement, but the country, can be reclaimed from the self-seeking avarice of recent years.
And now, happily, we have the unexpected emergence of Occupy
Wall Street. Every new poll shows an increasing percentage of the
young taking up progressive positions. They're more likely than the
general public to favor, among other issues, a government-run universal health care system and an open-door policy on immigration.

One 2005 *NBC News–Wall Street Journal* poll even found that
53 percent of *all* Americans disapprove of the Bush tax cuts on the
grounds they'll lead to further curtailments in government social
services. None of which means that major social change is around
the corner: the corporations still go unchecked; the gap between
the rich and poor continues to widen; membership in labor unions
continues to slide; the feminist movement seems in disarray.

And in June 2012, Eli and I gave another QEJ fund-raiser in our
apartment—and raised a measly $3,500. *Can* hope spring eternal?

—from *Waiting to Land* (2009)

Class Is a Queer Issue

Here are some facts you might not know:

1. Most gay people are working class (whether "class" is defined by income, educational level, or job status).
2. Class identity is an amalgam of identities: one's place within the economic structure is deeply inflected by race, ethnicity, gender, and sexual orientation.
3. Most people in this country, including many with poverty-line incomes, identify themselves as "middle class."
4. The workplace remains strongly defined by heterosexual norms. Most straight workers believe gender comes in two, and only two, packages: male or female. And most would claim (at least officially) that lifetime, monogamous pair-bonding is the best guarantee of a contented, moral life.
5. Within certain segments of organized labor, there's been a growing understanding of the effect of homophobia on gay workers and also a willingness to address it.
6. There has not been a comparable growth in understanding within national gay organizations about class issues. Nor any notable concern or announced agenda to deal with the economic plight and deplorable workplace conditions of many working-class LGBT people.

Here are a few myths that commonly pass for facts among many *non*-working-class people, gay as well as straight:

1. The typical worker is a male in industry who heads a family.
2. Minorities are now well represented in union leadership positions.
3. The national gay movement is dominated by people holding radical social and political views.
4. Many labor union leaders are either stealing from their treasuries, in bed with the bosses, or both.
5. Organized labor's politics are strictly centered, and properly so, on issues relating to wages and working conditions.

Such "facts" are widely held, dominate public discourse, deeply affect the culture of the workplace, the attempt to organize unions, and the personal lives of workers. These interconnected issues clarify why progressives active in class, gender, and sexual orientation politics need to recognize their linkages and combine their forces to a far greater degree than has been the case to date. The result could be a strengthened new engine of social reform.

The national LGBT movement must, if it has any hope of becoming genuinely representative of the majority of gay people, broaden its agenda to include working-class issues. And the union movement must—if it hopes to increase its numbers much beyond its current enrollment of 12 percent of the workforce—take far greater cognizance than it currently does of the oppressive conditions that dominate the lives of workers who are gender and sexual nonconformists.

Specifically, unions need to assume the responsibility of creating a climate in the workplace where those who are not straight white men can feel comfortable in being open about their lives and can be assured that their needs will be represented forcefully during contract negotiations with employers. The traditional union agenda of fighting for higher pay and better working conditions needs to be broadened to include such issues as homophobic harassment at the workplace and domestic partnership benefits for LGBT employees.

Any sustainable alliance between the LGBT and union movements must be preceded or accompanied by a considerable amount of transformative work *within* each movement. The dominant ideology of most of the large national gay organizations, such as the Human Rights Campaign, would require a profound shift in emphasis away from their traditionalist, centrist concerns (the legal right to marry and serve openly in the military, for example), a shift that their middle-class constituency—and this is a huge sticking point—might not support.

The political scientist Cathy J. Cohen explains why such a shift is nonetheless urgent. In her brilliant essay, "What Is This Movement Doing to My Politics?" Cohen argues that ever since the demise of Queer Nation and the refocusing of ACT-UP on issues relating to *global* AIDS, there's no longer a radical domestic wing of any import in the national lesbian and gay movement (with the exception, I'd add, of the transgender movement; small though it is in numbers, its challenge to binary notions of gender is of potentially huge importance).

Otherwise, most of the numerically and monetarily significant national gay organizations appear indifferent to a genuinely transformative politics. In 1998, for example, the Human Rights Campaign endorsed Alfonse D'Amato for the Senate; the Log Cabin Republicans honored a black politician who has worked *against* affirmative action in California; the National Gay and Lesbian Task Force accepted (though later did return) a sizeable contribution from Nike, which employs sweatshop labor; and the Gay and Lesbian Alliance Against Defamation accepted (and did not return) a gift from the right-wing, union-busting Coors corporation.

Cohen's disgust with the national gay movement's efforts to "sanitize, whitenize, and normalize the public and visible representations" of the gay community—to embrace and focus on mainstream assimilation—has led her to ask, with justifiable anger, "Can

I have [radical] politics and be a part of this [gay] movement?" "In-creasingly," she concludes, "I am sorry to say, I'm not sure."

Cohen doesn't minimize the importance of continuing to work through traditional political channels, such as electioneering and lobbying, in order to win much-needed civil rights legislation. But she does worry, rightly in my view, that a focus on civil rights alone has thus far been of most benefit to those gay people who are com-paratively privileged and has closed the door to the less conforming members of the community—people of color, say, or cross-dressers, or S/M devotees, or those who self-identify as transgendered. What heightens concern is that so little discussion is taking place within the major gay political organizations about the right to a living wage and to decent working conditions. As Cohen pointedly puts it, "Without dialogue and debate about what greater good we are working for, we may in fact achieve inclusion, but inclusion in an oppressive society."

There's some ground for hope in the emergence of smaller, more radically minded lesbian and gay organizations—for example, the Audre Lorde Project and Queers for Economic Justice in New York, Esperanza in San Antonio, and the national Black Radical Congress. The hope is that they will grow in strength, influence, and resources. But as matters stand, those who control the gay community's major resources and organizations are currently, one might even say smugly, committed to assimilationist goals that have little to do with gay working-class grievances and a lot to do with making it easier for the already privileged to "join up." And the bit-ter truth, as gay progressives well know, is that these organizations are powerful because their assimilationist goals accurately reflect the values and hopes of the majority of gay people.

Patrick McCreery demonstrates this point clearly in his superb essay in the anthology *Out At Work* on the politics of the federal Employment Non-Discrimination Act (ENDA). McCreery shows that the outpouring of mainstream gay support for ENDA is, on one level, understandable, since it *would*, if ever passed, extend needed workplace protection. But those benefits would come, McCreery forcefully argues, "through an unabashed privileging of normative sexuality—meaning non-fetishistic sexual relations between two adults in a monogamous, committed relationship." And this, in the long run, would *strengthen* the hetero-normative environment of the workplace.

If we turn to organized labor's side of a potential gay/labor alliance, we find a comparable picture: a formidable set of obstacles to cooperation, in tandem with some recent developments that provide at least limited grounds for optimism. Among the obstacles, the foremost is the still significant amount of homophobia in the workplace. A mere thirty years ago, homophobia was so fierce and endemic that only a rare homosexual would *think* about "coming out"—knowing that the consequences would almost certainly include being fired, verbally harassed, or physically assaulted. Today homophobia continues to run deep in the workplace, and gay bashing remains a constant threat. But harassment is now *somewhat* contained by the existence of gay caucuses within some unions, as well as by the determination of various union leaders, preeminently the head of the AFL-CIO, John J. Sweeney, to put gay rights and gay safety at the forefront of their agendas. Still, there's a very long way to go in combating homophobia.

Some of the worst offenders in the workplace, sadly, are members of other minorities. Their own experience with oppression hasn't automatically translated into sympathy for other oppressed people. And especially not those people who, by their very being, offend against deeply held religious beliefs and ingrained notions of "proper" gender behavior.

The inability of minority workers to join hands in solidarity has led some activists to feel that if further inroads against homophobia in the workplace are to come, they will have to be initiated from the top, from those in union leadership positions. Yet other activists deny this; they argue that the general increase over the past few decades in public understanding about homosexuality has already, at the workplace level, changed a significant number of hearts and minds: gays are now more willing to come out, and their straight counterparts are more supportive in their response.

Those who hold to an optimistic view can point to the recent emergence of such bottom-up formations as the Lesbian and Gay Issues Committee (LAGIC) in District Council 37 (the union of New York City employees), as well as the creation of Pride at Work, a national caucus of gay, lesbian, and transgendered trade unionists, which in 1998 became an official constituency group of the AFL-CIO. In a deeply researched and closely reasoned essay in *Out At Work*, Tamara Jones illuminates the dynamics at play in these new groups. Using the formation and history of LAGIC as a case study, Jones demonstrates how the rules-driven bureaucratic structures of many unions thwart decentralized decision making and power sharing. In particular, they constrict the ability of gay and lesbian organizers to increase their numbers and leverage in the struggle to redefine "workers' rights" in a more expansive way.

Jones persuasively shows how LAGIC itself has adopted some of the formalistic features of its parent union, D.C. 37, and has become more traditional over time; it now largely forgoes the radical inclusivity that had marked its early days, and no longer addresses the significant variations in lifestyle and belief that exist among its highly diversified queer membership. The key lesson Jones draws from LAGIC's evolution is that "the existence of a lesbian and gay union caucus does not automatically pose a radical challenge to the status quo, nor is it inherently conservative."

One has to look to the specific conditions in which a particular gay caucus is operating, Jones argues, and has to recognize that "often, mobilization and organizing occur within organizational fields and institutional settings that were not designed to support transformative or collectivist politics." Jones's insights are persuasively stated and will hopefully be taken to heart. But we need to recognize, too, that—as with all social movements that are genuinely progressive—the struggle for gay rights in the workplace will inevitably pass through alternating cycles of advance and retreat.

As for the specific question of whether it's possible to create an expanded alliance between gay and nongay workers that could serve as an important agency for social change, there's evidence available to feed both optimism and pessimism. The pessimists would emphasize the ongoing homophobia at most workplaces. As AFL-CIO head John J. Sweeney has put it, promoting the rights of gay and lesbian workers has "been a slow and painstaking process. . . . And we still have quite a long way to go. Historically, unions have had to be challenged and prodded before opening the door to people their members view as 'different.' For gay and lesbian workers, in particular, that remains a hard reality to this day." (Sweeney doesn't mention transgendered workers, but should have, since their travails are often severe and usually go unacknowledged.)

There's additional fuel for pessimism in the way those national gay and lesbian organizations with the greatest resources and the most visible public presence continue to ignore or marginalize economic issues. Many LGBT activists and organizations remain aloof from the union movement, in deference to a politics of assimilation that ignores any radical analysis of class. Transgender organizations stand apart from "a politics of assimilation" or any process of normalization—but the two largest LGBT organizations, the Human Rights Campaign and the National Gay and Lesbian Task Force, have in my view committed far too much time and money to assimilationist issues such as the right of gays to marry or to serve openly in the military.

Those who hold to an optimistic view of the prospects for an expanded gay/worker alliance can also cite a significant amount of evidence to bolster their hopes. Certain unions, particularly the American Federation of State, County and Municipal Employees (AFSCME) and the Service Employees International Union (SEIU) have taken the lead in supporting strong LGBT caucuses and in educating straight workers about the significant amounts of fear and discrimination that gay workers experience in the workplace. Increasingly, straight workers recognize the material importance *and* the ethical rightness of making sure that domestic partnership benefits for gay people are negotiated into contracts with employers.

It's also true that an increasing number of gay and lesbian workers are casting aside their doubts about the value of unions and are beginning to recognize that organized labor, for all its shortcomings, could well become a significant force in the struggle for gay rights, benefits, and safeguards.

Not only might unions transform the workplace for gay people, but as gay workers take their place at the table, they, like women and people of color before them, could help to transform union culture. Once social identity issues join economic ones as an intrinsic part of union demands, hetero-normative standards could then, over time—probably over a *lot* of time—give way to a far more inclusive embodiment of the exceedingly varied lives, the amalgam of identities, that unions, like it or not, do in fact represent, even if, until recently, they mostly preferred not to notice. A reconfigured working class would fully acknowledge not merely the geographical and economic dimensions of its struggle, but also its racial, gender, and sexual ones.

Think of it: an economic-justice movement that included gay people, and a gay movement that concerned itself with a more equitable distribution of wealth. Emerging in tandem, they could engineer a revitalized workplace *and* a reinvigorated politics. With so much at stake, it's hard not to go with the optimists—and after all, how but through optimism have social justice movements ever come into being or been able to sustain themselves?

—from the *Progressive*, August 2001

Coda: Acceptance at What Price? The Gay Movement Reconsidered

Acceptance Speech for Kessler Award from the Center for Lesbian and Gay Studies (CLAGS), CUNY Graduate Center, December 5, 2012

I'd like to begin by defining my personal political position in order to help you better evaluate the subsequent argument I'll be making.

First, to state the obvious, I strongly believe that gay people are entitled to all the rights and privileges of other citizens in this country, including marriage.

Second, and perhaps less obvious: I'm speaking to you as someone who self-identifies politically as radical, not liberal. "Isn't 'radical' the same as 'liberal?' " people often ask me. No, it isn't. Liberal and radical are often lumped together, usually to be denounced, but to explain my own politics, I think it's important and necessary to distinguish between the two. Both *do* share a belief in the need for progressive social change in this country, but there the similarity ends. Liberals struggle to integrate increasing numbers of people into what's viewed as a beneficent system. Radicals believe that the system does have beneficent aspects, but also believe that it requires substantial restructuring.

Social justice movements in this country have often been started by radicals who have then, and usually in short order, been repudiated and supplanted by liberals. Thus in the nineteenth century, the Garrisonian abolitionists gave way to the Free Soil Party—meaning that the call for the immediate abolition of slavery slid into the mere refusal to allow slavery to expand further. Thus, too, the Knights of Labor—"One Big Union," skilled and unskilled combined—mutated into the AFL, which catered only to skilled workers and denied admission to people of color. A final example might be the broadgauged Seneca Falls declaration of womens's rights, with its open challenge to male domination; that got transmuted into the suffragists' single-issue concentration on winning the right to vote.

Over and over, the deeply conservative undertow of American ideology has undermined and diminished progressive goals. Central to that ideology is the conviction that any individual willing to work hard enough can achieve whatever he or she desires. It follows from this pull-yourself-up-by-your-own-bootstraps assumption that all presumed barriers based on race, class, gender, or sexual orientation automatically evaporate or are reduced to insignificance when confronted by the individual's determined drive for success. And if you believe that, there's this little bridge in Brooklyn for sale that I'd like to interest you in.

Those in this country who self-identify as left-wing, as I do, have never been able to solve the conundrum of how to prevent a radical impulse from degenerating into reformist tinkering—which comes down to how to mobilize a large constituency for substantive change when most of its members (think the Human Rights Campaign here) prefer to focus on winning certain kinds of limited concessions (like, for gay people, the right to marry or to serve in the military) and show little interest in joining with other dispossessed groups to press for a broader social reconstruction.

Perhaps the Occupy Wall Street movement—the radical element in *this* generation—will manage to solve this conundrum. I dearly hope so, though I have my doubts, given the history of radical protest in this country.

Part of the problem, as all the surveys I've seen agree, is that Americans are twice as likely to blame *themselves* rather than structural obstacles if their income and status remain low—that, in other words, we're a good deal less class-conscious than Europeans. Thus in the 1970s it proved impossible to draw together the class-based politics of the labor unions of the 1930s with the demand for racial justice of the 1960s into what we most need—an inter-racial class identity. Yet there is hope, and it resides, in my view, in the eighteen- to twenty-five-year-old cohort, the generation that spawned Occupy, which is far and away the most progressive force on the scene today.

In describing how liberalism—with much help, of course, from conservatism—has historically swallowed up any fragile shoots of radicalism in this country, I make no exception for the gay rights movement itself, in which I've been periodically active for some forty years.

Following the Stonewall riots in 1969, which inaugurated the modern LGBT movement, the radical Gay Liberation Front (GLF) initially emerged as the dominant political force. It offered a far-ranging critique of traditional notions of gender and sexual behavior. And it emphasized the ideal of androgyny—that is, combining in every individual the characteristics and drives previously parceled out as "natural" to one gender or the other. It also aimed at making alliances with other oppressed groups, like the Black Panthers and the Young Lords.

Today GLF has long since disappeared. It has been replaced by national LGBT organizations—of which the Human Rights Campaign is currently the largest—that work toward assimilationist goals like gay marriage and the right of gays to serve openly in the military. And it's precisely this agenda that for twenty years has swept the field, pushing aside and ignoring a host of other issues and insisting that we're "just folks," exactly like you mainstreamers in our perspectives and values, with the sole exception of this insignificant little matter of sexual orientation.

It isn't true. Gay people are *not* carbon-copy straight people— just as black people aren't carbon-copy whites. Gay radicals insist that our special historical experience has provided us, just as it has black people, with special perspectives and insights into mainstream American culture—insights we feel should be affirmed, not denied.

Gay radicals, then and now, oppose reducing our critique of mainstream values to an agenda that pledges allegiance to them, as is currently the case. That critique ranges from economic to sexual issues, from the demand for a genuine safety net for all citizens to a questioning of the universal superiority of lifetime monogamy.

More than sixty years ago, the (heterosexual) philosopher Herbert Marcuse wrote in his classic work *Eros and Civilization* a sentence that has become a kind of mantra for me: "Because of their rebellion against the subjugation of sexuality under the order of procreation, homosexuals might one day provide a cutting-edge social critique of vast importance."

It's precisely the loss of that "cutting-edge social critique" that so much bothers me and others on the left. For us to reach the potential Marcuse envisioned for us, it seems to me that we need to assert our differentness from the mainstream rather than continue to plead for the right to join it.

We need to assert the fact that, despite enormous variations in our individual lifestyles, a distinctive set of perspectives—reflecting our distinct historical experience—exists among gay people in regard to how they view gender, sexuality, primary relationships, friendships, and family. Gay "differentness" isn't some second-rate variation on first-rate mainstream norms, but rather a decided *advance* over them. Gay subcultural values could richly inform conventional life and could open up an unexplored range of human possibilities for *everyone*. Could, that is, if the mainstream were listening, which it isn't. And the reason it isn't is due in part to *us*—to our denial or concealment of our own specialness in the name of being let into what is essentially a middle-class white male clubhouse.

When I speak of our specialness, I mean the challenge the radical GLF presented in the years following Stonewall. I mean the challenge to the gender binary, to the assumption that everyone is either male or female and that certain biologically induced traits adhere naturally to each gender—that women, for example, are *intrin-*

sically emotional, men *intrinsically* aggressive. That gender binary is *not* true of gay people in general.

But what *is* true, as a number of studies have shown, is that gay people score consistently higher than straight people in empathy and altruism. Also true is that lesbians as a group have been shown to be far more independent-minded and far less subservient to authority than straight women.

Many gay men, moreover, put a premium on emotional expressiveness and sexual innovation. Studies have shown that lesbians and gay men hold a view of coupledom that is far more characterized by mutuality and egalitarianism than is true of straight couples.

If you don't believe me, surely you'll believe the *New York Times*. Back in 2008 the *Times* published an article summarizing recent scholarly evidence that (in the words of the *Times*) "conclusively shows that same-sex couples are far more egalitarian in sharing responsibility both for housework and finances than are heterosexual ones, where women still do much more of the domestic chores (and live with a lot of anger as a result) and where men are more likely to pay the bills." As a result, the *Times* concludes that same-sex couples "have more relationship satisfaction" and—hold on to your beads—"have a great deal to teach everyone else."

In other words, there really *is* a gay subculture, a way of looking at life and coping with its joys and sorrows that has much to offer the mainstream—and also to offer the multitude of gay people who prefer to claim that we're just like everybody else. Those of us on the left feel much the way James Baldwin did when he asked why blacks were begging to rent a room in a house that was burning down. Wouldn't it be better, Baldwin asked, to build a new house?

In the same spirit, gay radicals denounce the killing machine known as the military and have no wish to become part of it. Nor are we interested in having our primary relationships sanctioned by church or state. *Not* being carbon copies, we at least *aim* at equality in our unions, rather than at the privileging of one partner's personal, sexual, and career needs over the other's. And we do not believe that being part of a couple should convey special status and reward, for that reduces the vast number of single people in our midst to some sort of second-class, second-rate status.

We are, of course, entitled to all the rights and privileges of everyone else in this country. But the recent concentration of our resources and energy on the narrow agenda of marriage and the military has implicitly denigrated both the *un*married state *and* the refusal to maim and kill in war. Our current national organizations for the most part have not only failed to challenge mainstream American values, but also have ignored the actual needs of most gay people themselves. Organizations like the Human Rights Campaign speak primarily to a middle- and upper-class white constituency and all but ignore the gay world's black, Asian, and Latino members; the plight of its own poor; and the history of our challenges to traditional gender and sexual norms.

Though you'd never know it from the current gay agenda, most gay people are *working class*—and that's true whether "class" is defined by income, educational level, or job status. The chief concern these days of gay working-class people is finding a job with decent wages and benefits—and keeping that job, since in half the states employers still can legally fire workers simply because they're gay.

The workplace itself remains strongly defined by heterosexual norms. Most straight workers believe gender does and should come in two, and only two, packages: the traditionally defined male *or* the traditionally defined female. The heterosexual norm also explicitly claims—at least officially—that lifetime, monogamous pair-bonding is the sole guarantee of a contented, moral life. Of course official rhetoric and actual behavior are often far apart, as you might have noted recently with a certain high-ranking general.

The large majority of working-class gay people, like most straight ones, have *non*union jobs. The union movement currently enrolls less than 12 percent of the workforce. Even where a union exists, gay people often don't feel comfortable talking openly to fellow workers about their lives. Nor are their needs, like domestic partnership benefits, forcefully represented during contract negotiations with employers. The gay employee feels fortunate if homophobic harassment—literal physical assault—is absent from his or her workplace.

Under the leadership of John J. Sweeney, the AFL has made some strides in including and protecting gay union members, but homophobia in the workplace, unionized or not, is still formidable. Alas, the national LGBT organizations, enamored of the marital arts and traditional marriage, have shown scant comprehension or interest in the hidden wounds of class and the open wounds of race.

In a brilliant essay entitled "What Is This Movement Doing to My Politics?" the lesbian political scientist Cathy Cohen has argued that, ever since the demise of Queer Nation and the refocusing of ACT-UP on issues relating to *global* AIDS, there is no longer a radical domestic wing of any import in the national lesbian and gay movement—which is to say, the gay movement no longer represents a genuinely transformative politics.

Remember, if you will, that as far back as 1998, the Human Rights Campaign endorsed Alfonse D'Amato for the Senate, and later GLAD—the Gay and Lesbian Alliance Against Defamation—accepted money from the right-wing, union-busting Coors Beer corporation.

The national gay movement's efforts, in Cohen's words, to "sanitize, whitenize, and normalize the public and visible representations" of the community—to focus, in other words, on mainstream assimilation—has led her to ask, with what *I* feel is justifiable anger, "Can I have radical politics and be part of this gay movement?" Her answer *and* mine, I'm sorry to say, is, "We're not sure."

Why? Because we're deeply concerned that the gay movement in its current incarnation is essentially devoted to winning inclusion into an unequal, greed-haunted, oppressive society.

There are currently 46 million Americans who subsist on food stamps, an increase of more than 14 million over the past four years. More than a quarter of blacks and Latinos in this country—compared to 10 percent of whites—live *below* the government-defined poverty line of $11,000 a year for an individual and roughly $22,000 a year for a family of four.

One in every five children lives in a family below the poverty line, and they often go to bed at night hungry; again, if you doubt me, have a look at the recent *Frontline* television program "Poor Kids." One in every four adult black men are either in jail or have recently been released from it, often for minor drug charges. Again, don't take my word for it: read Michelle Alexander's recent book, *The New Jim Crow*. In sum, for 46 million Americans—*which includes many gay people*—basic human needs and minimal levels of security are going unmet.

Surely, it's long past time for the gay movement, and for the country as a whole, to refocus its agenda. What is needed is nothing less than a massive antiracist, pro-feminist, economic justice movement. I know—easier said than done. But easiest of all is to continue to do nothing about the country's gross inequities.

Do we see any signs in the national LGBT movement that it seeks coalition with others suffering oppression, that it must cease to be a one-issue movement and instead must stand with those suffering from assorted forms of racial, class, and gender discrimination? Yes, on the local level there *are* a few struggling LGBT organizations centered on dealing with the plight of its own poor people, and also on creating bridges to others. Here in New York City, there's Queers for Economic Justice. How many of you have even *heard* of QEJ? It attempts, with a small budget and staff, to deal with the multiple issues of the gay poor, including those living in shelters.

In closing, I have to tell you that I think it's a disgrace that our country as a whole is far more entranced with improving the technology of drone strikes, those anonymous killers in the sky, than with the plight of the poor. And I'm afraid I have to add that I also consider it a disgrace that our assimilationist-minded national gay movement does a far better job at representing the white middle- and upper-class elements in our community than it does representing those of *our own people* who suffer from a variety of deprivations—to say nothing of the nongay multitude who are also afflicted.

It is time, in my view, to reassess and revise our goals as a movement. To do otherwise is to implicate us in the national disgrace of caring much more about the welfare of the privileged few than the deprived many. We are in danger of becoming part of the problem. My hope is that we may yet become part of the solution.

Permissions